The New Jackals

The New Jackals

Ramzi Yousef, Osama bin Laden and the future of terrorism

SIMON REEVE

Northeastern University Press

BOSTON

Northeastern University Press

Copyright © by Simon Reeve 1999

Published in England by André Deutsch Ltd, London.
Published in the United States of America by
Northeastern University Press, by arrangement
with André Deutsch Ltd.

Library of Congress Cataloging-in-Publication Data
Reeve, Simon.
The new jackals : Ramzi Yousef, Osama bin Laden
and the future of terrorism / Simon Reeve
p. cm.
Includes bibliographical references (p.   ) and index.
ISBN 1-55553-407-4 (cl. : alk. paper)
1. World Trade Center Bombing, New York, N.Y., 1993.
2. Yousef, Ramzi Ahmed. 3. Bin Lādin, Usāmah, 1957–   .
4. Terrorism—New York (State)—New York. I. Title.
HV6432.R42   1999
364.1'09747'1—dc21   99-37245

MANUFACTURED IN THE UNITED STATES OF AMERICA
03 02 01   5 4

For my family, Alan, Cindy, James, Lucy and Ian

Ramzi Yousef, Osama bin Laden and the 'Afghan Arabs' have 'dominated international terrorism as it relates to the United States and Europe [in the 1990s]. At the international level the only terrorist apparatus that the United States has had to deal with over the past several years has been Osama bin Laden and before that Ramzi Yousef.'
  Oliver 'Buck' Revell, *former Deputy Director of the FBI*[1]

'Ramzi Yousef is an evil genius.'
  Senior Pakistani intelligence officer[2]

'Ramzi Yousef was probably the most dangerous and prolific terrorist since the heyday of [Carlos] the Jackal'
  Judge Kevin Duffy[3]

'Yousef was a pretty unique person. He liked the bar scene, he liked women, he liked moving around. Yousef was very good. He was well trained, very clever. He'll certainly be ranked right up there with the all-timers. Even to this day, he is a very shadowy figure that we really don't know that much about, even after all that's been done and all that's been investigated on him.'
  Neil Herman, *the FBI Supervisory Special Agent who led the New York Joint Terrorist Task Force during the hunt for Yousef*[4]

'Yes, I am a terrorist, and I'm proud of it.'
  Ramzi Yousef[5]

'In the past, we were fighting terrorists with an organizational structure and some attainable goal like land or the release of political prisoners. But Ramzi Yousef is the new breed, who are more difficult and hazardous. They want nothing less than the overthrow of the West, and since that's not going to happen, they just want to punish – the more casualties the better.'
  Oliver 'Buck' Revell, *former Deputy Director of the FBI*[6]

'He's a cold-blooded terrorist. He doesn't care who he kills. He may be the most dangerous man in the world.'
  Superintendent Samuel Pagdilao *of the Philippines National Police describing Yousef*[7]

'One man said to me, "Remember there will only be those who believe and those who will die. There will only be the dead and the believers".'
   Benazir Bhutto, *former Prime Minister of Pakistan*[8]

'If Russia can be destroyed, the United States can also be beheaded.'
   Osama bin Laden[9]

'In my personal view [Osama bin Laden] is very much interested in obtaining weapons of mass destruction and he has the money to pay for them. It's certainly a credible threat.'
   Peter Probst, *Pentagon terrorism expert*[10]

'We don't consider it a crime if we tried to have nuclear, chemical, biological weapons. If I have indeed acquired these weapons, then I thank God for enabling me to do so.'
   Osama bin Laden[11]

'Terrorism is changing. We expect biological attacks in the future.'
   Marvin Cetron, *author of the Pentagon's secret Terror 2000 investigation*[12]

References

[1] Author interview with Oliver Revell.
[2] Author interview.
[3] Duffy speaking to Yousef before he sentenced him to 240 years in prison.
[4] Author interview with Neil Herman.
[5] Yousef speaking before he was sentenced.
[6] 'Symbol of a New Generation of Terrorists', *International Herald Tribune*, 7 September 1996.
[7] Nicholas Cumming-Bruce, 'Manila turns "terrorist" over to US', *Guardian*, 15 April 1995.
[8] Author interview with Benazir Bhutto.
[9] Hamid Mir, interview with Osama bin Laden, Pakistan, 18 March 1997.
[10] Author interview with Peter Probst.
[11] Rahimullah Usufzai, 'Conversation with Terror', *Time*, 11 January 1998.
[12] Author interview with Marvin Cetron.

CONTENTS

INTRODUCTION

Targeting Terror

THE SECRET attack was code-named Operation Infinite Reach. On 27 August 1998, 80 Tomahawk cruise missiles were launched from five US warships in the Arabian Sea and two in the Red Sea. They were sent towards two targets: one, an apparently innocuous pharmaceutical plant in Sudan. The other was a scattering of buildings in Afghanistan. This was the lair of Osama bin Laden, the shadowy figure orchestrating global Islamic terrorism.

For America, it was a chance to strike back at terrorists who had made the nation look impotent on the world stage. President Clinton gave a 3 a.m. 'green light' to the operation after being shown evidence of bin Laden's involvement in bomb attacks on US embassies in Kenya and Tanzania which killed 224 people. The President was also told that bin Laden had supported Ramzi Ahmed Yousef, a figure best described as a 'modern-day Carlos the Jackal', who was sentenced to life imprisonment in 1998 for a devastating campaign of terror.

'Our target was terror,' said the President. 'Our mission was clear: to strike at the network of radical groups affiliated with and funded by Osama bin Laden, perhaps the pre-eminent organizer and financier of international terrorism in the world today.'

Initially the American cruise missile attacks were deemed a complete success. The Sudanese factory, suspected of producing ingredients for deadly VX nerve gas, was completely destroyed, while bin Laden's camps in Afghanistan suffered heavy damage. However, bin Laden himself was unhurt, unrepentant and soon feeding off his new global notoriety. 'By the grace of Allah, I am alive!' he said in a radio broadcast to his legions of supporters.

Few in the West had heard of bin Laden before the embassy

1

bombings, but suddenly his photograph was plastered across global television screens and his anti-American rhetoric filled the airwaves. The world's media had found a new hate-figure to occupy their attention, and military commanders and radio talk-show hosts thumped tables and called for bin Laden to be hunted down and killed.

America might eventually capture and jail Osama bin Laden, just as it captured and imprisoned Ramzi Yousef. But others will follow in their wake, because the two men are just the first of a new breed of terrorist unleashed against the West. Poisoned by political hatred and religious fervour, these 'New Jackals' have no qualms about mass killing and are as deadly and committed as any group of terrorists the world has ever faced.

The roots of this new wave of extremist terrorism can be traced to the arid mountainous regions of Afghanistan. After Soviet forces invaded the country in 1979 thousands of young Muslims from around the world travelled to Afghanistan to fight a holy war alongside the muja-heddin rebels, their Muslim brothers. For more than a decade they were pawns in the Cold War, encouraged, armed, trained and supplied by America, Britain and the Gulf states. But when the Soviets were defeated this support ceased and thousands of young militants, known by then as 'Afghan Arabs', were left to fend for themselves. Highly politicized and charged with religious zeal, they sought new enemies, both in their own homelands and around the world, under the influence of new leaders. 'It's rather ironic given that the United States provided logistical support and training and weapons for at least part of the mujaheddin,' said Oliver 'Buck' Revell, the former Deputy Director of the FBI.[1]

Ramzi Yousef was one young man who trained in Afghanistan and then launched himself against the world. Osama bin Laden was one of the leaders. Together they epitomize the new terrorist threat facing the West.

'It is all a consequence of the Afghan war, where a lot of indoctri-nation took place,' said Benazir Bhutto, the former Prime Minister of Pakistan.[2] The Islamic fighters in Afghanistan 'were told that if you have your faith you don't need anything else to demolish all the superpowers. They were brought up to believe you can demolish both the Soviet Union and the United States and all the world. And having driven the Soviet Union out of Afghanistan they feel they have the power to drive America out as well.'

The US Central Intelligence Agency (CIA) has a term for such unpredictable events: they call it 'Blowback'. At the end of the war the Afghan Arabs became, in euphemistic spook parlance, a 'disposal problem', and officials who helped support the mujaheddin during the 1980s now acknowledge their mistakes. 'We did spawn a monster in Afghanistan,' admits Richard Murphy, the Assistant Secretary of State for Near East and South Asian Relations during the Reagan administration, and former US Ambassador to Syria and Saudi Arabia.[3] 'Once the Soviets were gone [the Afghan Arabs] were looking around for other targets, and Mr Osama bin Laden has settled on the United States as the source of all evil.'

Charles G. Cogan, the CIA's operations chief in the Near East and South Asia between 1979 and 1984, admits: 'It's quite a shock. The hypothesis that the mujaheddin would come to the United States and commit terrorist actions did not enter into our universe of thinking at the time. We were totally preoccupied with the war against the Soviets in Afghanistan. It is a significant unintended consequence.'[4]

Estimates of the total number of Afghan Arabs vary. One source, formerly a senior CIA official, claims the number is close to 17,000,[5] while the highly respected British publication *Jane's Intelligence Review* suggests a figure of more than 14,000 (including some 5,000 Saudis, 3,000 Yemenis, 2,000 Egyptians, 2,800 Algerians, 400 Tunisians, 370 Iraqis, 200 Libyans, and scores of Jordanians).[6]

Some of these men are now responsible for much of the global terrorism threatening the West, while others returned from the Afghan war to start or lead guerrilla movements in their own countries against governments they perceive as being un-Islamic, corrupt or despotic. These veterans of the Afghan jihad have taken the war home to more than 25 countries, including Algeria, Azerbaijan, Bangladesh, Bosnia, Britain, Burma, Chechnya, China, Egypt, France, India, Morocco, Pakistan, the Philippines, Saudi Arabia, Sudan, Tajikistan, Tunisia, the USA, Uzbekistan and Yemen.

Perhaps the greatest impact has been felt in Algeria. After the government cancelled the 1992 general election, which Islamic fundamentalists were predicted to win, approximately 900 battle-hardened Afghan veterans returned to Algeria, in three waves up to 1994. They formed the core of Algeria's Muslim extremists, responsible – along with government troops – for horrific massacres. More than 65,000 souls are believed to have perished in political violence and terrorist attacks in Algeria since 1992.

The fanaticism of these fighters is terrifying. Terrorism in the 1970s and 1980s consisted largely of radical left-wing groups in Europe and South America with definable goals – however unattainable. The new breed of terrorist attacking the West has few aims. They just want to kill and punish for what they believe is Western imperialism and the global oppression of Muslims. In their eyes it is guilt by association.

When Osama bin Laden was asked why he targets American and British civilians around the world, when Islam prohibits its followers from killing civilians in war, he replied: 'If the Israelis are killing the small children in Palestine and the Americans are killing the innocent people in Iraq, and if the majority of the American people support their dissolute president, this means the American people are fighting us and we have the right to target them.' Any American taxpayer is a target, he says, 'because he is helping the American war machine against the Muslim nation'.[7]

Bin Laden has been responsible for a covert war against the West which began at the beginning of the 1990s and shows little sign of abating. America may think it has prevented future bomb atrocities by attacking bin Laden, but its cruise missiles have started a virtually unwinnable war with the world's principal sponsor of terrorism. 'Our answer will be deeds, not words,' said bin Laden's spokesman after the Afghan bases had been bombed.

Bin Laden commands an army of some 5,000 terrorists, all of whom seem willing to kill and die for the Islamic cause. His soldiers are men such as Ramzi Yousef, the prototype for the new breed of terrorist: young, full of zeal, technically skilled to a high level, and determined to bring terror to the West. Where Yousef led, many more will follow. Thousands of young Islamic militants are now being trained to fight a jihad, or holy war. 'The majority come from universities, they're modern and they use modern methods. Americans imagine these people come from the Middle Ages and that's not true,' said Diaa Rashwan, an analyst at Egypt's Al-Ahram Centre for Political and Strategic Studies.[8]

Many of the militants are massing under Osama bin Laden's command, but if he is killed or captured they will not be deterred from their mission. Extremists will still rally to fight against 'American imperialism' and the 'Great Satan'. They know their task is simple: to attack and punish the West with bullets and bombs.

References

[1] Author interview.

[2] Author interview.

[3] 'War just started, says bin Laden', Associated Press, 23 August 1998.

[4] Tim Weiner, 'Blowback from the Afghan Battlefield', *New York Times*, 13 March 1994.

[5] Author interview.

[6] James Bruce, 'Arab Veterans of the Afghan War', *Jane's Intelligence Review*, 1 April 1995.

[7] Jamal Ismail, 'I am not afraid of death', *Newsweek*, 11 January 1999.

[8] Anthony Shadid, 'The next generation of militant "Islamic International" equipped for the '90s', Associated Press, 21 August 1998.

ONE

The Twin Towers

JUST BEFORE 4 a.m. on 26 February 1993, a yellow Ford Econoline van bearing the markings of the Ryder hire company emerged from a driveway beside a scruffy apartment block at 40 Pamrapo Avenue, New Jersey, and turned slowly on to the deserted streets of Jersey City, just across the Hudson River from the bright lights of Manhattan. With a dark blue Lincoln and a red Chevrolet following closely behind, the three vehicles drove the short distance down J. F. Kennedy Boulevard to the Shell petrol station at the junction with Route 440 and pulled up by the pumps.[1]

From the passenger seat of the Ford van, a dark-haired man called Ramzi Yousef watched as Willie Hernandez Moosh, the forecourt attendant working the graveyard shift, left his small booth between the pumps. Yousef lowered his window as Moosh approached.

'What do you want?' asked Moosh.

'Fill it up,' replied Yousef.

As Moosh began filling the tank, the passenger door opened, and Yousef slid out on to the forecourt, bracing himself against the cold. Yousef was a tall, wiry man with large ears and a bulbous nose. His eyes flicked over the cars behind and then swept up and down the street. Then, as if a nagging thought was preying on his mind, he began inspecting the yellow van. Moosh removed the petrol cap and watched idly as Yousef began checking the sides and glancing underneath.

Yousef knew the van was designed to hold 2,000lbs in its 295 cubic feet of space. It had been carefully selected as the perfect size for carrying a massive terrorist bomb to attack a target on American soil. Yousef had travelled thousands of miles and spent six months in

America plotting and then building a 1,200lb bomb, which was resting in the back of the van with several heavy tanks of hydrogen. But was the cargo pushing the van low on its springs? Nothing could be left to chance.

Moosh was too busy watching Yousef to notice anything suspicious about the van. He had a long, pointy face, thought Moosh. The face of a horse surrounded by a beard.[2]

The 22-gallon tank on a yellow Ford Econoline van takes a few moments to fill, and Moosh left the nozzle in the tank and walked back to the Lincoln. 'Fill it up,' said Mahmud Abouhalima from the warmth of the driving seat. A tall, stocky, red-headed man, Abouhalima had no desire to brave the bitter cold. Ramzi could handle any final inspection – after all, he was in charge.

Moosh pumped petrol into the vehicle, then walked back to the van to ask who was paying. Mohammad Salameh, a lean young man with a straggly beard, turned to Moosh from the driving seat and motioned to the Lincoln behind.

'He will pay,' said Salameh.

The Lincoln's window lowered again to let in the icy air, and Abouhalima handed Moosh a $50 note – $18 worth of petrol for the van and around $13 for the car. Abouhalima took the change, gave Moosh a $2 tip, then Yousef jumped back into the van and the drivers of all three vehicles gunned their engines.[3]

There were few cars on the streets that night, and Moosh watched the convoy as it pulled slowly out of the forecourt. Suddenly the lead van jerked to a halt. A white Jersey City police car was coming into view, driving slowly along J. F. Kennedy Boulevard. The van quickly swung round into a parking space behind the petrol station's office, with the two cars close behind, and Yousef and Salameh jumped out and opened the bonnet.

'Can you bring us some water?' Yousef shouted to Moosh, pretending there was a problem with the van. Moosh grabbed a jug of water and walked over to the two men. Yousef and Salameh were peering into the engine bay and shooting glances at the police car cruising slowly along the street. It must have been a nerve-racking few moments for the men.

Earlier that night Salameh had calmly rung the police from near the Pathmark supermarket at the Route 440 shopping plaza and told them the Ryder van had been stolen from the car park. It was a clever ruse to avert suspicion: Yousef was planning a heinous act of terrorism – he did not want detectives investigating his handiwork to trawl around rental centres and discover a group of Arabs had failed to return a large van. Yousef decided they would report it as stolen and give police a false licence-plate number. But even without a stolen vehicle report, many police officers might consider a three-vehicle convoy driving slowly around Jersey City before dawn vaguely suspicious.

Yousef and Salameh held their breath, but the car cruised by. Perhaps the officers did not see the small convoy. Perhaps they had not been given the report of a stolen yellow Ryder van. Moosh noticed a man in the red car motioning to the others and pointing at the road. Yousef and Salameh left the water untouched, slammed the bonnet shut, climbed back into the van, and the convoy turned back on to the streets of Jersey City.

By 8 a.m. the van was nosing through the New York rush-hour towards Manhattan. With Yousef giving directions the van arrived at a hotel in midtown Manhattan where an old friend of his called Eyad Ismoil, a baby-faced Jordanian college student, was staying for a few days. 'They were knocking on the door at 9 a.m. and saying "Hurry up, we are going to be late",' said Ismoil. 'I took a bath and went with them and he [Yousef] asked me [to] drive; he said, "You are a taxi driver and a driving expert in the street." I laughed and told them I was willing to drive.' Ismoil climbed behind the wheel of the van, and the group drove towards southern Manhattan. 'In the middle of a major street we stopped at a traffic light; he [Yousef] said "Go to the right from here" in the direction of an underground tunnel,' said Ismoil. 'I did and we went down underground. I was surprised . . . He said "Park here" . . .'[4]

At the southern tip of Manhattan island, dominating the New York skyline, the twin towers of the World Trade Center stand proud, symbolizing commercial power and the core American values of hard work and success. New Yorkers are rightly proud of the vast buildings, which rise 107 storeys or a third of a mile into the sky and are served by 250 different lifts. Tower One hosts a huge antenna which pushes the total height to 1,710 feet above sea level. The entire World Trade Center complex comprises seven huge buildings, and even the underground basement boasts impressive statistics: a subterranean world of cooling pipes, parking garages and offices, bigger than the Empire State Building, it houses a small army of 300 mechanics, electricians, engineers and cleaners who keep the towers alive for the daily working and visiting population of nearly 150,000.

On 26 February 1993, Monica Smith was one of those working in a small office on level B-2 in the town under the ground. Monica was a pretty, dark-haired, 35-year-old woman from Ecuador, a secretary whose main responsibility was scrutinizing time-sheets submitted by cleaning contractors. She had met her husband Eddie in the World Trade Center when he had gone to the building for a sales meeting, and now she was seven months pregnant with little Eddie, their first child. Her colleagues adored Smith, fussing around her attentively from the moment she announced her pregnancy. Just a few days previously Stephen Knapp, a 48-year-old maintenance supervisor, had even asked his wife Louise to bake Monica a special dish of aubergine parmigiana.[5]

At noon the room next to Smith's office was being taken over for lunch. A meeting about maintenance services had finished with the arrival of Robert Kirkpatrick, the 61-year-old bespectacled chief locksmith for the towers, closely followed by Bill Macko, a 47-year-old maintenance worker. Kirkpatrick always sat in the same large oak chair for lunch and no meeting would get in his way. Macko unfolded a newspaper, pulled out a knife from his pocket and slowly began peeling an orange. Stephen Knapp, the next to join the group, cracked open an illicit beer from a refrigerator in the corner of the room and flopped wearily into a chair.

Bill Lavin, who worked for the chief maintenance contractor for the Trade Center, eyed his friends, then decided he wanted to see daylight, and perhaps catch a glimpse of the snow forecast on the television that morning. It was falling lightly outside, dusting Manhattan in white. Lavin told the others he would be back in a few minutes and walked down the corridor towards the elevators.

A solid concrete wall separated the lunchroom from a ramp to the public car park. It was supposed to be a no-parking zone, with signs warning off anyone tempted to stop, but it was so close to the offices that nobody took any notice of the rules. As Knapp, Macko and Kirkpatrick ate their lunch, a yellow Port Authority van was parked in the zone. One of the basement army, a purchasing agent leaving the maintenance meeting, grabbed a set of keys to the van and drove off to buy some lunch. There were no windows through which the three workers could see another yellow van glide slowly down the ramp and into the same space. Nobody saw the driver and passenger slide out a few minutes later and disappear. There was no one to stop them, no one to question them, and certainly no one to tell them they were illegally parked. Even if a guard had seen them, he would have assumed the van was owned by a maintenance company. Yellow vans were often left on the ramp while heavy boxes were loaded or unloaded.

Nobody was planning to unload the contents of this yellow Ford Econoline bearing the markings of the Ryder hire company. In the back, Ramzi Yousef used a cheap cigarette lighter to ignite four 20ft-long fuses. They would take just 12 minutes to burn down to his massive bomb. Yousef clambered out of the van, jumped into the red car that had followed him into the garage, and then drove carefully out towards West Street. Then he had a shock: another van was blocking the exit, barring his escape from the car park. Yousef must have felt like a character in a Hollywood disaster movie, with the seconds ticking down to oblivion. The van driver shouted to Yousef he would move in a few moments, and within two minutes Yousef was out of the Trade Center and back on the crowded streets of southern Manhattan.

In her office Monica Smith was carefully checking time-sheets. Next door the lunching workers were indulging in a little verbal sparring, joking and gently teasing each other. In the back of the Ryder van the fuses, encased in surgical tubing to limit smoke, were burning down at the rate of an inch every two and a half seconds. The critical moment came at 12.17 and 37 seconds. One of the fuses burnt to its end and ignited the gunpowder in an Atlas Rockmaster blasting cap. In a split second the cap exploded with a pressure of around 15,000lbs per square inch, igniting in turn the first nitro-glycerine container of the bomb, which erupted with a pressure of about 150,000lbs per square inch – the equivalent of about 10,000 atmospheres. In turn, the nitro-glycerine ignited cardboard boxes containing a witches' brew of urea pellets and sulphuric acid.

In the split second that followed the huge explosion blasted in all directions, tearing the van to shreds and ripping through the nearest office, stamping the patterned imprint of Monica Smith's green sweater into her shoulder. It killed little Eddie, tore apart her lungs, arteries and internal organs, fractured her pelvis and broke her leg. Concrete blocks pummelled her head. She died instantly, 'blunt impact trauma' extinguishing her life.[6]

Bob Kirkpatrick was the next to die. A veteran of the Korean war, just six months from retirement, he was hurled across the room, his skull rent apart by a piece of piping; the left side of his body flattened on impact.

Bill Macko, another ex-military man, was sitting next to Kirkpatrick: small chunks of concrete, moving faster than speeding bullets, ravaged the left side of his face. The blast ripped apart his vertebrae, tore his intestines from the side of his abdomen, and ruptured his arteries, spleen and kidneys. Before Stephen Knapp had time to close his eyelids tiny particles of concrete peppered his eyes, then his body was thrown backwards.

One floor above, Wilfredo Mercado, the 37-year-old receiving agent for the Windows on the World restaurant (that sits a quarter of a mile above the basement at the top of One World Trade Center), had been having a quiet snooze. Mercado studied engineering in his native Peru before moving to New York, and his short nap was a daily ritual, a brief moment of rest in a busy day. For most of the week Mercado worked in the twin towers checking that all the fruit and vegetables for the restaurant were delivered correctly. The other two days he returned to the building to work as a security guard. His wife Olga and two young daughters were his life. Mercado probably never woke from his brief slumber. Like a giant hand rising from below, the explosion plucked the Peruvian out of his room and sucked him down five floors. He landed head first, still in his chair, and his body was crushed under tonnes of concrete.

Back in the car park 45-year-old John DiGiovanni, a dark-haired, olive-skinned dental products salesman from Valley Stream, New York, had just parked near an underground ramp when the bomb went off. He was thrown around 30 feet, his body crumpled and bloodied. Paramedics eventually reached him and took him to St Vincent's Hospital, but it was already too late. John DiGiovanni died of traumatic cardiac arrest, caused by the extreme nature of his injuries and deep smoke inhalation.

Timothy Lang had been waiting to get into the car park behind DiGiovanni. A successful young stock-trader, Lang parked his car underground just moments before the explosion. Now he found himself dazed and barely conscious. He crawled through piles of rubble, his neck bleeding profusely, his lungs hacking from the smoke, and collapsed. Such are the vagaries of life. DiGiovanni had cut in front of Lang as their cars entered the building. Lang survived; DiGiovanni died.

The blast-wave roared upwards, passing through five reinforced

concrete floors and severing all power. For a brief moment the buildings were plunged into darkness. In an underground station below the
twin towers commuters screamed as the blast blew out a hole 180ft by
12ft in the side of the wall on level 2. Concrete and twisted metal flew
through the air, ripping through legs and arms, and lacerating spines.

Outside on the street, several hundred feet from 'ground zero', the
centre of the blast, the back window of a car waiting at traffic lights on
West Street blew out. The shockwave spread out from its source, and
within seconds tourists one mile away on Liberty and Ellis Islands in
New York harbour felt the ground shudder gently. Many New Yorkers
thought there had been an earthquake.

'There was a big boom, the building shook and I looked out of the
window across the Hudson River to see if New Jersey had disappeared,' said Lisa Hoffman, a worker in the nearby World Financial
Center.[7]

The first call to the emergency services came within five seconds of the
explosion.

'Police operator five. Is this an emergency?' queried the operator.[8]

'Yes, there is an emergency,' said a male caller at precisely 12.17 and
42 seconds. 'Something just blew up underneath the parking garage
tunnel between World Trade Center Tower One and the World
Financial Center, across the street.'

'Okay, it's in the World Trade Center?'

'No, it's an underground parking garage, the entranceway down
there.'

'Hold on a minute,' said the operator. 'What street is it on?'

'On West Street.'

'And what?'

'West,' said the caller, 'near Vesey, just toward the FDR from Vesey.'

'Okay, hold on for the Fire Department, you're in Manhattan,
right?'

The operator decided the caller was genuine and transferred him to
the Fire Department operator.

'Fire Department, Fletcher, 191.'

'Hi,' said the man, 'there was a big explosion in the underground
entranceway to the parking lot on West Street between World Trade
Center Tower One and the World Financial Center across the street on
West.'

'Okay, would that be, like, by the Vista Hotel?'

'Exactly.'

'Okay, and it's what number are you calling from?'

'I'm calling from 298 6020.'

'Okay, Fire Department is on our way, sir.'

The Fire Department were already there. Lieutenant Matt Donachie, 36, was standing just around the corner on Liberty Street, watching Fire-Engine 10 backing into its bay, when he heard the explosion.[9] Donachie jumped up into the front seat of the tender and radioed his dispatcher. A 12-year veteran, Donachie was convinced it was an electricity transformer explosion – a routine call. The tender drove around the corner and slowed to look for signs of damage. As it cruised past the 22-storey Vista Hotel, which stood between the twin towers, Donachie saw a wisp of smoke curling out into the street from a ramp leading down to the underground car park. He radioed for more units.

While the Fire Department moved into action, workers on the upper floors of the towers were already smelling smoke in their offices. Car fires in the basement were pumping out thick, acrid smoke, which spiralled up through stairways, elevator shafts and ventilation pipes as if the towers were giant chimneys.

During construction of the building safety and union officials had wanted the stairways pressurized, so the air pressure inside would be higher, preventing smoke entering during a fire. Their advice was ignored: now tens of thousands of people had to escape from one of the world's tallest buildings through thick smoke and down blackened stairwells.

Many people were crushed underfoot as panic began to spread. Hysterical men and women punched and kicked their way down the stairs. In a country fed a regular diet of disaster movies, it was almost inevitable that many would think they were facing death. Denise Bosco, a secretary, was working on the 82nd floor when the bomb exploded: 'The whole building shook. The lights flashed on and off, the computers went down. Then, instantly, there was smoke. I was terrified. People panicked. They started pushing and shouting to get out. Some of them were throwing up. I said, "Oh, dear God, what is it? Is it my time? Is this the way?"'[10]

Many of those in the towers evidently thought so. Rescue workers on the ground saw people hanging out of windows, apparently considering whether to jump. One man threw a hastily written note from one of the upper storeys addressed to his family. It said simply: 'I love you and will always love you.'[11]

Amid the panic there were great acts of heroism. Two men carried a female lawyer in a wheelchair down 66 storeys. Debbie Matut, a pregnant transmitter technician, was plucked off the roof of one tower by a police helicopter hovering 50ft above in powerful crosswinds.[12] But for most there was just a seemingly endless ordeal.

Peter Stanhope, a British banker working on the 85th floor, was trapped for hours. Many of his colleagues tried to escape down the stairs, only to find the lighting had been turned off to prevent electrical fires. 'We had very little communication from the outside world, bar what came in on the emergency telephone line,' he said. 'We closed the doors and put wet towels across the bottom of them.'[13] More than 200 five-year-old children were caught in the panic. One group of 70 children from a Brooklyn school was trapped in darkness in lifts for five hours before rescue arrived. Anna Marie Tesoriero, their teacher, sang 'This Old Man' and used her cigarette lighter to keep spirits high while children wept and vomited with fear.[14]

Calls flooded into emergency control rooms, television stations and radio programmes. The thousands of workers stuck in the towers were terrified. Was the basement on fire? Should they stay where they were? Should they brave the smoke and try to navigate the pitch-black stairways? In a panic, many smashed windows, showering lethal shards of glass on to the emergency services hundreds of feet below, and feeding the fires inside the building with oxygen. Flames began to roar out of control at the base of the building.

The New York City Fire Department sent a total of 750 vehicles to the explosion, and did not leave the scene for the next month.[15] It took hundreds of firefighters two hours to extinguish the blazes and more than five hours to evacuate both towers.

Christopher King walked down dozens of flights of stairs from the Dean Witter brokerage. 'Once we made that decision [to leave], some panic set in,' he admitted. 'There were no lights, so we put our hands on the person in front of us to see and made a human chain. As we headed down the stairs, it became hotter and hotter and you never knew if, when you turned a corner, there would suddenly be a wall of flames. *Towering Inferno* was in our minds all the way. When I reached the ground, my face was dark and sooty from the smoke, I was drenched in sweat, but all I cared about was being alive.'[16]

Among the last to leave was Peter Gseslad, a 26-year-old trader at Sumitomo Bank on the 96th floor. 'We were still trading after the explosion,' he said. 'We thought it was just lightning. We were told by the brokers we were doing deals with; they said, "Hey, there's smoke coming out of your building." '[17] Gseslad and his colleagues struggled down the stairs, some of them talking and conducting deals on their cellular phones on the way, but by the time they reached the 60th floor, 'people started freaking out': 'Lots of them just couldn't breathe. By the time we got down to 24 it was like a race. We just ran for it.'

Gasping for breath, their faces blackened by soot and muck, thousands of workers and visitors staggered out on to the street and collapsed into the snow, many of them hacking up blood from their lungs.

The bombing took six innocent lives. It also caused 1,042 injuries and more hospital casualties than any other event in domestic American history apart from the Civil War.[18] Many of those who escaped without apparent physical injury will be scarred mentally for life, and yet it is almost miraculous that in such a huge bomb attack even more were not killed or injured. More certainly would have perished had the bomb not been detonated during lunchtime, when many workers had left the twin towers. If it had exploded in the early evening, as thousands were returning to their cars in the underground garage, many hundreds might have died.

A persisting mystery is why the terrorists did not drive straight to the twin towers after leaving Willie Moosh's gas station and detonate the bomb earlier in the morning. Several of the gang were religious Muslims, indoctrinated by mullahs preaching hatred and murder, and some American investigators believe they went to another safehouse – one that has never been uncovered by the Federal Bureau of Investigation (FBI) – to pray and prepare.[19] Another theory is that Yousef tried to attack the headquarters of the United Nations, further up the east bank of Manhattan from the World Trade Center, but was prevented from getting close to the building by security officers.[20] The gang instead turned to their fall-back target – the twin towers.

As it was, some of the most serious casualties were found in the Port Authority Trans-Hudson (PATH) station underneath the Trade Center. One victim had three inches of bone exposed as rubble penetrated his back. 'We crawled under pipes when we arrived and everything was on fire,' said Edward Bergen, one of the first firefighters to enter the station.[21] 'Suddenly a guy came walking out of the flames like one of those zombies in the movie *Night of the Living Dead*. He was a middle-aged man and his flesh was hanging off.'

Neil E. Herman, the 46-year-old senior FBI Supervisory Special Agent in charge of the FBI-led Joint Terrorist Task Force (JTTF), was at his desk on the 28th floor of the FBI's New York headquarters when Yousef's bomb exploded.[22] A veteran anti-terrorist specialist with the appearance and demeanour of a seasoned poker player, Herman was brought up in St Louis, Missouri, briefly followed his father into journalism after leaving college, and then joined the FBI during a recruiting drive in the early 1970s. He spent 14 weeks at the FBI training academy in Quantico before transferring at the age of 25 to the Bureau's office in Miami, Florida – the 'Super Bowl of Crime'.[23] A year later Herman was transferred up the eastern seaboard to New York, and arrived in the city the day President Richard Nixon resigned from office.

New York has always been a theatre for terrorism. Within a few months of Herman's arrival in the Big Apple a wave of bomb attacks rocked the city, most perpetrated by the Puerto Rican independence movement. 'One thing led to another and I pretty much stayed in this programme [anti-terrorism] my whole career,' he said.[24]

Herman worked on terrorism cases throughout the 1970s, but it was not until May 1980 that a decision was taken to form a special Joint Terrorist Task Force to pool the resources of the FBI and New York Police Department (NYPD). The reason was simple: 'We were getting the hell kicked out of us,' said Herman. 'Basically we were competing with and against the NYPD, instead of working with them. It wasn't cost effective.'

The JTTF was formed with 25–30 investigators, originally just from the FBI and NYPD. Herman took over as supervisor in 1990, and by the time of the World Trade Center bombing the squad numbered 40–50 and comprised agents from the FBI, NYPD, the State Department, the Secret Service, the Immigration and Naturalisation Service (INS), the Federal Aviation Administration (FAA), the US Marshals Service, the Bureau of Alcohol, Tobacco, and Firearms (ATF), the New York State Police and the Port Authority of New York and New Jersey.[25]

The team was permanently on call from its Manhattan offices. 'We had police radios with us at all times and within about five to ten minutes of the [World Trade Center] blast we began to hear a series of communications,' said Herman. 'There was a flurry of activity that indicated there might have been a fire or a transformer explosion or something like that. Within about 15 minutes the activity began to increase. I walked down to the World Trade Center – about six or seven blocks away – with about half a dozen investigators, to determine the extent of the damage and see what happened.'[26]

Herman arrived at the scene around 12.45 p.m., less than half an hour after the explosion. 'It was a total madhouse,' he said. Hundreds of fire-trucks, police cars, ambulances, Port Authority vans and cars were blocking the roads around the massive complex. Herman and his team pushed through the crowds, flashed their identification, and conducted a quick survey of the scene. He could see that the Vista Hotel had been badly damaged, and that the road had buckled outside the complex. Gut instinct told him it was more than a transformer explosion, and within an hour of the blast he had issued instructions to open the command centre at FBI headquarters in the massive federal government building at 26 Federal Plaza.[27]

Herman's boss James Fox, the FBI Assistant Director in charge of the New York bureau, had been eating swordfish and chips for lunch at Harry's restaurant, a short walk to the north-east of the World Trade Center complex, when his pager began to bleep.[28] The veteran agent was walking to a public phone to respond when a friend who happened to be in the same restaurant told him a PATH train had derailed under the WTC. His office at 26 Federal Plaza gave him a few more details: they initially thought it was a transformer explosion.

Fox was a wily character. The lawyer son of a Chicago bus driver, he had spent most of his FBI career working in Counter-Intelligence and battling the KGB. He moved from smaller FBI offices in New Haven, Connecticut and San Francisco, to the larger bureaux, Chicago and Washington, before joining the New York bureau in 1984.[29] 'Some guys get into FCI [Foreign Counter-Intelligence] and it gets in your blood. It got in mine. Others want to break down doors and put handcuffs on people and get scumbags off the streets,' he said.[30]

Fox had spent so much time working in the shadows that the high-profile role of heading the FBI's New York bureau must have come as a shock. But he was still a reassuring figure, best known to New Yorkers for his comments the previous April on the conviction of John Gotti, the legendary mobster who strutted around New York in silk suits. Gotti, known as the 'Teflon Don', because prosecutors could never get anything to stick to him, was finally convicted on charges of murder and racketeering. 'The Teflon is gone,' Fox had told the cameras. 'The Don is covered with Velcro, and all the charges stuck.'

Like Herman, Fox was instantly suspicious of the reports that a transformer had exploded under the World Trade Center. 'I thought, "If this was a transformer explosion, it's the biggest one I've heard of." In this business, you wonder if it is an accident, or is it terrorist inspired?'[31]

Yet even among senior FBI agents there was still a natural reluctance to believe New York had joined the roll-call of international cities synonymous with terrorism. 'This sort of thing just doesn't happen in New York' seemed to be the prevailing wisdom. But violent death had hardly been a stranger in the city over the preceding couple of decades. Two weeks before the bombing six residents of the Bronx were lined up in an apartment block and shot through the head. A seventh victim of the same feud was shot dead outside the Bronx courthouse. Nor were terrorists strangers in southern Manhattan. Forty people died and more than 200 were injured when a bomb exploded during lunchtime on Wall Street in September 1920.

Fox wasn't taking any chances. He left his lunch in Harry's, walked quickly to his car, switched on its flashing red strobe-light, and drove the short distance to the World Trade Center. By the time he arrived the scene was already cluttered with dozens of fire-engines and ambulances. Fox decided the FBI command centre at 26 Federal Plaza would be the best place for him to direct the agency's response.[32]

Neil Herman had also made his way back to FBI headquarters and took a lift up to the command centre on the 26th floor. Although an adjoining operations centre is open all the time, the command centre, with video screens lining a wall and banks of desks and telephones, is only activated during a major crisis. From that moment the FBI command centre was manned 24 hours a day for the following six weeks.

As reports of the explosion circulated on TV and radio news, a spate of copycat hoax phone-calls were made to the police and FBI. At 4.25 p.m. a bomb warning sent police cars scurrying to the Empire State Building. Tens of thousands of visitors and workers were evacuated and the police spent hours checking for bombs. The state National Guard was put on full alert, and security was tightened at the United Nations, the Port Authority Bus Terminal, which received a 'general bomb scare' at 5.45 p.m., and New York's three airports – Newark, JFK and La Guardia. On a 'normal' day in New York City, the police expect to receive less than 10 bomb threats. Between 2 p.m. and 9 p.m. on 26 February 1993, they received 69.

Herman monitored the situation for several hours from the command centre, then rallied a group of senior agents and bomb technicians and headed back down towards the twin towers to try to examine the site. The damage was enormous: great slabs of masonry the size of small cars were still falling into a massive crater at the bottom of the complex, and by early Friday evening Herman had still seen only the periphery of the explosion.

Yet by 5 p.m. the FBI and NYPD were confident the damage had been caused by a bomb. Leslie E. Robertson, the original structural engineer of the World Trade Center, had been rushed down to the complex by police car from his office on East 46th Street, and was certain it was sabotage. Agents from the JTTF had also studied plans of the complex; there was nothing in the area of the explosion that could possibly have caused such devastation. There was no electrical transformer, no hidden gas-storage depot. It was a public parking area – it must have been a bomb. But nobody could be absolutely sure, because getting to the heart of the explosion was 'like finding a route down to hell'.[33]

The JTTF swung into action. A moment wasted could have given the bombers precious time to escape. Herman's investigators began by analysing the calls claiming responsibility for the bombing. At first there were rumours one had been received from the Serbian Liberation Front (SLF) a few minutes before the explosion, but when time-sheets were checked agents discovered the call was received at 1.35 p.m. – more than an hour later. A man with a foreign accent had rung the NYPD First Precinct, which houses the twin towers within its boundaries, and said the SLF was responsible. Out of more than 20 calls claiming responsibility in the hours following the attack, this was the only one treated seriously, partly because of the speed with which it was received (at that time the emergency services still thought there had been a transformer explosion) and partly because the caller took the trouble to ring a police station rather than the 911 emergency line.

There were other reasons to suspect Balkan involvement: the Pentagon had just announced it would start parachuting aid supplies into Bosnia, and America had been targeted before by Balkan extremists taking their internecine war across the Atlantic. Between 1968 and 1993 Croatian extremists conducted 26 separate attacks within the

United States in support of their claim for independence from Yugoslavia.

However, each call still had to be considered and analysed. Another 17 callers to 911 during Friday evening and Saturday morning claimed to know who was responsible, with blame attached to everyone from the Black Liberation Front to Colombian drug cartels. Neil Herman's team was not short of help; even Nita Lee, a 'psychic counsellor' from Oklahoma, contacted the authorities to offer details of 'mental images' she claimed to have about the bomb and the suspects.

The agents assembled in the FBI's command centre began to formulate theories. Perhaps the explosion was a botched presidential assassination attempt, suggested some agents. The US Secret Service, which guards the President, has its New York headquarters in the World Trade Center. Three Secret Service agents were injured – one of them, Pamela Russillo, was literally blown out of her shoes – and several Secret Service cars, including the bullet-proof limousine used by President Clinton during visits to New York, were destroyed. President Clinton had travelled in the car when he had visited the United Nations headquarters in eastern Manhattan the previous Monday. Perhaps, suggested one FBI agent, it was a device planted in the car that had detonated at the wrong time.

The theory was dismissed as the scale of the devastation became clear. The bomb would have been huge and conspicuous – it could never have been missed in security checks. There must have been another vehicle. Perhaps Mario Cuomo, New York's Governor, had been the target, suggested one agent. He had been due to leave his state car in the garage on level B-2 on Friday, but had cancelled a meeting in the Center only hours before the explosion.

'What about the Macedonians?' suggested another agent with a grasp of Balkan politics. An anonymous claim of responsibility had been received from a group acting 'for a former-Yugoslav republic'. That was part of the new name for Macedonia.

Later it was proposed that the bombing was a quick retaliation for the US bombing of the Al Rashid hotel in Baghdad, Iraq, on 17 January 1993. The Iraqi leader Saddam Hussein had invited a number of Islamic fundamentalist leaders from around the world to the hotel for a conference when the building was struck by a US missile. The Pentagon apologized for the attack and said it had been an accident, but CIA analysts thought one of the fundamentalists staying in the hotel could have decided to exact revenge and sent supporters to bomb the Vista Hotel.[34] 'They suggested the real target had been the actual hotel, and not the [twin] towers,' said a retired CIA official.[35]

Officials from the CIA and the State Department were soon channelling other theories into the FBI's command centre. On the same day as the World Trade Center explosion a bomb had been placed in a small coffee shop in Cairo, killing four people. It was one of the worst acts of political violence in the Egyptian capital for years – perhaps there was an Egyptian connection.

Another possibility, barely perceived in the immediate aftermath of the bombing, was that the motive might have been purely criminal. The bomb blew open the underground vaults of the Bank of Kuwait. An FBI agent tasked with checking this theory soon dismissed it: unless the robbers had been hopelessly inept such a device would never have been designed to break open a vault. Perhaps then, suggested another agent, it was just the building that was the target. The New York police were taking no chances. They began questioning Port Authority workers to see if anyone had a serious grudge against his or her employer.

Then there were Islamic militants, responsible for massive bombings in the Middle East. 'The modus operandi of the bombing was very similar to what we'd seen with Islamic extremists overseas, but we really didn't know. We looked at several different groups that we thought were capable of doing something like this,' said Neil Herman. 'We started to get a series of investigative leads, none of which really took us anywhere. And we were also analysing classified intelligence from overseas.'[36]

The FBI was initially drawn to the theory that Balkan extremists were responsible, and the hypothesis was bolstered when Herman's command centre was informed by agents of the Diplomatic Security Service, part of the State Department, that a bomb had been found in front of the American embassy in Zagreb, the Croatian capital, five hours before the World Trade Center explosion. The prevailing evidence was enough to establish a tenuous link to the Balkans. On Friday night four agents from the JTTF were sent to upstate Rockland County to watch the homes of Balkan activists already known to the FBI. Phone records were checked by 'pattern-searching' computers. JTTF agents back in Manhattan began trawling through a special computer database, containing more than 185,000 names of men and women from around the world suspected of involvement in terrorism.

Within 12 hours of the explosion the investigation was mushrooming, but technicians had still not found forensic evidence that confirmed the cause was a bomb. 'The massive amounts of communications and paper were almost overwhelming,' said Herman. 'Then there were regular briefings to people in Washington and of course to the White House.' Managing the investigators became a priority. 'One of the big mistakes in some of these investigations is that you have to be careful. You can burn people out very quickly. You have to put people in shifts and send them home. It has to be seen as a marathon – as a long run. On the first night by 4 a.m. we decided we wanted people to go home, change – if not get any sleep, and then be back by 6 or 7 a.m. People were wearing suits and ties, and they needed to be dressed down.'[37]

Herman himself rang his wife from his mobile phone to tell her he would be home 'when he could', then finally drove at around four in the morning to his home just outside Manhattan. He had a quick shower, changed, and was back in his office by 6 a.m.[38] His marathon was only just beginning.

References

[1] Information for this section comes from author interviews with US federal and state investigators, and Neil Herman, the FBI Supervisory Special Agent who ran the New York Joint Terrorist Task Force; also testimony given at the trial United States of America v. Mohammad A. Salameh et al., S593CR.180 (KTD), and Jim Dwyer, David Kocieniewski, Deirdre Murphy and Peg Tyre, *Two Seconds Under the World*.

[2] Moosh's testimony at the trial US v. Mohammad A. Salameh et al.

[3] Ralph Blumenthal, 'Fitting the Pieces of Terrorism', *New York Times*, 26 May 1993.

[4] Interview with Ismoil conducted by Jordanian police investigator Fayez Mohamed Qablan, 2 August 1995. US Government Exhibit 221-T, S593CR.180 (KTD).

[5] Dwyer et al., op. cit.

[6] Testimony of Dr Jacqueline Lee at the second World Trade Center bombing trial, 7 August 1997.

[7] Tony Burton, 'Disaster in the skyscraper', *Daily Mail*, 27 February 1993.

[8] 911 tape. Sourced from author interview with American investigator. Transcript of call also entered as evidence in the trial United States of America v. Mohammad A. Salameh et al., S593CR.180 (KTD), and reprinted in Dwyer et al., op. cit.

[9] Dwyer, op. cit.

[10] Peter Pringle and Patrick Cockburn, 'The Storming of Fortress America', *Independent on Sunday*, 28 February 1993.

[11] Jim Gallagher, 'Killer terror bomb traps 10,000 in World Trade towers', *Today*, 27 February 1993.

[12] Geordie Greig, 'The Two Faces Of Terror', *Sunday Times*, 27 February 1993

[13] 'I was trapped on level 85', *Today*, 27 February 1993.

[14] Greig, op. cit.

[15] Author interview with investigator, and Hugh Davies, 'America wakes up to the full horror of terrorism', *Sunday Telegraph*, 28 February 1993.

[16] Greig, op. cit.

[17] Ibid.

[18] Judge Kevin Duffy speaking during the first World Trade Center trial.

[19] Author interviews with American investigators.

[20] In a later tape-recorded conversation between Emad Salem, an undercover informant for the FBI, and Siddig Ibrahim Siddig Ali, a leader of another terrorist plot involving militants connected to Yousef, Salem said: 'I learned they originally wanted to bomb the Big House [a code they were using for the United Nations], and then it was changed to the World Trade Center.' Ali replied: 'Yes, exactly.' While awaiting trial Mahmud Abouhalima, one of the men arrested for the World Trade Center attack, told his cell-mate they had planned to detonate the bomb earlier in the morning but 'something went wrong'.

[21] Colin Smith and Yaroslav Trofimov, 'Terrorism comes to America', *Observer*, 28 February 1993.

[22] Author interview with Neil Herman.

[23] Ibid., and Ronald Kessler, *The FBI*.

[24] Author interview with Neil Herman.

[25] Ibid.

[26] Ibid.

[27] Ibid.

[28] Kessler, op. cit.

[29] James Fox left the FBI in 1993. He died in May 1997.

[30] Kessler, op. cit.

[31] Ibid.

[32] Ibid.

[33] Author interview with American investigator.

[34] Author interview with retired CIA official.

[35] Ibid.

[36] Author interview with Neil Herman.

[37] Ibid.

[38] Ibid.

TWO

Ground Zero

EVEN AS smoke rose from the World Trade Center, covering southern Manhattan like a light shroud, a lone figure stood watching from the Jersey City waterfront. Ramzi Yousef, a young Kuwaiti-born man known to many of his friends and conspirators as simply 'Rashid', had driven to a vantage point in New Jersey after leaving Manhattan. As tens of thousands of people in the twin towers choked on smoke and prayed for their lives, Yousef must have felt a stab of disappointment. The towers were still standing. Half a dozen men and women had perished in the bombing and America had been shaken to its core, but the towers were still there.

Yousef had planned differently.[1] In his reasoning, there was only one way of making America realize it was 'at war': the 'Great Satan' must suffer casualties similar to those inflicted on the Japanese at Hiroshima and Nagasaki.[2] His plan, stunning in scale, had been to topple one of the towers into the other, causing perhaps 250,000 fatalities in the entire WTC complex.[3] According to Yousef, only carnage on such a level would be sufficient punishment for supporting Israel, America's friend and ally, and the fundamentalists' sworn enemy because of its treatment of the Palestinians.

The US nearly paid the ultimate price for its friendship with Israel.[4] Each side of the twin towers is supported by 21 steel columns, and Yousef had tried to direct the explosion towards them by parking the van next to a wall in the basement that shielded a quarter of the support columns for Tower One, the northern building.[5] Yousef also designed a bomb that could shear through the columns: normal high explosives have a velocity of at least 3,000ft per second; Yousef's bomb exploded with a velocity of at least 15,000ft per second. At that speed

24

a person standing in southern Manhattan would be blown into Jersey City in less than a second.[6]

Yousef is an explosives genius. He enhanced his bomb's destructive force by adding aluminium azide, magnesium azide and by including bottled hydrogen bought from the AGL Welding Company. The blast sent one 12ft-long diagonal brace, used to lash the steel columns together, shooting through the room where Bill Macko, Robert Kirkpatrick and Steve Knapp were quietly enjoying their lunch. The brace weighed 14,000lbs. It landed 75ft from the steel columns.[7]

The towers swayed and reverberated, but despite the ferocity of the blast, they absorbed the explosion. To Yousef's lasting disappointment, neither crashed to the ground.

The people of New York should also thank fate that other elements of Yousef's plan went awry. Some investigators allege that he incorporated a container of sodium cyanide into the bomb in the hope it would be sucked up through ventilation pipes, stairwells and lift shafts in the north tower. This would have dramatically increased the number of fatalities, causing thousands of deaths, but the explosion incinerated rather than vaporized the sodium cyanide.[8]

Yousef wanted to buy more hydrogen tanks to increase the size of the bomb and make it 'more effective'.[9] He also wanted to use hydroxide gas and considered buying a truck, rather than a medium-sized Ryder van, to carry a larger bomb. But more tanks and a bigger van would have required more cash. His plans were stymied by nothing more than a lack of available funds.[10]

As it was Yousef's bomb came shockingly close to causing devastation. The carnage that would have resulted from one of the towers toppling into the other is barely imaginable, but the bomb nearly wreaked havoc in more subtle, insidious ways. The basement of the World Trade Center complex descends seven storeys into the earth, keeping out the dark waters of the Hudson River. Yousef's bomb weakened the internal structure of the protecting walls to such an extent that one of the crucial concrete slabs protecting the building slid down by several feet. There was consternation among the engineers who discovered the drop: they feared that the walls could have punctured, allowing millions of gallons of water to flood into the basement, rust the structural support columns and force the abandonment and destruction of the towers. Engineers worked quickly to brace the lowered concrete slab.

As he stood watching the smoking World Trade Center from the

Jersey City waterfront, Yousef could only imagine the havoc he had caused. For many terrorists the urge to wait and evaluate the scale of the damage would have been overwhelming, but Yousef was a professional: the young terrorist might have started one of the largest investigations in the history of the FBI, but he remained calm. He went home to his safehouse in Jersey City, packed his bags, and made his way to JFK airport. Most of southern Manhattan was still in utter chaos, but a $30 cab ride away the Pakistani International Airlines passenger lounge was an oasis of calm. Ramzi Yousef settled back into a comfortable chair in the first-class lounge and waited for his flight to Karachi, Pakistan.

It was Saturday morning before investigators managed to get deep inside the bowels of the World Trade Center to see the full extent of the damage. Leslie Robertson, one of the building's original designers, was one of the first, going in alone early in the morning. The guts of the building made an awesome sight. The air was choked with dust and oil particles, while great slabs of concrete dangled into the crater, suspended on the remnants of their internal reinforcing wire mesh; sections of floor still intact near the 200ft-wide crater were crumbling away, as if they had aged a thousand years overnight, and lumps of concrete slipped and crashed down into the dark void. The smell was appalling: 'We had two million gallons of sewage water pumped in on top of this. All of the fire extinguisher systems and the 30-inch sewer lines for the entire complex ruptured directly over the scene of the blast,' said David Williams, the FBI's senior bomb expert.[11]

Williams had arrived in New York that morning with the rest of the bomb squad from the laboratory at the FBI's Washington headquarters. Within hours he told James Fox and Neil Herman he was convinced the explosion had been caused by a bomb.

James Fox wanted to be sure and asked Williams how he could be so certain.

'I have examined ten thousand bombings,' said Williams simply.

'That's good enough for me,' replied Fox.[12]

As the man who would soon become the supervisor of the investigation into the bombing, Neil Herman also donned a helmet and protective equipment and crept inside the building. He had never seen anything like it. 'I don't think any of us had,' he said.[13] 'I got down fairly deeply into the crater area and had a good look at the lower levels. It was a case of crawling around on your hands and knees with a flashlight. I had seen some pretty horrific bombing scenes in the past, notably the La Guardia airport bombing in 1975, when 13 people were killed and 100 injured. But in my career, nothing came close to the World Trade Center.'

After the La Guardia bombing Herman had driven out from Manhattan along Grand Central Parkway on a cold December night to get to the airport. 'The traffic was backed up for about seven miles, and the last four or five miles I had to walk to get to the scene. It was total chaos.' Yet the state of the World Trade Center still came as a shock to him. 'It was immediately apparent to me when I got into the basement that, based on the several hundred cars destroyed, there had been a tremendous explosion that blew out and up. No way was it a transformer explosion.'

At 10 a.m. on Saturday 27 February, within 24 hours of the bombing, the senior representatives of more than a dozen city and federal agencies met in a briefing room at 26 Federal Plaza, the second-largest federal building in the United States.[14] Governor Mario Cuomo of New York was present, as was Ray Kelly, the avuncular Police Commissioner, a man who once worked in Macy's department store as a stock boy. James Fox from the FBI had a seat, as did officials from the Secret Service, the Bureau of Alcohol, Tobacco and Firearms (ATF), the Port Authority, the NYPD bomb squad and the US Attorney's office just across the road.

Officially, the explosion was still under the jurisdiction of the NYPD, but everyone at the meeting knew that it was a bomb and the case would soon be turned over to the FBI and Neil Herman's Joint Terrorist Task Force. 'It looks like a bomb. It smells like a bomb. It's probably a bomb,' said Governor Mario Cuomo that Saturday. 'There is an immense crater. It's difficult to imagine what did that if not a bomb.'[15] Experts on terrorism around the world were already warning that the bombing might have been the first major external attack on the American mainland. Bruce Hoffman, a terrorism expert working for the Rand Corporation who would later take over as director of the Centre for the Study of Terrorism and Political Violence at the University of St Andrews, Scotland, issued a chilling and remarkably prescient warning: 'We may be talking about the opening salvo of a new conflict for a New World Order.'[16]

Opening salvo or not, the bombers had to be caught, and the senior officials present at that meeting, and their legions of agents and investigators, all knew they could be in for a long slog. So the initial priority, as in any bombing, was to get to ground zero, the heart of the explosion, as quickly as possible. Without an obvious suspect, investigators need clues, and bombs, especially large bombs, always leave traces of their maker. The evidence may be microscopic, it may be buried under tonnes of concrete or dust, but dedicated investigators will sift through that rubble until they find it.

It is a process that can take months, even years. After 270 people died when Pan Am flight 103 exploded over Lockerbie in Scotland in 1988, police officers, soldiers and bomb technicians searched hundreds of square miles of countryside with simple instructions: 'If it's not alive or a rock, bag it.'[17] Bogs were drained, trees chopped down and leaves checked for wreckage. Eventually a fragment of a circuit-board the size of a small fingernail was found and matched to an identical board found in the timing mechanism of a bomb seized in Togo in 1986. The Swiss electronics firm that made the board admitted they had sold 20 to Libya, and two Libyans were eventually charged with the crime and finally flown to Holland to face trial in April 1999 – more than a decade after the bombing.

As Neil Herman sat in the FBI command centre after the WTC bombing he considered the likely course of his investigation. Agents might first find a few fragments of a mystery vehicle; perhaps part of a door, or chassis. If they were lucky, very lucky, they might find fragments and identify them as being part of the bombers' vehicle. Then, if their luck still held, they might be able to identify the vehicle, perhaps even its approximate age, and appeal to the public for help in tracing it. They would produce an identikit picture of the vehicle, based on an old library photograph of the make and model, and hope someone remembered selling such a van to some suspicious figure. But then, the van might have been stolen, and senior FBI agents would be running around the country like rookie cops looking for car thieves. It might take weeks, months, years; they might never find the car; they might never find the bombers. The greatest international terrorist assault on the United States might go unpunished. It was enough to keep senior investigators awake in their beds.

But luck would appear to be on the side of the detectives. On Sunday 28 February 1993, the day of the infamous raid on the Mount Carmel complex of Waco cult leader David Koresh, two days after the WTC bombing, a hastily convened meeting was held in the ballroom of the Vista Hotel. James Fox from the FBI stood up and announced that based on chemical analysis of the blast site, his agency had decided the cause of the blast was a bomb and would be taking over the investigation. All the evidence and any clues would be passed to the FBI, he said.

'I spent the first weekend down there at the scene,' recalls Neil Herman. 'And then by Sunday afternoon Mr Fox made the announcement that we'd determined it to be an act of terrorism, and then I moved back to Federal Plaza to co-ordinate the investigation.' At the time of the WTC explosion, there were between 40 and 50 investigators working for Herman on the JTTF. The core group of investigators he then assembled to handle the 'Tradebom' investigation, as it was code-named, was separated from their colleagues and reinforced with other staff. The total number of agents working on the case swelled to more than 70, with 'many more' helping from within the FBI and other agencies. 'There were several hundred people involved in the case at the beginning. When you have a major investigation, you really have to separate the team investigating it and sanitize them from everything else,' said Herman.[18] 'You can't convolute everything.'

David Williams, the head of the FBI's explosives team, immediately took responsibility for the bomb-site. He knew that Herman's team needed solid leads to pursue if they were to have any hope of catching those responsible, and more than 30 investigators from the NYPD, ATF and FBI were divided into several groups and sent into the building over the next few days in the hunt for clues.

Joseph Hanlin, a senior explosives enforcement officer from the explosive technology branch of ATF, was partnered up with Donald Sadowy, a detective from the NYPD bomb squad who happened to be one of the department's two resident experts on car-bombs.[19] The two men also had a chemist, a photographer, several technicians and even a sketch artist. After wrapping their bodies in two-piece white jumpsuits, helmets, respirators and gloves to protect against harmful chemicals, asbestos and leaking sewage, Hanlin's team began their descent into hell.

'It was controlled chaos,' said Neil Herman. 'You have to be really careful. You have to ensure that evidence you find can be retrievable two months, two years afterwards, perhaps for a prosecution.'[20]

Hanlin had spent more than 20 years as a bomb technician in the US Army before joining ATF, and had been trained on all types of bombs, including high explosives and rockets, toxic chemical bombs and even nuclear devices.[21] He had disarmed air bombs in Lebanon, helped dismantle dozens of Israeli high-explosive shells abandoned after the 1967 Six Day War, and was about as experienced a bomb technician as it is possible to find in a nation at peace.

His team began its search on the west side of the blast area, moving down to the lowest point in the building, the B-6 level. Slipping and sliding around amid the debris, Hanlin led the group around that level and over to the east side, where they then climbed back up to the B-2 level – 'ground zero'. 'What we were trying to do was just skirt the crater and get a feeling for the size of the crater and the amount of damage and what we were going to have to deal with . . . and also looking for likely places where there may be some explosive residues on vehicles . . .' said Hanlin.[22]

With the crater on their left, the team emerged on to B-2 level in the 'red' parking area and walked north past a ticket booth towards what was once the Secret Service parking area and the exit. Hanlin was now near the source of the explosion, standing at the end of a ramp leading down to where the Secret Service had parked the Presidential limousine. 'If I had gone to my right, I would have gone down into the Secret Service parking area. Had I gone to the left, I would have gone off the concrete and into the crater. It was an area where there were some vehicles parked against the wall, and there was an old escalator.'[23] The team could hear the sound of ticking (which must have been particularly eerie on a bomb-site), as many of the cars' indicator signals had been activated and were still working.

Guided by light from torches and lamps, Hanlin's team gingerly negotiated several piles of rubble and moved closer to the centre of the blast. Ahead of them were the shells of four or five cars. 'The car nearest the edge of the crater had suffered extensive blast damage, and it was severely crushed. Hoods were blown off, portions of fenders and doors were blown away,' said Hanlin. 'That vehicle had burned quite extensively. All of the rubber and most anything that was combustible in that vehicle had burned. The vehicles farther away had suffered – I believe, the one next to the severely burned vehicle was also burned, but the ones farther away had suffered just blast damage. They were crushed and pushed up against one another.'[24]

The area was still potentially lethal for the investigators. Great chunks of concrete were falling from the roof, but Hanlin was concentrating on finding the area closest to the blast. 'I wanted a vehicle that I thought was closest [to the explosion] . . . where we might be able to swab for possible residues. These residues would be taken back to a laboratory and analysed by a chemist,' he said.[25]

Hanlin was walking along the edge of the crater area when he spotted vehicle parts that looked slightly out of place. 'Most of the parts we had found had come from the blast-wave hitting the vehicles, so it would rip a hood off or crush the vehicle, or it would rip a fender or door handles, mirrors. The parts I found along this area were internal components for a vehicle.'

The first to catch Hanlin's eye was part of a gear assembly that was just lying on the ground. The second was the housing or cover for a gear assembly, and Hanlin realized the two parts must have been from the same unit. 'So when I saw these parts, I knew that they had to be right at the point of the explosion or blast, that they were not something that was ripped or removed from a vehicle that was parked in the garage; rather, they were exploded away from it.'[26]

A short distance away from these two parts, Hanlin spotted a crucial third bit of the vehicle – an actual differential housing. Before the bomb explosion the three components had all formed a single unit. 'This is forged steel,' Donald Sadowy said to Hanlin. 'Never in my life have I seen it ripped apart like this. To get blown apart this violently, they had to be sitting right underneath the bomb!'[27] Hanlin and Sadowy were breathless with excitement. They knew the parts must have been from the vehicle that had carried the bomb into the World Trade Center.

While other members of the team gathered around and shone their torches on the metal, Hanlin and Sadowy held it up to the light and looked for any identifiable marks. Gradually, as Hanlin ran the side of his glove across the metal, a series of dots and digits became visible. 'I think that's a VIN [vehicle identification number]!' shouted Sadowy through his mask. Hanlin and Sadowy had found the proverbial needle in the haystack – this one comprising more than 6,000 tons of debris. The two agents found a stretcher and carried the frame out of the building. They carefully put it into the back of an NYPD car, and sent it off to the FBI's laboratory on East 21st Street. It was a crucial breakthrough.

Finding that VIN so quickly can be attributed to a combination of skill and a fair amount of sheer luck. A small army could have spent weeks searching the rubble for clues, and then found only unidentifiable fragments of the bombers' vehicle. 'I vividly remember getting a phone-call from one of our bomb technicians who was working with

Hanlin, Jimmy Lyons, a very experienced bomb technician, and he called me and said we had a major break and gave me the information on the VIN number,' said Neil Herman.

It took Herman's agents just a few calls and computer checks to establish that the yellow van had been bought by Ryder, a vehicle hire firm with branches across the country. 'From that we determined through Ryder from where it had been rented,' said Herman: the DIB Leasing Agency at 1558 Kennedy Boulevard, Jersey City. 'Then I briefed Jim Fox and various other management people, and we immediately notified our office over in New Jersey and set up surveillance.'[28]

With every piece of good news the investigators wondered how long their luck would last. Surely anyone who bombed the World Trade Center would have stolen the van, or at least ensured it would be untraceable. But the van had not been stolen. It had been hired by a man called Mohammad Salameh with an address in Jersey City. From his command centre in 26 Federal Plaza, Neil Herman contacted his colleagues in the New Jersey FBI bureau, who raced to Jersey City to interview employees at the branch.

Surely the name Salameh was false, thought the agents – he must have used an alias and false documents. But when JTTF agents ran a check on his name they found Salameh appeared on their massive computer database as someone who had demonstrated on behalf of a convicted terrorist a few years previously. Then staff at the leasing agency told the agents Salameh had actually returned to the office since the bombing to claim a refund on the van, which he said had been stolen the night before the explosion. Staff had told him to get an incident number from the police, and he was due back in a few days.

Salameh, it would later transpire, needed the deposit money to upgrade an airline ticket and escape from New York.[29] With his last few dollars Salameh had bought a $65 infant's ticket for Royal Jordanian flight 262 to Amman in Jordan, via Amsterdam, dated 5 March. The ticket had helped earn him a Dutch visa, but he needed the cash from the van deposit to upgrade his ticket and pay for an adult fare.

'Why would anyone try to claim their money back on the van?' wonders Neil Herman. 'Well you have to understand there was not a vehicle left. People think we put it together, but anyone who was involved in this [bombing] would not have thought there would be anything left. Having said that I think it shows the brazen side of some of these people, plus Salameh was not necessarily one of the brightest people in the world.'[30]

On the morning of 4 March 1993, Mohammad Salameh, a simple and impressionable militant who had fallen under Ramzi Yousef's control, shuffled through the car park of the DIB Leasing Agency and pushed open the door of the rental office. He looked tired, with a wisp of a beard, and was walking with a slight hunch.[31]

'Hello,' said Patrick Galasso, the manager.

Salameh greeted him in return and began stammering through a story about leaving the key to the van at his home. Galasso just nodded politely, and led him over to FBI agent William Atkinson, who was working undercover – posing as an area manager of the rental company.

'I'm with the, erm, loss prevention unit at, erm, Ryder,' said Atkinson, 'and I work out of New Brunswick and we try to settle claims without . . .'

'Yes,' interrupted Salameh.

'. . . a lot of problems,' continued Atkinson. 'But what we've done, we, there's a lot of stolen cars in New Jersey . . .'

'Yes,' said Salameh again.

'. . . more than any other state in the union.'

'Yes,' said Salameh. 'And New Jersey I called.'

This was going to be difficult, thought other agents who were listening in on the conversation. 'What we're trying to do, we're trying to put an end to that, and we're doing it by help of our customer representative and our customers. Maybe you can help us, if I can just get some information,' said the FBI agent.

'I will tell you now what's happened?' asked Salameh, in his heavily accented English.

'All right, let me, let me just run through this and it will take you . . .' said Atkinson before Salameh interrupted. The little Arab was determined to state his case.

'Today's Thursday,' said Salameh.

'Yeah.'

'Like this day, but in the night, ah, I go again to increase my language,' Salameh said.

This was farcical, thought other agents.[32] Atkinson struggled on regardless. He moved a form across the desk, and prompted Salameh to explain that he had rented the van on 23 February, and that it had then been stolen from the car park of the Pathmark plaza shopping centre just two days later. Salameh had only realized the van had gone when he came back from his shopping laden with parcels.

'How many parcels did you have?' asked Atkinson.

'In, inside it?' queried Salameh.

'Were you carrying.'

'Ah, three. Three bags. Three small, small, eh.'

'Three bags,' repeated Atkinson, apparently trying to make this sound suspicious.

'Yeah.'

Perhaps he was trying to lighten the mood, but Atkinson then thought he would try a joke. 'Three bags full, sorta like, ah . . .'

'What you . . .' interrupted Salameh.

'Baa, baa, black sheep, have you any wool . . .' said the agent.

The joke bombed.

'Yeah,' said Salameh, without the slightest understanding of what this strange man was talking about. Atkinson decided to let Salameh do the chatting. It took a few minutes, but eventually he told his garbled story, claiming he had hired the van to help a friend move home. When it had been stolen it was loaded with a few chairs and a table. Atkinson took notes. Confirming Salameh's name took another minute, but then Salameh decided he wanted extra money because he had filled the van's petrol tank just before it had been stolen.

'I want justice,' said Salameh defiantly.

Atkinson decided to try a few more questions.

'But what did you do after the van was stolen? How did you move?'

'Well, I didn't.'

'You didn't move?'

'Move for what?'

'You didn't move after the van got stolen?' asked Atkinson.

'No, I moved now.'

'Oh, did you? How did you do it?'

'Yes.'

'Did you get another van?'

'By my friends, yeah,' said Salameh.

'Okay.'

'Yes.'

'All right. Moved aided by . . .'

'Yeah, by my friends.'

'Okay.'

'Yeah, I want [to] tell you one . . .'

'Okay, just give me . . .'

'His name is Adel. A-D-E-L.'

'Adel?'

'Yes. Mohammad.'

'Uh-hum.'

'His last name Mohammad. Yeah.'

'Okay.'

Now it was down to a discussion about money. Atkinson said he was prepared to offer $200 for a refund.

'Is not justice!' said Salameh. 'This is not justice!'

'Well, but it's business,' said Atkinson helpfully.

'I know business, but eh, eh, I need justice, some justice. I paid $400, he told me I need deposit. No justice! We need justice now!'

'All right,' said Atkinson, 'how about $250? Would that get you out of here, $250? Now we're taking, we're taking the burden.'

'Now listen to me,' said Salameh. 'Now. I have a good idea. Eh, two days and a half, two days and a half.'

'Is $200,' said Atkinson. 'Half of four hundred dollars is two hundred dollars.'

'That's good.'

'Okay.'

'I see this is justice.'

'Okay, that makes sense,' said Atkinson, as Salameh argued himself out of the extra $50 the FBI agent had just been offering.

There were more discussions about how much petrol had been in the tank, when the key to the van would be returned, and then finally Salameh started to leave. 'This is, I see this is justice,' he said. 'Thank you for, ah, see, what's your name?'

'Bill,' replied Atkinson.

'Bill, thank you very much,' said Salameh with conviction. Atkinson would be the last person Salameh ever spoke to as a free man.

Neil Herman wanted to wait and watch, in the hope Salameh would lead the FBI back to where he was living, but news of the operation had leaked to local TV news stations and the press. One New York newspaper even printed a story that morning identifying the bomber's van as a Ryder vehicle and naming the DIB Leasing Agency as the hire centre. Even as armed FBI agents were hiding and waiting for Salameh, a TV news crew appeared at the front gate. Patrick Galasso ran out and told them they had the wrong address, and the van drove off, but the FBI knew they had no hope of keeping the operation secret or tailing Salameh for more than a few hours. 'The decision was made to arrest him,' said Herman. 'We still don't know if there was another safehouse that he was at we don't know about. I always felt that there was probably one or two other safehouses out there that we may have missed. You never know.'

Salameh walked out of the office carrying his money, and all hell broke loose. Radios quietly crackled, van doors flew open, and dozens of FBI agents leapt from their hiding-places. 'FREEZE!! FREEZE!! DON'T MOVE!!' they screamed at the bewildered Arab. Salameh was cuffed, bundled into the back of a waiting FBI car between two burly agents, and driven off. The FBI had made its first arrest on the case.

'We knew that catching Salameh was a significant turn,' said Neil Herman. 'The key was what Salameh had on his person, because they spring-boarded us down other investigative avenues. He had identification on him, he had a driver's licence, he had addresses of locations where phones could be traced, bank cards which gave us details of bank accounts. We were off to the races.'

Even as the operation at the DIB Leasing company was being prepared, the staff of another rental company in Jersey City were uncovering more damning evidence of Ramzi Yousef's sophisticated bombing operation.

Yousef and Salameh had rented locker no. 4344 at the Space Station storage centre in New Jersey in the weeks before the bombing. It became a central 'spare parts' repository for the World Trade Center bomb, but staff at the centre had become suspicious of the two men. Just days before the attack on the twin towers, David Robinson, the assistant manager of the storage station, had spotted Yousef and Salameh accepting delivery of a consignment of several 4ft-tall hydrogen gas tanks, which for safety reasons featured prominently on a list of items prohibited from storage. After remonstrating with the men Robinson had eventually relented and allowed them to keep the tanks on the site for half an hour while they waited for a friend to arrive in a yellow Ryder van. They loaded them into the van and left.

Staff at the Space Station were highly trained, had a sense of duty and took pride in their work, describing themselves as 'self-storage consultants'.[33] One of Robinson's colleagues mentioned he had seen them carrying what appeared to be containers of chemicals into the centre a week before. Robinson mentioned his concerns to Doug Melvin, the manager of the Space Station, who decided to resolve the issue. Headquarters at Tennessee had a master-key for the locker. Melvin rang his superiors, explained the situation, and arranged for the key to be delivered to his office.

Melvin and Robinson were still waiting for the key when they heard news of the World Trade Center bombing. They watched from outside their New Jersey office as black smoke billowed out of the massive buildings just across the Hudson River. Later that night, several news reports mentioned that a bomb could have been responsible; then there was talk of the culprits – perhaps they were from the Balkans, said one report. 'No,' said another expert, 'more likely they're Middle Eastern – Arabic.' Melvin's blood ran cold.

'I'm thinking: "It couldn't be them, could it?"' he said. 'But something told me it probably was.'[34]

Melvin rang his friend John Pelesko, who had some understanding of physics and chemistry, and had worked previously as an engineer. Melvin wanted to get some idea of whether his suspicions were well founded before dragging the FBI down to the storage station. On the night of Thursday 4 March, Pelesko finished teaching classes in applied mathematics at the New Jersey Institute of Technology, where he worked as a graduate student, and drove down to see Melvin for a chat.[35] Late that night Pelesko and Melvin opened the door of locker 4344 and discovered a makeshift laboratory.

Pelesko remembers: 'We found several containers in the space containing ... [or labelled] ... nitric acid, sulphuric acid, urea. We found a garbage can filled with chemical-looking glassware, tubes, some bags. There were several boxes or crates in there that I did not see any labels on, but we didn't lift them up to look at them.'[36] There were also several strangely discoloured rings on the floor of the locker. The men looked around for ten minutes, then locked the door and left. Pelesko was hungry after spending all day in classes, so they went to a restaurant for dinner, discussed what they had found, then parted company just after 11 p.m. When Pelesko arrived home an hour later he looked up the chemicals they had seen in his chemistry and science reference books.[37]

When Melvin and Pelesko next spoke on the phone, John Pelesko had no doubts. 'This shit is dangerous,' he told Melvin.[38]

The following morning Melvin rang the New Jersey office of the

FBI, and agents arrived at the storage centre within an hour. Based on an affidavit provided by Special Agent Eric Pilker, a magistrate judge in the District of New Jersey issued a search warrant for the shed on 5 March. Inside the FBI found sodium azide, sodium cyanide, two bottles of methenamine, seven glass bottles, beakers, shotgun powder, funnels, glassware, urea, wire, sulphuric acid, 13 bottles of nitric acid, a transfer pump and potassium nitrate. Salameh's fingerprints were found on a bottle of shotgun powder, a 50lb (23kg) bag of ammonium nitrate, a glass beaker, a clear plastic bottle, duct tape, and on a brown bottle of a chemical known as aniline reagent. Yousef, as was his way, had been more careful. Only two of his fingerprints were found in the locker: on a brown bottle of sodium azide, a propellant.

The first concern for the agents gingerly examining the contents of the locker was that they might explode and pump poison gas into the air over New Jersey. After discussing the various options with the police and other explosives experts the FBI loaded the chemicals into bomb-containment vessels and took them to Liberty State Park in New Jersey to be destroyed. Fifteen bomb technicians from the FBI, ATF and police arranged for a secure cordon to be thrown around a quiet area of the park, then they rigged three explosive charges to destroy the chemicals, and retired to a safe distance. When the agents and technicians were about three-quarters of a mile away, the devices exploded. 'We heard a tremendous explosion and a tremendous vibration on the ground,' said FBI Agent Don P. Haldimann, a bomb technician.[39] The blast completely destroyed a precious $18,000 bomb-containment vessel.

Now the dominoes started to fall. Just after 2 p.m. on 4 March the FBI searched Mohammad Salameh's tiny apartment at 34 Kensington Avenue, Jersey City, an area hosting a large number of expatriate Arabs.[40] The raid yielded the young radical's briefcase, photographs of him and his friends and a telephone: 'Once we had the location we found the telephone records,' said Neil Herman. JTTF agents quickly subpoenaed the local phone company to provide detailed records of all calls made on the phone.

With the computerization of telephone exchanges massive files can be kept by phone companies detailing calls made and received. For law enforcement agencies these records are a goldmine. They can provide other addresses, other contacts and suspects – particularly helpful in massive and complicated investigations such as the World

Trade Center bombing. 'There are several things you can do; you can get a toll record of the calls for say six months or a year, that the people used, who they called and what calls came in. That's stored at the phone company and we can get them with a subpoena,' said Herman.

FBI agents in Federal Plaza checked the calls made from Salameh's apartment, then ran pattern-searching computer programmes to identify suspicious numbers, and obtained more subpoenas to check telephone numbers called from those addresses. JTTF agents obtained lists of telephone calls made from the safehouses where Ramzi Yousef and his gang had lived, and even from payphones in the streets outside their houses and at JFK airport, in case any of the gang had made calls as they fled.[41] All of those numbers – both prior to and subsequent to the bombing – were then 'dumped' into the pattern-searching computers.

As well as obtaining toll records and court authorization to tap the phones of some of those they suspected of being linked with Salameh, Herman's team also took out more basic 'Pen' registers on some phones. 'A "Pen" register records all the calls that are made from a particular phone while it's still active,' explains Herman. So when anyone made a call on a phone tagged with a 'Pen' register the number would be recorded and given to the FBI. The telephone database created during the WTC investigation eventually became 'rather massive', according to Neil Herman, so huge that three or four agents worked full time uploading numbers into computers, '… running those leads out, identifying who the calls went to, running their names. We had databanks on the WTC that are probably unparalleled.'[42]

Ramzi Yousef spent thousands of dollars on phone-calls during his time in the US, ringing terrorist contacts in the Middle East, the Philippines and Pakistan. Even now, many years after the bombing, the FBI is still using the database of telephone numbers from the World Trade Center investigation to track terrorists in America and across the world. 'Even up to this point it's a database that's been very helpful,' admits Herman.

The Feds quickly identified other addresses and suspects. They then searched those properties, arrested suspects, interviewed witnesses and found local people who could identify other suspects. 'We did about 17 searches in the next few weeks, and each location opened up more addresses – sort of like compounded interest.' After

Salameh's capture one of the first names to crop up was that of the red-haired giant, Mahmud Abouhalima.

'By the middle of the first week we were beginning to fan out with names from ticket manifests on people that had fled.' Abouhalima had flown from New York to Saudi Arabia four days after the bombing, and then flown to his parents' home in Egypt. 'We traced him through a series of investigative leads, and tickets, and people that he had worked with at his car service, and then the Egyptian authorities did the rest – in more ways than one,' said Herman. Abouhalima was taken into custody by the Egyptians and viciously tortured because of his connections to Islamic militants campaigning against the Egyptian government.

By the time he was flown back to New York, several more of the principal conspirators involved in the World Trade Center bombing were also in custody. Nidal Ayyad, who had procured chemicals for the bomb, was arrested on 10 March, and Ahmed Ajaj, a friend of Yousef's (they would later learn) who had offered advice on building the bomb, was arrested shortly after he was released from jail for other offences.

The FBI did, however, make some mistakes. At 34 Kensington Avenue they interviewed Abdul Yasin, a graduate student in engineering at City College, New York, who was born in Bloomington, Indiana, to Iraqi parents. He appeared to be shocked by what had happened, and gave the FBI another address at 40 Pamrapo Avenue, New Jersey, which the FBI raided the next day. Yasin told the FBI he had taught Salameh to drive the Ryder van just a few days before the bombing, and he impressed the agents with his helpful attitude. They thanked him and let him go, thinking he was on their side as a 'co-operating witness'. Instead Yasin flew to Jordan the next day, then travelled across the border and on to Baghdad.

In August 1993 Yasin was indicted on charges of plotting the attack with Yousef and of helping to mix the bomb. He is now believed to be living with his family and working for the Iraqi government. Since he returned to Iraq Yasin has spoken to FBI agents on the telephone, but he refuses to return to New York. The FBI have put a $5 million reward on his head.

'[Yasin] was not a major player . . . but he was someone that was part of the team,' said Neil Herman. 'I don't want to use the word gopher, but I think he was more of a helper, soliciting and helping. But with hindsight allowing him to move around was a mistake.'

It was a rare error in the investigation. Cuffs were snapped on to militant after militant and the evening news and the morning papers were full of stories of FBI successes – but Neil Herman and his agents knew their probe was far from over.

They had uncovered a small cabal of Muslim militants who had assembled and detonated a massive bomb in the World Trade Center, but there was still someone missing: Herman's agents were sure there was a mastermind of the operation who had escaped their dragnet. When they began checking through interviews with other residents of buildings containing the gang's safehouses they began to hear rumours of another mysterious young man, an 'Iraqi', a man called 'Rashid'. It was the first reference to the man who would become known to the world as Ramzi Yousef.

'Yousef's name first cropped up in interviews at some of the locations, where people were able to come up with names and we produced sketches of Salameh and his friends,' said Herman. 'People in the apartment blocks were coming up with names, and Yousef appeared to be one of the major players right from the beginning.'

When Abouhalima was returned to America from Egypt he was also able to provide a little more information. The bearded giant realized he was in serious trouble and during an interview on the plane back with Louis Napoli, a NYPD detective on the JTTF, he asked if the US agents knew someone called 'Rashid'. As with each name or alias they discovered, Herman's team checked it against the ticket manifests for all flights leaving airports near New York for several weeks before and after the bombing. 'We were able to see that Yousef left on the night of the 26th and we were able to trace him back to Pakistan,' said Herman. 'After we traced his exit from the ticket stubs we could trace back and find when he arrived. It took some time for us to digest the results of some of the searches and some of the forensic examinations, but we knew by mid-March that he was a key player.'[43]

Although the JTTF investigation was still in its infancy, Herman's team had gathered enough material to charge Yousef with the bombing and circulate details of his aliases and crimes around the world. 'At that stage we put out all the information, descriptive data on Yousef, to include his fingerprints, his known aliases, his history and set out leads throughout the world, emphasizing the places we knew he had been to in the past. We set up our teams and started co-ordinating with the law enforcement services in those countries, Pakistan, London, and other countries where we had leads.'

Neil Herman then began going through the evidence. By the second week of the investigation the massive amounts of paperwork and documents flooding into his office in 26 Federal Plaza had become 'overwhelming'. 'I can remember many times going home at around four o'clock in the morning and coming back at seven or eight [a.m.] and the incoming communications were really in their thousands,' said Herman. 'It's not like you'd have a stack of mail and you'd go through it and not have any more mail for the next few days, you're talking about every field division in the FBI in the US – 59 offices – and every LEGAT [FBI Legal Attaché] around the world was involved. There was a tremendous amount of intelligence being developed by every foreign government and every foreign intelligence service on this.'

One of the priorities was to obtain a photograph of the prey. Because Yousef used his own passport when leaving the United States after the bombing the FBI was able to establish exactly when he had arrived in the country. Yousef had entered the US the previous year and claimed asylum; a copy of his passport had been taken and filed away. When Immigration and Naturalisation Service (INS) agents found it they discovered visas and stamps which indicated Yousef had travelled to Britain several times between 1986 and 1989. Stamps from Swansea police station (aliens department) in South Wales, dated 19 September 1988, confirmed he had been a student in the city, and detectives from Scotland Yard and South Wales Police Special Branch were asked to uncover his life in the country. Herman recalls: 'We got photographs of him from his educational background, some of which were dated. Some came back from Swansea. Some came back from when he attempted to claim political asylum, from the INS and the State Department. You would be surprised how many times a person is photographed as they come and go around the world.

'We were also able to pin-point a number of phone-calls that had been made, and we began computerizing all the phone-calls that had been made from the safehouses leading up to the incident. And those phone-calls became very important in identifying Yousef's associates. We wanted to identify where the calls had been made to, and then identify the people they had been made to, and then we would make contact with the law enforcement agencies in those countries and see if the people were known to them.'[44]

Neil Herman's team notified Interpol and issued a special international 'Red Notice' for their new suspect, alerting other governments to the hunt for Yousef. On 2 April 1993, the FBI's famous 'Ten Most Wanted List' was extended to 11 to accommodate the new quarry. Ramzi Ahmed Yousef instantly became the most wanted man in the world.

References

[1] According to Secret Service Agent Brian Parr, who interrogated Yousef in February 1995.

[2] Yousef's comments during his trial for the WTC bombing.

[3] Author interview with an American investigator.

[4] During the trial United States of America v. Mohammad A. Salameh et al., S593CR.180 (KTD), Judge Kevin Duffy said: 'If the bomb had the explosive force that you envisioned, placed as it was at the base of the north tower next to a diagonal brace, you might have succeeded in your nefarious plot to topple over the north tower into the south tower just like a pair of dominoes.'

[5] Yousef and Parr, op. cit.

[6] Comments of Judge Kevin Duffy, 24 May 1994, United States of America v. Mohammad A. Salameh et al., S593CR.180 (KTD).

[7] Jim Dwyer, David Kocieniewski, Deirdre Murphy and Peg Tyre, *Two Seconds Under the World*.

[8] During his summing-up in United States of America v. Mohammad A. Salameh et al., S593CR.180 (KTD), Judge Kevin Duffy said: '... death is what you really sought to cause. You had sodium cyanide around, and I'm sure it was in the bomb. Thank God the sodium cyanide burned instead of vaporizing. If the sodium cyanide had vaporized it is clear what would have happened is the cyanide gas would have been sucked into the north tower and everybody in the north tower would have been killed. That to my mind is exactly what was intended.' Neil Herman, however, does not believe cyanide was included in the bomb.

[9] JTTF interview with Yousef.

[10] Yousef and Parr, op. cit.

[11] Quoted by J. Gilmore Childers, Senior Trial Counsel, in a memorandum to Mary Jo White, US Attorney, dated 26 February 1997.

[12] Ronald Kessler, *The FBI*.

[13] Author interview with Neil Herman.

[14] The Pentagon is the largest.

[15] Geordie Greig, 'America's confidence shattered by bomb blast', *Sunday Times*, 28 February 1993.

[16] Michael Pye, 'No longer safe as houses in America's frontyard', *Scotsman*, 1 March 1993.

[17] Author interview with US investigator.

[18] Author interview with Neil Herman.

[19] Dwyer et al., op. cit.

[20] Author interview with Neil Herman.

21 Testimony of Joseph Hanlin at the first World Trade Center trial.
22 Ibid.
23 Ibid.
24 Ibid.
25 Ibid.
26 Ibid.
27 Dwyer et al., op. cit.
28 Author interview with Neil Herman.
29 Ibid.
30 Ibid.
31 Sourced from author interview with American investigator. A transcript of the recording was also entered as evidence in the trial United States of America v. Mohammad A. Salameh et al., S593CR.180 (KTD). A longer version can be found printed in Dwyer et al., op. cit.
32 Author interview with US investigator.
33 Testimony by the storage consultants at the first World Trade Center trial.
34 David Kocieniewski, 'Something Cooking', *New York Newsday*, 5 March 1994.
35 Court testimony of David Robinson and John Pelesko, United States of America v. Mohammad A. Salameh et al., S593CR.180 (KTD).
36 Ibid.
37 Testimony of John Pelesko.
38 Dwyer et al., op. cit.
39 Testimony of FBI Agent Don P. Haldimann to the second World Trade Center trial.
40 Court testimony of FBI agent James A. Kyle.
41 Author interview with Neil Herman.
42 Ibid.
43 Ibid.
44 Ibid.

THREE

Manhunt

AFTER RAMZI Yousef was identified as the likely mastermind of the World Trade Center bombing, a team of senior FBI investigators was assembled in New York to track him down. Neil Herman split his Tradebom unit into sections so that each defendant was investigated by a team of Joint Terrorist Task Force agents. 'We wanted to know who they had come into contact with, who they had touched, their history, their associates, where were they from, where they had travelled to, everything,' he said.[1]

Yousef was given special treatment: half a dozen agents were assigned to his case, their task to build up the evidence against Yousef, find him, capture him, arrange an extradition, get him back to the US and secure a conviction in a US court. It was a tall order, but the agents were still required to give Herman daily briefings and explain and justify the leads they had been following.[2]

Herman was lucky to have several senior investigators on the Yousef team, including Frank Pelligrino, an outstanding FBI Special Agent with a dry sense of humour, and Brian Parr, an agent with the Secret Service ('a rock of Gibraltar – a real solid investigator', according to one colleague on the JTTF),[3] which is traditionally more famous for guarding the President.[4] The two men were joined by Charles 'Chuck' Stern, a youthful FBI agent and former bomb technician who distinguished himself in the investigation for his thorough and meticulous work. 'We had a few key people on him,' confirms Herman.[5] The lead investigators were backed up by detectives and agents from the NYPD, INS, State Department and Port Authority.

However, by the time the team had assembled, Ramzi Yousef was safely ensconced in a safehouse in Quetta, the capital of the wild

Pakistani province of Baluchistan, and a virtual oasis enclosed by bleak and arid mountains.

Yousef had left New York using a passport bearing his real name: Abdul Basit Karim. He landed in Pakistan's largest city, Karachi, flushed with the success of his operation, and boarded a connecting flight to Quetta, where he had left his young wife and baby daughter.[6] The mastermind was returning home, and it was, for anyone seeking security, a near-perfect destination. Nestling 1,700 metres above sea level on the main trade routes between Iran, Afghanistan and the subcontinent, Quetta is the legendary stronghold of the western frontier, a city of nomadic traders just across the border from the Afghan town of Kandahar. It is a city without proper maps, road signs or government; the police would never notice another transient soul in a city of half a million strangers.

Yousef also had plenty of friends in Quetta who were happy to shield and protect him from inquisitive outsiders. There was Haji Akhtar Mohammad Bareeh, who owned a suburban timber depot,[7] and Abu Safian, a young Pakistani who was brought up in Jordan, where his father worked until 1984. Safian, then in his late twenties, had fought alongside the mujaheddin in Afghanistan, but by the time Ramzi returned to the city he was living in a slum area of Quetta with his two younger brothers, and heading the United Arab Emirates Red Crescent Society in the city.[8]

It would be weeks and months before Neil Herman's team could begin piecing together Yousef's background. But they quickly realized many of the leads went back to Pakistan, and the agents knew they needed to establish healthy relationships with Pakistani law enforcement agencies and those of other countries where they suspected Yousef might be hiding. From Washington, senior FBI agent John Lipka began forging alliances overseas.

Lipka was the perfect man for the job. A former minor-league baseball player who joined the FBI, founded the Joint Terrorist Task Force in the Washington Metropolitan Field Office, and then became a senior figure in the FBI's Counterterrorist Section, Lipka had travelled in Asia and studied Farsi and Arabic.[9] His top priority was developing links in Pakistan, where the authorities are not always renowned for co-operating with the US. Luckily for the FBI, one of Pakistan's most senior policemen, Rehman Malik, a Director of the Federal Investigation Agency (FIA), the Pakistani equivalent of the FBI, was assigned to the case.[10]

'As time went on and we became more knowledgeable of [Yousef's] background, travel and aliases, more and more information was being disseminated around the world,' said Herman. 'We were trying to develop information on him that had to be checked and tracked down. Many of the leads we followed were in Pakistan and on the Afghan border, and all roads seemed to lead back to the Baluchistan area.' Herman sent his JTTF out to the area on several trips. 'It was very difficult. Many of the leads turned out to be fruitless, but they had to be pursued.'

Rehman Malik proved crucial.[11] A dogged and tenacious investigator, known for working 24-hour stretches on difficult cases, Malik soon made headway.[12] Through his contacts among young militant Muslims, Malik traced some of Yousef's relatives and had them interviewed by agents from the FIA. The relatives disclosed details of Yousef's home in Quetta, and Malik sent a C-130 plane with a crack team of officers and two agents from the US Diplomatic Security Service to raid the house. They arrived just a few hours too late. Yousef had slipped away the day before.[13]

Yousef's immediate movements after he left his Quetta home remain unclear. However, a CIA official and Pakistani intelligence sources claim he was hidden in a safehouse and received help and financing from two Quetta-based senior representatives of one of the wealthiest and most powerful men in the militant Islamic world: Osama bin Laden.

American intelligence files on Osama bin Laden date back to the 1980s, when the US viewed him as an ally and funded him and other rebels battling against Soviet troops in Afghanistan. But in the weeks after the World Trade Center bombing Neil Herman's JTTF agents began to uncover evidence he had started plotting against the United States.

The links between Yousef and bin Laden have always been shrouded in secrecy and confusion. Bin Laden himself has claimed that he never knew Yousef before the World Trade Center explosion. 'Unfortunately, I did not know him before the incident,' he has said.[14] Perhaps he did not know Yousef personally, but investigators believe Yousef received support and funding from bin Laden via his relatives and associates. Neil Herman certainly remembers that bin Laden's name cropped up early on in the Tradebom investigation.

'The first connection with bin Laden came in connection with some phone records overseas, connecting either Yousef or possibly one of his family members,' said Herman. 'That's my recollection of the first connection with Osama bin Laden.' Five years later FBI investigations into bin Laden would develop into a massive operation involving hundreds of FBI agents and intelligence officials, but after the World Trade Center bombing in 1993, says Herman, bin Laden's name and reference was just 'one of thousands of leads that we were trying to run out'.[15] Initially the connection appeared tenuous.

Dozens of court orders for wiretaps and Pen registers were taken out by Herman's team during their investigations, enabling agents to retrieve phone records 'to see what calls were made and to what location'. After a thorough analysis the FBI discovered that calls had been made between the safehouse where Yousef was living during his preparations for the World Trade Center bombing and Osama bin Laden.[16]

There were other close connections between the two men. After raiding Yousef's home in Quetta, Rehman Malik's FIA agents traced his uncle Zahid Al-Shaikh, a brother of Yousef's mother, to the town of Peshawar, where he was working as a senior figure within Mercy International, a Saudi-funded charity providing aid and assistance to Afghan veterans and refugees. Al-Shaikh had lost one brother – Abid – during the Afghan war, and 'actively participated' in the fighting himself, according to FIA sources. When FIA agents arrived at Al-Shaikh's house, he had allegedy fled the country (he is now believed to be in Kuwait), leaving behind documents and a 'stack' of photographs. The photos included shots of Osama bin Laden taken during the Afghan war, and investigators believe there were close links and even a friendship between Yousef's uncle and the Saudi militant.

When FIA agents checked records in their Immigration and Passport office they discovered that Yousef's embarkation card and other documents had mysteriously disappeared. Javed Iqbal, head of the records room, told senior officers from the FIA that as several Pakistani federal agencies had access to the room, including the FIA, Intelligence Bureau (IB) and powerful Inter-Services Intelligence agency (ISI), any number of officials could have stolen the file. An explanation for the disappearance of the file has never been provided, although the FBI has since given the Pakistani government the names of officials they suspected of colluding with terrorists.[17]

'Bin Laden had friends in the ISI who had funded him during the war in Afghanistan,' said one investigator. 'The same contacts were cultivated by Yousef and members of his family.'[18] Photographs now in the possession of senior Pakistani intelligence officials are reported to show close associates of Nawaz Sharif, the current Prime Minister of Pakistan, with Ramzi Yousef's maternal uncle Zahid Al-Shaikh and one of his brothers. Pakistani intelligence officials working closely with the FBI discovered further links between government figures close to Nawaz Sharif and Zahid Al-Shaikh as a result of his charitable work, although there is no suggestion they have done anything wrong.

However, it is easy to imagine Yousef's attraction to Pakistani militants, even to the few in positions of power in the government and intelligence services. Yousef was a terrorist celebrity, he was the man who had bombed the World Trade Center and wreaked death and destruction in the heart of Manhattan. After his house in Quetta was raided, Yousef flitted around Pakistan, visiting friends and making contacts, and travelling to the 'Wild West' city of Peshawar, where he stayed in Osama bin Laden's Bait-Ashuhada (House of Martyrs) hostel, and frequently attended weddings and parties in the town. 'They [wealthy militants] were queuing up to sponsor Yousef, asking him to launch further attacks [on America and the West],' said an American investigator.[19]

Among those wanting to congratulate Yousef on his 'success' in America was Munir Ibrahim Ahmad (*aka* Munir Madni, *aka* Abdul Majid Madni), a businessman with offices in Karachi. According to intelligence sources, Ahmad knew Yousef through mutual acquaintances before the World Trade Center bombing, and renewed his friendship on Yousef's return to Pakistan. Both men were followers of the Sunni Muslim faith and allegedly shared a hatred of Shiite Muslims (which springs from the centuries-old dispute over who was the proper successor to the Prophet Mohammad). The intelligence sources also claim that Ahmad eventually decided to fund some of the young militant's operations.[20] 'We never had that much on [Ahmad],' said an American intelligence source. 'He's kind of an enigma . . . a mysterious guy, rarely seen even by some of Yousef's closest conspirators.'[21]

Ahmad's current location is unclear, but officials who investigated Yousef's background discovered that during the mid-1990s he was living in Bahadurabad, Karachi, and would tell people euphemistically that he worked in the 'import–export' business. In fact Ahmad imported holy water (known as 'Abe Zam', or 'Aabe Zam Zan') from Mecca in Saudi Arabia, the holiest Muslim site in the world, into

Pakistan for sale through a company called Al-Majid Importers and Exporters. Several intelligence sources believe the relationship between Ahmad and Yousef went beyond a simple financial arrangement where the older businessman funded the younger terrorist.

Yousef seems to have joined Ahmad in his business, perhaps as a partner making an investment in the company. The source of Yousef's funds is unclear, but many officials believe it was – directly or indirectly – Osama bin Laden. It was a useful investment for Yousef: when Pakistani intelligence officers investigated the firm they found that in the middle of 1994 it had a turnover of approximately 7,000,000 Pakistani rupees a year, roughly £100,000 or $160,000.[22] Yousef may have been one of the most wanted men in the world after the World Trade Center bombing, but with the money from Al-Majid Importers and Exporters he could have laid low and stayed hidden until the FBI and Pakistani investigators had exhausted every line of inquiry.

Ramzi Yousef, however, had an ego as vast as his crimes: ambition and arrogance drove him on. Even as the FBI was launching a manhunt for him from New York, Yousef was rekindling his contacts with Pakistani extremists, most notably with senior figures from Sipah-e-Sahaba (Army of the Companions of the Prophet) – an extremist group founded a few years previously in the Pakistani province of Punjab by poor Sunni Muslims angry with Shiite landowners in the Jhang area. With funding from Saudi Arabia the group had infected entire neighbourhoods of Karachi with divisive hatred, turning much of the city into a battleground between Sunnis and Shiites.[23] Yousef's first contact with the group had almost certainly occurred before he travelled to the US for the World Trade Center bombing, in terrorist training camps in Pakistan where he occasionally 'studied' and taught, learning guerrilla tactics and lecturing other students on bomb-making and the delights of militancy.

With an unprecedented terrorist attack on American soil under his belt, Yousef's terrorist star was in ascendance, and in July 1993 he was approached in Karachi by representatives of a militant Islamic group and asked to assassinate Benazir Bhutto, the secular candidate for Prime Minister in Pakistan's October 1993 elections. It is unclear, even now, exactly who was sponsoring the attack, but it would probably be harder to establish which militant Islamic group did *not* want Bhutto killed: most of them were fervently opposed to the very concept of a woman, let alone a pro-Western woman, leading an Islamic nation. 'The Islamists [militant Muslims] produced pamphlets which they distributed saying that it was the duty of believing Muslims to assassinate me because as a woman I had usurped a man's place,' said Benazir Bhutto.[24]

The mysterious men funding the attack are understood to have offered Yousef more than 3,000,000 Pakistani rupees (roughly £41,500 or $68,000) to plan and lead the assassination.[25] Emboldened by his success in New York, and by ideology, hatred and healthy funding, Yousef accepted. Some Pakistani investigators believe he may also have seen the proposed hit as revenge for past wrongs. Yousef's family roots are in the province of Baluchistan (a region, culturally defined, that stretches across the borders with Iran and Afghanistan) and Bhutto's father, Zulfiqar Ali Bhutto, a former Prime Minister of Pakistan, ordered the military to suppress a major tribal uprising in the region in 1973 which resulted in the deaths of at least 10,000 Baluch.[26] Yousef set about recruiting a small terrorist gang who would form his core group of accomplices.

His first move was to recruit two of his oldest friends: Abdul Hakim Murad, a trained commercial pilot who had grown up with Yousef in Kuwait and was then living in Pakistan; and Abdul Shakur, another old friend from his early years in Kuwait. Yousef knew and trusted these people; he knew their families, their way of life, he understood their troubled sense of identity. Their families also had roots in Baluchistan, but had been transplanted to the suburbs of Kuwait City, where they became 'guest workers' and were treated like serfs by the wealthy families of the Gulf state.

Murad was a small, slight man with a beard and bushy brown hair. Shakur, by contrast, was taller with an air of youthful energy. Born in Karachi in 1972, Shakur was the son of a stout, tough, Baluch from the Iranian side of Baluchistan. When his father was offered a job in Kuwait the whole family moved to the Gulf emirate to settle and work.[27] After the Iran–Iraq war Shakur's family left Kuwait and returned to Pakistan to live in Lyari, a bustling section of Karachi, where his father took a job in a workshop. It was a restless time for young Shakur. Soon after returning to Karachi he met up with Abu Hudefa, a Palestinian friend of his who had also spent years in Kuwait and was a student at Karachi University, then a hotbed of militant activity.

The two young men would talk late into the night about the situation in Afghanistan, and how Muslims should work together with the mujaheddin to defeat the Soviets.[28] Abu Hudefa was so inspired that he gave up his studies and went off to fight and later die in Afghanistan. Abdul Shakur eventually followed his friend, travelling to an Afghan camp called Bait-ul-Ansar in Peshawar, just over the Pakistan side of the Afghan border, where most of the population during the Afghan war seemed to be either spies or fighters.

The instructors at the camp spotted the young Pakistani's fighting spirit, and took him to a military training camp called Al-Faruq, where he was trained – not to fight conventional battles, but to wage an urban war for Islamic supremacy. There would be no trench warfare in the coming campaign: instead Shakur was taught about bombs, detonators, plastic explosives, small arms and even hijacking.[29] 'I spent four months in that camp and after that came back to Karachi,' said Shakur during a later interrogation.[30] 'But in early 1993 I went to Afghanistan again for further training.'

When Shakur returned to Karachi, he met up with Yousef (who would later claim he thought Shakur 'mentally sick', 'schizophrenic' and 'a liar and a thief')[31] and was persuaded to join his small group. Under Yousef's leadership, and with Murad helping, the three men began plotting Benazir Bhutto's assassination. After more than a week of planning and scouting, Yousef concluded the best way to kill Bhutto was with a large remote-controlled bomb placed near the gate of her official home, Bilawal House (a white, two-storey building in Karachi's wealthy seafront Clifton district).[32] It was an audacious plot: apart from the risks posed by placing a bomb outside the home of a prominent politician, Yousef then wanted to position himself near by and personally detonate the device as Bhutto's car drove past.

Working from a base in Karachi, Yousef told Shakur to contact Yaqub al-Bakr (*aka* 'al-Bakri'), a Saudi national, and Khalid Baluch, an Iranian – who Pakistani and American intelligence agents allege were prominent leaders of the group that was financing the plot – and give them a list of the tools and weapons Yousef would require.[33] Khalid is understood to have flown to Saudi Arabia to obtain more money for the plot; he then returned to Pakistan to buy the equipment.

A few days later Yousef sent Abdul Shakur to an Afghan refugee camp in Pabi, in Pakistan's North-West Frontier province, to collect the equipment. On 23 July 1993, Shakur returned to Karachi and took two detonators and one wireless set to Yousef, who was hiding in a safehouse at 402, Nidia Towers, Nanakwara, in Karachi; a small, simple flat allegedly owned by Murad.

Yousef worked quickly, fitting the explosive into a box and attaching a simple remote-control device and a detonator – an outdated piece of Soviet technology left over from the Afghan war. Then it was just a matter of placing the bomb outside Bhutto's home and waiting for the right moment to murder their target.

Early one morning in late July Yousef, Murad and Shakur parked outside Bhutto's home in the Clifton district, and carried the bomb over to the drain cover where they had decided to place the device.[34] Benazir Bhutto remembers the details well: 'There was a police patrol which saw this car and stopped and they said to the men [Yousef and his accomplices] "What are you doing?", and the men said they had dropped their keys in the gutter, and they were looking for them. And at this stage they were putting a bomb down there. The patrol car went away and [Yousef] tried to pull the bomb out.'[35] Yousef apparently feared the police would return to investigate further, but as he was kneeling on the ground pulling the bomb out of the drain, its ageing Soviet detonator exploded directly in his face. Although the main explosive did not detonate, tiny fragments of metal shot into Yousef's left eye and knocked him unconscious. 'It didn't explode properly, but Yousef still injured himself and damaged his fingers,' said Bhutto. He collapsed in the street, blood pouring from the side of his face.

Fearing for the life of their friend, Murad and Shakur rushed him by car to Karachi's Civil Hospital for treatment. They told doctors that Yousef's name was Khalid Ali, but when medical staff began asking difficult questions about how he had received his injuries they promptly hustled him into the back of a taxi and left within an hour of arrival.[36]

Murad and Shakur transferred Yousef to Karachi's elegant Aga Khan Hospital and Medical College and admitted him under the name Adam Baluch.[37] By this time Yousef was conscious, if a little groggy, and he told staff a butane gas canister had exploded in his face. Doctors at the busy philanthropic teaching hospital, which has 721 beds and often treats more than 1,500 emergency cases a day, had no reason to believe the injured young man was not telling the truth, but Murad and Shakur were still concerned the Pakistani police would be along to ask questions. His friends stood guard near Yousef as he waited for a minor operation, and then one slept in a chair near his bed as he recuperated afterwards.

By the time of the accident Yousef was a well-known but shadowy figure among militant organizations in Karachi, and there was consternation as news of his injuries spread. Murad quickly warned several of Yousef's friends about the accident, and within 24 hours Munir Ibrahim Ahmad had arrived at the hospital for a short visit. Another of his visitors is believed to have been Abdul Wahab, the owner of the Junaid Bakery in the Lyari area of Karachi, who was alleged to be a senior figure within the Sipah-e-Sahaba terrorist gang.

Yousef spent at least two days in the hospital. Then his wounds were dressed and bandaged, and he left, disappearing first on to the streets of Karachi, and then slipping back into hiding in Baluchistan.[38] Although he spent several weeks recuperating, and his injuries apparently made him irritable and aggressive ('He was like a wounded animal', according to one Pakistani investigator who later interviewed Yousef's associates), the accident did not deter Yousef from continuing with his plot to kill Benazir Bhutto before the October elections.

Within two months of the failed attempt, Yousef formed a plan to assassinate her with a sniper's rifle while she addressed a public meeting.[39] 'It was around the time of the election campaign, I don't remember the exact month, but I remember the day,' said Benazir Bhutto.[40] 'I was supposed to be addressing a public meeting in Karachi, and I got a report from one of my party people that according to police sources there was going to be an assassination attempt on me that night.'

Bhutto still went along to the meeting, but by the time she arrived it was 'complete chaos'. 'There were people everywhere and armed men on the stage. In the midst of all this my mother also arrived. So I decided to go up, but the police were not coming to clear the stage. So I had a choice of leaving or taking the risk. So we took the risk and went up there, and it was absolute bedlam. I don't know how I spoke on that stage, or how I got out unscathed, but I did.' Several months later when she had been elected into office as Prime Minister, Bhutto discovered that Ramzi Yousef had been supposed to assassinate her that night. 'He was supposed to have shot me. He had gone and done a recce of the place and with his associates he had got on top of the building.'

Fortunately for Bhutto, however, a rifle that was supposed to be delivered to Yousef had not arrived in time. 'So in other words Ramzi Yousef would have shot me if he had got the weapon in time,' said Bhutto. 'As you can imagine, I was quite shocked by this.'

While Yousef was trying to kill Benazir Bhutto in Pakistan, back in New York Neil Herman's JTTF agents had been building thick files on the Tradebom suspects. Although Yousef was still seen as the mastermind of the attack, the FBI knew that several other militants were equally culpable.

As Pelligrino, Parr and Stern concentrated on tracking Yousef, the rest of the agents on the JTTF were producing detailed dossiers on the other terrorists. After investigating the background of each suspect the agents all came to the same conclusion: a disparate group of 'Afghan Arabs' – men who fought alongside the mujaheddin Afghan rebels after the Soviet invasion of Afghanistan in 1979 – formed the bulk of the group behind the bombing.

For senior officials in the CIA's Counterterrorism Center it was an appalling realization. The CIA had funded and trained the Afghan Arabs during the war, and now their former 'assets' appeared to be turning on their old ally. While the FBI began their own massive criminal investigation, Admiral James Woolsey, then head of the CIA, realized his agency needed to dust off its intelligence files on other Afghan Arabs and check that more were not planning to attack landmarks in New York or Washington.

On 13 April 1993, Woolsey flew to Cairo with more than 20 CIA Middle East specialists for extensive meetings with Egyptian intelligence and to read their files on hundreds of Afghan Arabs, compiled by the Egyptians because of Afghan Arab involvement in attacks in Cairo.[41] Another small team of agents from the FBI and CIA flew in to Islamabad three days later to meet with Rehman Malik of the FIA, who had already been heading investigations into the Afghan Arabs. The American team also met other Pakistani intelligence officials and agents from the Egyptian Mukhabarat al-Amat – the so-called political police – who had compiled lists of Afghan Arab suspects living on the border between Pakistan and Afghanistan thought to be involved in militant activity.

The World Trade Center bombing had mobilized intelligence services around the world: several realized the bombing might be a signal that the Afghan Arabs had decided to take their war from the refugee camps of Pakistan to the cities of America, Europe and the Middle East. The Egyptian and Algerian security forces were particularly concerned, and within two weeks of the New York bombing a mysterious Colonel 'Ismail' – responsible for counter-espionage in the Algerian Sécurité Militaire – and General Omar Suleiman – head of the Evaluation and Prospection branch of Egypt's Mukhabarat al-Amat – had organized a 'census' of Afghan Arabs still in Pakistan through their network of informants.[42] This list was whittled down to identify 30 Afghan Arabs deemed to be a serious threat to Middle Eastern and Western security; eight of them were 'tagged' as being senior militants. But this did little to help Neil Herman's team in its hunt for Ramzi Yousef.

So in Washington senior FBI officials began negotiating with the State Department to develop an innovative project which they hoped would lead to Yousef's capture. 'We wanted to smoke him out of hiding,' said an agent involved in the case.[43] They turned to 'the Heroes program'. In 1984 the State Department had established an international rewards scheme in a desperate attempt to combat terrorist bombings in Beirut. Informants who offered information leading to the capture and arrest of wanted terrorists could expect generous cash rewards of up to $500,000 through this 'Heroes program', as well as the offer of a new identity, American citizenship and a place in the US witness protection scheme. At least that was the theory: for the first five years the program was under-funded and under-resourced, and thus a spectacular failure. It did not manage to attract a single decent informant.

Then in 1989 an official called Brad Smith took over the department and increased the standard reward money. Smith began advertising the awards in television and radio advertisements featuring famous actors such as Charlton Heston, Charles Bronson and Charlie Sheen. Brochures and leaflets were printed in up to 15 languages, including Arabic and Greek, and distributed around the world.[44] The operation was both high-tech, using the Internet as it emerged as a global communications highway, and low-tech, using matchboxes printed by a firm called George W. King of Baltimore, with photographs of wanted terrorists on the outside and details of the rewards program on the inside. Brad Smith was diagnosed with Lou Gehrig's disease in 1991, usually a terminal nerve illness, but he continued to work, alternating between his office and home in northern Virginia, where a respirator kept him alive and the Internet kept him in touch with contacts around the world.

With Yousef on the run the FBI and State Department knew they would have to offer major inducements if they were to have any hope of attracting an informant. After lengthy consultations a reward of up to $2 million was offered for information leading to his capture, then posters were printed and details of the reward were circulated to newspapers in countries where the FBI suspected Yousef had connections: Pakistan, India, Malaysia, the Philippines. More than 37,000 matchboxes were printed bearing Yousef's photograph and dropped by plane over Baluchistan, Yousef's homeland, and along the porous border between Afghanistan and Pakistan. 'They smoke a lot in that part of the world,' said one FBI official.[45]

Yousef's name and photograph were shown to thousands of police officers, detectives, intelligence agents and informants, and dozens of people came forward claiming to have information, all of which had to be investigated, but most of which proved fruitless. The matchboxes distributed around Asia bearing Yousef's photograph were a particularly clever idea and an ingenious way of reaching the masses. 'But they also invited people to come off the wall, and we had to evaluate all of them,' said Neil Herman. 'This wasn't a case of getting someone out there to go and flippantly [investigate]. We had to work very closely with the governments of Malaysia, the Philippines and Pakistan, and other countries in the region. Whether it was phone records or associates, we had to run down the leads.' As the $2 million reward for Yousef became public knowledge, the JTTF agents were contacted by people who were basically con-artists: '. . . there were people wanting money up front and we had to explain to them that it didn't work like that,' said Herman.

Perhaps the greatest concern for the JTTF, and eventually the State Department, was that normal American citizens might try to locate Yousef to earn the reward money and get hurt or killed in the process. Journalists, mercenaries, members of the public, and agents from the CIA and other less public American and foreign government agencies all had a go: '. . . there were people trying to do things on their own, sometimes on an amateur level, going into different countries, and we had to try and temper that because we didn't want them to be representing our government,' said Herman. 'Some of the people thought they had information, some were interested in the money, some were interested in helping, some were not even close, and some had little bits of the puzzle.' Most were gently warned to go home.

While the FBI and the State Department were employing overt methods to capture Yousef, and making contact with governments and officials in Asian countries where Yousef was thought to have links or be hiding, agents at the CIA's Counterterrorism Center in Langley, Virginia, began to consider more secretive measures. 'If he couldn't be brought back using extradition treaties or the goodwill of governments in the region, then a decision was taken at a senior level that we would try to snatch him,' said a former CIA agent.[46]

For several decades America has followed an aggressive anti-terrorist policy designed to hunt down those responsible for atrocities. Once opened, a file on an attack or bombing is never closed while a perpetrator remains alive and free. 'They're pursued to the ends of the earth,' said the CIA official.[47] The logic behind the policy is that terrorists will realize America has a long memory and will be dissuaded from attacking American targets. As an anti-terrorist policy it is now touchingly naïve: the new breed of terrorist attacking the West often has little fear of death, let alone the prospect of spending the rest of his or her natural life in a small American cell. In fact, many extremists view imprisonment, torture or death as part of their holy duty: they reap the rewards as martyrs in heaven. As a visible, political indication of American determination to stamp out attacks on its nationals, however, the policy has been far more successful.

In 1973 terrorists planted powerful bombs in rented cars left outside two Israeli banks in Manhattan and at the El-Al airline terminal at JFK airport. Crude and faulty wiring prevented the bombs from exploding, and the FBI was able to detect 60 fingerprints left behind by the terrorists. The prints were carefully filed – first on to card, and then, as the years ticked by, on to powerful computers.[48] In the 1990s the Israeli Mossad identified one of the bombers as Khalid Duhham al-Jawari, an Iraqi. Further investigations revealed al-Jawari had changed his name and was working as a PLO official based in Cyprus. In 1993 al-Jawari, unaware of the continuing American interest in his movements, left Cyprus for Italy, where he landed at Rome airport. His name was matched to that on a terrorist 'watch list', and he was arrested and extradited to the US, where he was convicted of the 1973 bombing plot and incarcerated.

Another terrorist to suffer from the long arm of American justice was Fauwaz Yunis, who hijacked a Royal Jordanian jet in 1985 with 70 passengers on board, including four Americans. Yunis may well now regret not checking the passenger list and politely asking the Americans to leave the plane, because in 1987 the CIA tracked down a former friend of his who was living in Cyprus, and persuaded him to ring Yunis to chat about drug dealing. The man talked Yunis into admitting his role in the hijacking on a phone bugged by the CIA. Yunis then joined the man for a 'drugs deal' on board a yacht in the Mediterranean rented by the FBI. Agents appeared and nabbed Yunis, who was whisked back to the US in a Navy jet and sentenced to 30 years in prison.

Every possible method of getting Yousef back to the United States was considered in the Counterterrorism Center, including kidnapping him or luring him into a 'honey-trap' by preying on his weakness for pretty women, which was becoming apparent from investigations underway in Pakistan and also in Wales, where Yousef had been a student in the late 1980s.[49] However, every plan, both overt and covert, required precise knowledge of Yousef's location, and the pressure was building on Neil Herman's JTTF agents to make headway.

The investigation began to strain even the hardiest agents. 'Over the years I really learned in working these cases never to underestimate your adversaries,' said Herman. 'It's not that you learn to respect them, but in trying to track people down you really had to understand that to many of these people there really was commitment. The people who do things like this, whether it's blowing up a car or killing people in a bombing, generally speaking they're really committed; they're not people who waitress during the day and go out and kill people at night. [For] these people, generally, terrorism is their life.'

According to Herman: 'those of us who were tracking them ... have to become almost more fanatical than the fanatics. There were times that I would stay there [in his office] two or three or four days and sleep in the office.' The investigation began to take a heavy toll on both Herman and his family. 'I have two daughters; one is now 18 and one is 10. The younger one doesn't really remember much about this, other than that I was gone for long periods of time, because these cases are very, very long.'[50]

John Lipka, who was working on the case in the Washington FBI office, concurs. 'I know agents that have retired, had strokes, heart attacks,' he said.[51] 'These cases go on for years, and years, and years.' According to Herman the work can 'overwhelm your life'. 'People do tend to get very burned out by that, working six or seven days a week. I have done that over and over and over. It had an effect on my personal life, and it's very frustrating. Six people lost their lives [in the World Trade Center bombing], and you can't let that go. With these cases you do tend to get to know the victims and their families. You do tend to associate yourself with the people involved.'

Herman also worked on the Pan Am 103 bombing, and still keeps in touch with a number of families who lost loved ones in the skies over Lockerbie in Scotland. 'You can't help but identify with the families,' he said. 'The people who work the cases also suffer. If you want to do it well and successfully then you have to get that involved.

59

There's a downside to staying in the program, because it can't help but affect you, and sooner or later it does. It does take a toll. You bleed to death with these cases.'

While dozens of Herman's JTTF agents were investigating the men already arrested for the World Trade Center bombing and hunting for Yousef around the world, a further terrorist conspiracy linked to Yousef had been unravelling in New York.

After the arrest of Salameh, Abouhalima, Ayyad and Ajaj, Yousef's co-conspirators in the WTC attack, the FBI realized one of the main threads connecting the men was a cramped room above a toy store in Jersey City. There, in a makeshift Jersey City mosque behind a locked chipboard door, several of the men had met to hear the violent, rabid sermons of a blind Muslim preacher called Sheikh Omar Abdel-Rahman, who would urge his congregation to '. . . hit hard and kill the enemies of God in every spot, to rid it of the descendants of apes and pigs fed at the table of Zionism, communism and imperialism.'

Sheikh Omar, who was blinded by diabetes when he was 10 months old, had built himself a huge following among militants in America, Europe and the Middle East. In Egypt he was considered an enemy of the state for his role in fomenting anti-government propaganda and his open support of terrorist gangs, and in May 1990 he left Cairo for Sudan. In Khartoum he managed to obtain a visa for the United States from a US consular official, despite being listed on the American Automated Visa Lookout System as a suspected terrorist, and being sentenced in absentia by an Egyptian court for the 1989 murder of a police officer and for plotting to overthrow the Egyptian government.

The CIA, it is now clear, arranged the visa to try and befriend the Sheikh in advance of a possible armed fundamentalist revolution in Egypt. CIA agents, still regretting mistakes they made before the Iranian revolution in 1979, were trying to win the Sheikh's trust.[52] 'The US thought that Omar was going to be like the [Ayatollah] Khomeini in Iran and that Omar was going to take the state. They wanted to . . . make contacts with the new government,' said Abdullah Omar Abdel-Rahman, the Sheikh's son.[53] The FBI was left to pick up the pieces.

The Sheikh's rhetoric in the New Jersey mosque was an open incitement to violence, and he had been monitored by the FBI since one of his followers murdered a racist rabbi called Meir Kahane in 1990. The great fear for the FBI was that if the four men they had already arrested were capable of bombing the World Trade Center, what might the rest of the Sheikh's followers be planning?

They were right to be concerned. After arresting Nidal Ayyad, one of Yousef's conspirators, the FBI uncovered a letter on his computer written on behalf of the 'Fifth Battalion' of the 'Liberation Army' which stated: 'If our demands are not met, all of our functional groups in the army will continue to execute our missions against military and civilian targets in and out of the United States. For your own information, our army has more than [a] hundred and fifty suicidal soldiers ready to go ahead.'

When details of the letter were made public it caused consternation – 150 suicidal soldiers? James Fox, the head of the FBI in New York, was quick to offer assurance, but privately he was said to be deeply concerned.[54] The problem for the FBI was gauging the scale of the threat. They had no agents on the inside and no clear intelligence, so Fox took the decision to re-activate Emad Salem, a former lieutenant-colonel in the Egyptian army who was close to the Sheikh and had been working as an informant for the FBI. In the months before the twin towers were bombed Salem had been warning the FBI that militants close to the Sheikh were trying to obtain explosives and were discussing assassinations and bombings. If the FBI had taken his warnings seriously they could probably have prevented the World Trade Center attack, but senior agents at the Bureau decided Salem was unreliable and was probably working simultaneously for the Egyptian security services. They thought he was exaggerating the threat from Muslim extremists in New York and stopped his FBI salary of $500 a week. After the bombing he was rehired and told to infiltrate the Sheikh's followers. His payment was $1.5 million.

Salem was genuinely disgusted by the six deaths in the twin towers and was eager to help. With the help of microphones concealed in the zipper of his trousers, he helped to expose a terrorist web around Sheikh Omar led by a Sudanese man called Siddig Ibrahim Siddig Ali. By April 1993 Salem was reporting back to the FBI that a series of simultaneous massive bombings were planned: two in the Holland and Lincoln tunnels that connect southern Manhattan to New Jersey; one on the George Washington Bridge, which spans the Hudson River between upper Manhattan and New Jersey; one next to the Statue of Liberty; and another in the United Nations (placed in the basement with help from diplomats at the Sudanese mission to the UN). Finally another bomb would wreck the massive government building at

26 Federal Plaza, and yet another would be placed in the midtown Diamond District, where the largest percentage of workers are Hassidic Jews. The gang was also considering kidnapping former US President Richard Nixon.

The terrorist cell asked Salem to rent a building where they could make their bombs, and he promptly found an old warehouse in a poor area of Jamaica, Queens, which the FBI then stuffed with concealed recording devices and hidden video cameras. In mid-May 1993 the conspirators moved into the warehouse and began their work. Without Ramzi Yousef advising them the bombs they began preparing were not particularly sophisticated but what they lacked in quality they made up for in size.

After taping and recording hundreds of hours of evidence, the FBI surrounded the warehouse early on 23 June 1993 with dozens of heavily armed marksmen, and assault teams sneaked inside through a door Salem had carefully left unlocked. Twelve of the conspirators were inside mixing fuel and fertilizer into bombs with the help of vats and long wooden spatulas. 'The subjects were actually mixing the witches' brew,' said a jubilant James Fox. 'We entered so fast some of the subjects didn't know we were in the bomb factory until they were in handcuffs.'

Sheikh Omar took refuge in the Abu Bakr mosque in Brooklyn with dozens of his supporters. Several senior FBI officials did not want him arrested because he was a magnet for militants, drawing them out of the woodwork and helping the FBI keep tabs on extremist activity.[55] But political pressure was intense, and on the afternoon of 2 July the Sheikh was finally arrested.

A little more than two months after Sheikh Omar's arrest and the discovery of the second New York terrorist conspiracy, the first World Trade Center bombing trial of Mohammad Salameh, Mahmud Abouhalima, Nidal Ayyad and Ahmad Ajaj began. From the moment the trial started on 14 September, Ramzi Yousef was a ghostly presence in the New York courtroom. Dozens of witnesses walked through the court's heavy oak-panelled door, settled themselves into the green leather witness chair, and regaled the jury with tales of the mysterious young mastermind. In some cases it was just a fingerprint, a few spoken words, but it was clear Yousef had been the inspiration, the man who made it all happen.

The trial finished on 4 March 1994, and a masterly summation by

US Attorney Henry DePippo helped persuade the jury to return verdicts convicting the four men on 38 charges. On 24 May the four men were each sentenced to 240 years in prison, and taken to the high-security US Penitentiary at Lewisburg, Pennsylvania.

For the JTTF it was a rare moment for celebration. That evening a group of agents who had worked on the case gathered for a drink at the Paris Café near the South Street Seaport in downtown Manhattan, one of the oldest bars in New York, and took advantage of the bar's 4 a.m. liquor licence.[56] 'I remember a number of us went out and celebrated that night,' said Neil Herman.[57]

The JTTF had known they had the right men, but they had been worried the jury might not believe the prosecution case. 'The evidence [against all those prosecuted in the Tradebom case], to be perfectly honest with you, is not overwhelming,' admits Herman. All of those eventually arrested 'had differing degrees of complicity', he added. 'To have three of the four convicted and one acquitted would not be good enough. There would be a lot of finger-pointing. Everyone expects you to win because you have all these resources, you have all these prosecutors, you have all these agents and detectives, and in the end when you win, nobody's surprised. But the reality is that you have 12 jurors to convince.'

One of the major effects of the trial was to encourage the JTTF agents to redouble their efforts to capture Ramzi Yousef, who was still in hiding in Pakistan. 'The Yousef fugitive investigation was being very strongly pursued from the beginning, however it intensified again at the beginning of 1994, and we made an even bigger push,' said Herman. 'We were confident that he was in Asia and we knew that he was a timebomb waiting to happen.'

Herman was right: for Yousef the news from America must have been depressing. Whether as an act of revenge for the trial of his comrades, or simply because he was a committed terrorist now running loose across Asia, Yousef began plotting another devastating attack.

In late February or early March 1994 Yousef flew from Pakistan to Thailand and moved in with a group of Islamic militants living in Bangkok. He immediately began assembling a small terrorist cell for a major bombing attack, just as he had done in New York more than a year previously, but this time the target was to be either the US or Israeli embassy in Bangkok.[58]

In militant circles Yousef was a powerful character who managed to attract young extremists by sheer force of personality. 'Ramzi did not just talk, like so many hard-line Muslims. He was fully prepared, even willing, to take violent action in support of his beliefs. For many militants that made him a seductive character,' said a US intelligence officer.[59]

According to Pakistani and Thai police sources, Abdullah Salih, a Thai student in Bangkok, was one militant who saw Yousef as a teacher and leader. Salih was already considered to be a budding terrorist in militant Muslim circles when he met Yousef during the terrorist's time in Bangkok, and Yousef charmed him with stories of the jihad against the Soviets, and the new battle against the corrupt and evil empire of the United States.[60]

Yousef spent several weeks in Thailand planning his attack. He recruited a few supporters from among the thousands of Muslims living in the city, and built a 1-tonne bomb comprising plastic explosive, ammonium nitrate and fuel oil – similar to the bomb used in the WTC attack. One of his co-conspirators then rented a six-wheel hire truck, strangled the delivery driver, and stuffed his body into the back. On 11 March 1994, Yousef and his gang loaded the bomb into the van, pushing the dead body into a lockable trunk. One of Yousef's men then set off towards the Israeli embassy.

Yousef, however, seems to have had a knack of picking appalling drivers as his comrades. In New York Mohammad Salameh suffered several crashes during preparations for the World Trade Center bombing, even hospitalizing Yousef after one accident. The driver of the Bangkok truck bomb was even worse. On the way to his target he actually crashed the truck into a taxi-motorcyclist and another car at a busy intersection on Bangkok's Chitlom Road, just a few hundred yards from the Israeli embassy. It was a farcical event. The man panicked and tried to pay off the other drivers with foreign banknotes, but onlookers from a local department store crowded around the accident scene and police sirens began wailing in the distance. The amateur terrorist ran off down a side-street and disappeared.

When the Bangkok police arrived they found the abandoned truck and several incandescent drivers. The damaged vehicles were pushed to the side of the road and the van, with the bomb still undetected inside, was driven to a police depot and impounded.

The plot was discovered only when the police rang the truck's owner. He arrived at the depot on 17 March and opened the back of the truck to discover the decomposing body of the driver and a massive bomb linked to a detonating switch on the dashboard. Forensic experts from the Thai police then discovered Yousef's finger-prints on the bomb and launched a major hunt for the terrorists. A man suspected of being the driver was later caught and identified by one of the taxi-motorcyclists involved in the Chitlom Road accident, but by that time Yousef had fled Bangkok and returned to Pakistan.[61]

Yousef's trip to Thailand was not entirely wasted. Such was the lure of extremism that Salih, the young student, allegedly followed him several weeks later, expressing his commitment to Yousef's militant campaign, enrolling in the Islamic University in Islamabad and shar-ing a house with him.[62]

Yousef must have been furious at the failure of his latest plan, but he did not let it halt his burgeoning terrorist career. He returned to Islamabad and began plotting new attacks, dragging friends and other members of his family into his violent campaigns.

Early in May 1994 Abu Hashim, the brother of Yousef's wife, knocked on the door of an apartment belonging to Ishtiaque Parker, a young South African Muslim student at Islamabad's militant Islamic University. Parker recognized the man at his front door as a fellow student, and Abu Hashim told him he was looking for an old friend of his who had also been a student at the same faculty. The two men spent several minutes chatting politely, and during their brief conver-sation Parker told Hashim that the friend he was looking for had left several months previously.[63]

Hashim must have found their conversation interesting, because two days later he allegedly reappeared on Parker's doorstep with Ramzi Yousef.[64] The two visitors were friendly and charming, and the three men sat down to eat lunch together, giving Yousef a chance to quiz Parker on his background, claiming he wanted to marry a South African girl so he could get a South African passport and quickly obtain visas for foreign travel.[65] Yousef was fishing for information: a student with a South African passport could travel the world with ease, and Yousef was always looking for more recruits. After finishing their meal Yousef and Hashim left, promising to visit their new friend again.

Shortly after this – within two months of his return to Pakistan from Thailand – Yousef had another chance to launch a terrorist attack on his enemies. He was becoming increasingly vitriolic in his condemnation of Shiite Muslims, and he was approached by representatives of the Iranian rebel Mujaheddin-e-Khalq Organisation (MKO) – responsible for several terrorist attacks in Iran – and asked or paid to lead an attack against one of the holiest Shiite sites in Iran – the shrine of Reza, a great-grandson of Prophet Mohammad and the eighth Shiite Imam (he was allegedly poisoned by the ruling caliph in AD 817).[66]

For this attack, deep inside Iran, Pakistani and American sources allege that Yousef recruited his own father and one of his younger brothers, Abdul Muneem, into his terrorist cell.[67] Together with a small group of virulently anti-Shiite militants from the remote town of Turbat in Baluchistan (where some of Yousef's family still live), they travelled from Turbat across the border into Iran, and then on up to Mashhad ('Place of Martyrdom'), the largest city in Khorasan province in the north-east of the country.

Few details are known about the planning for the attack, but Yousef is believed to have spent several days building a small, easily concealed bomb containing around 5kg (11lbs) of a high explosive, probably C-4. 'We believe he was involved in the Mashhad bombing, but it's not as if we could just go in there [to Iran] and investigate,' confirms Neil Herman.[68] Pakistani investigators are also convinced of his involvement, and Yousef himself later told Ishtiaque Parker he was responsible.[69]

The attackers placed their bomb in the women's section of the mausoleum, and when it exploded on 20 June 1994, one entire wall and the prayer-hall dome caved in and huge ageing crystal chandeliers shattered above the heads of pilgrims. A young woman, interviewed later from her hospital bed, described the events to Iranian television: 'I was praying in the hall . . . I saw a bright yellow light. I was pushed strongly back, then down. When I opened my eyes I was surrounded by bodies all over the place.'[70] The same report went on to show workers, many in tears, clearing shattered glass from the blood-stained marble floor of the shrine. At least 26 pilgrims died in the attack, and more than 200 were injured. It was an appalling crime, all the more so because it took place on the anniversary of Ashura, the day of mourning for the martyrdom of Imam Hussein, Prophet Mohammad's grandson and the third Shiite Muslim Imam.

It was an adventurous attack for Yousef. His involvement, which appears to have been designed to inflame grievances between Shiite and Sunni Muslims, was not apparent to the Iranian security police until they caught and briefly interviewed Mahdi Nahvi, one of the leaders of the MKO terrorist group, after a shoot-out with him to the east of Tehran at the beginning of August. Bullets hit Nahvi in the abdomen and lodged in his spleen and collarbone. He died the next day.[71] Yousef's father, who was still in Iran, was apparently arrested by the feared Iranian security police, but his son escaped a dragnet and slipped back across the border into Pakistan, possibly travelling via Afghanistan.[72]

The bomb at Mashhad was not Yousef's only attack on fellow Muslims. During this period of his life he seems to have been motivated as much by hatred of Shiite Muslims as by hatred of America and the West. He was on a killing rampage, and even other Sunni Muslims were not safe. After returning from Iran Yousef decided to kill Dr Salim Qadri, a moderate Sunni religious leader from the Barelvi school of thought who had spoken out against the Sipah-e-Sahaba terrorist gang that Yousef supported. There would be no bombs or high-explosive for this assassination. It was to be a cheap, clinical hit: Yousef sent Abdul Shakur to buy a pistol and silencer for 8,500 Pakistani rupees (around £120 or $195) from another militant and he gave them to a killer called Arif Tajik – a hard-line supporter of Sipah-e-Sahaba whom Yousef had paid to do the job.[73]

Neil Herman and the FBI agents pursuing Yousef, meanwhile, were hearing little more than rumours about their prey, and were left chasing shadows in some of the most secretive regions of the world. In New York FBI agent Chuck Stern was working all the hours he could ('he never complained; he would work 100 hours a week, every Saturday and Sunday, and he would never bitch,' said another agent),[74] while Stern's colleagues on the Joint Terrorist Task Force were working abroad thousands of miles from home.

It was a complicated operation. 'New York identified the personnel they wanted to send, and my job was to facilitate the travel in the most professional manner with the appropriate clearances,' said John Lipka.[75] 'You can't just get on a plane and fly anywhere you want. It has to be extremely well co-ordinated with multiple agencies within the US government and overseas entities.'

In Asia Frank Pelligrino and Brian Parr befriended senior Pakistani and Filipino intelligence agents and began constructing a picture of Yousef's movements and background, using passport checks and information from sources, intelligence agents and police officers on the ground. From his base at the US embassy in Bangkok (which Yousef had hoped to destroy), Ralph Paul Horton, a senior FBI Legal

Attaché, was also helping to forge links between the FBI and Asian intelligence agencies. 'He isn't one of these wine and cheese guys,' said Neil Herman. 'Ralph gets things done. Part of the work by Frank Pelligrino, Brian Parr and Ralph Horton was developing a number of key sources in Asia.'[76]

Yousef was proving remarkably elusive, and the agents spent hours sitting on flights from New York to Islamabad and Karachi in pursuit of their man. 'I'd really like to have Frank's frequent-flier miles,' says Herman laconically. The pressure was building on the FBI agents: not only were they operating on foreign territory, but they were up against one of the most committed terrorists the FBI had ever faced. 'Neil [Herman] and I both spent a lot of hours without sleep; you can't catch these people working 8 a.m. to 5 p.m.,' said John Lipka.[77] 'You have to be available, you work into the weekends. It's very frustrating, but when you think of the people who lost their lives, and their families, and the phone-calls of the mothers, and the fathers, and the brothers, and the sisters, it keeps you going.'

References

[1] Author interview with Neil Herman.
[2] Ibid.
[3] Author interview with American investigator.
[4] Ibid, and author interview with another investigator.
[5] Author interview with Neil Herman.
[6] Author interview with Pakistani and American investigators.
[7] Haji Akhtar Mohammad Bareeh was arrested on 19 March 1995 by agents of the FIA and questioned over his friendship with Yousef. There is no suggestion he was involved in terrorist activity.
[8] Author interview with Pakistani and US intelligence sources. There is no suggestion he was involved in terrorist activity.
[9] Author interview with American investigator.
[10] Author interviews with John Lipka and a senior Pakistani investigator.
[11] Author interview with Pakistani investigators.
[12] Ibid.
[13] Ibid.
[14] John Miller, 'Talking with Terror's Banker', *ABC News*, 28 May 1998.
[15] Author interview with Neil Herman.
[16] Author interview with an American investigator.
[17] Ibid. Several senior Pakistani intelligence officers were later sacked or forced to resign because of their involvement in, or failure to stop, preparations for the World Trade Center attack.
[18] Ibid.

19 Author interview.
20 Author interview with Pakistani investigator and US intelligence agent.
21 Author interview.
22 Author interview with a Pakistani investigator.
23 Ibid.
24 Author interview with Benazir Bhutto.
25 Ibid. Much of this money is still believed to be sitting in the coffers of a Karachi bank.
26 Author interview with a Pakistani investigator.
27 Mohammad Mirza, 'Background of Accomplice Detailed', *Friday Times*, 30 March/5 April 1995.
28 Ibid. Also author interview with senior Pakistani investigator.
29 Shakur disclosed details of the training for hijacking during his interrogation by Pakistani intelligence officers in 1995.
30 Mirza, op. cit.
31 Interrogation of Yousef by Rehman Malik and Sajjad Haider of the FIA.
32 Details of the plot were discovered in 1995.
33 Author interview with a Pakistani investigator.
34 Author interviews with Benazir Bhutto.
35 Ibid.
36 Author interviews with Benazir Bhutto and Pakistani investigators.
37 Ibid. According to Bhutto, when the Pakistani Federal Investigation Agency later investigated the assassination attempt, Yousef 'told them that he had gone to hospital, and he named the hospital, and he said he went in at this time and went in under this name. So the FIA went to the hospital and they found that, indeed, there had been a man with that name, at that time, in that hospital, with that wound.' Source: author interview with Benazir Bhutto.
38 Ibid.
39 Author interviews with Benazir Bhutto, a retired CIA official, and American and Pakistani investigators.
40 Author interviews with Benazir Bhutto.
41 Author interview with American intelligence source.
42 'The Afghan Boomerang', *Intelligence Newsletter*, Indigo Publications, Paris, number 216, 28 April 1993.
43 Author interview.
44 Author interview with an FBI investigator.
45 Ibid.
46 Author interview.
47 Ibid.
48 Author interviews with an FBI investigator.
49 Ibid., and author interviews with Neil Herman.
50 Author interview with Neil Herman.
51 Author interview with John Lipka.
52 Author interview with a retired CIA official.
53 Richard Engel, 'Abdullah Abdel-Rahman hopes to follow his father's footsteps', *Middle East Times*, 27 June 1997.

[54] Author interview with an American investigator.

[55] Author interview with an American investigator.

[56] Ibid.

[57] Author interview with Neil Herman.

[58] Author interview with Pakistani and American investigators.

[59] Author interview.

[60] Author interview with a Pakistani investigator.

[61] A man was eventually caught, convicted of being the driver and sentenced to death, but he was then released in February 1998 by Thailand's Supreme Court.

[62] There is no suggestion Salih was personally involved in any terrorist action, although intelligence sources do allege that Yousef had recruited him into his broad circle of supporters.

[63] Based on a later interrogation of Parker by Pakistani investigators. Report obtained by author.

[64] Ibid.

[65] Ibid.

[66] Information taken from author interviews with American and Pakistani investigators and intelligence sources, and Kamran Khan, 'Ramzi's Terror Network', *The News*, 27 March 1995. Details of Yousef's role in the Iranian bombing came to light during the interrogation of Shakur by Pakistani intelligence officials. Shakur said one of Yousef's brothers told him he had been involved in the operation, which Yousef led.

[67] Author interviews with a former CIA official and Pakistani investigators.

[68] Author interview with Neil Herman.

[69] Interrogation of Parker by Pakistani investigators. Report obtained by author.

[70] Sharif Imam-Jomeh, 'Bomb blast kills 25 at Iranian prayer hall', Reuters, 21 June 1994.

[71] 'Detained Iran bomb suspect dies of bullet wounds', Reuters, 2 August 1994.

[72] Author interview with Pakistani investigator.

[73] Author interview with Pakistani investigator based on a later interrogation of Shakur. Something went wrong with the assassination attempt and the contract was not fulfilled.

[74] Author interview.

[75] Author interview with John Lipka.

[76] Author interview with Neil Herman.

[77] Author interview with John Lipka.

FOUR

The Bojinka Plot

AFTER RETURNING to Pakistan from the attack on Mashhad, and plotting to kill Dr Salim Qadri, Ramzi Yousef found himself much in demand. Pakistani intelligence sources believe that emissaries from several Sunni militant groups met with Yousef and tried to persuade him to conduct bombing campaigns or commit assassinations on their behalf.[1]

Yousef, however, seems to have spurned most of their advances in favour of making closer links with the terrorist financier Osama bin Laden. At the time bin Laden was living in a comfortable house in the suburbs of Khartoum, the capital of Sudan, and funding numerous campaigns against the Saudi government, which he accused of betraying Islam by allowing America to base thousands of troops in the kingdom. Pakistani investigators believe Yousef also began to develop links with groups connected to bin Laden that were committed to the overthrow of the Saudi regime.

According to one source a group of militant Saudi businessmen visited Pakistan in the middle of 1994 and had meetings with associates of Yousef and bin Laden.[2] The Saudis were given advice on the technology needed to install secret radio transmitters in the Middle East, which could be used to broadcast to the Saudi people from a location inside the kingdom. Their idea was to encourage dissent and ultimately encourage the overthrow of the House of Saud. Ramzi Yousef is understood to have been present at several meetings in Karachi between the businessmen and other militants, including two of bin Laden's senior representatives, when wider plots aimed at toppling the Saudi leadership were discussed.

71

The relationship between Yousef and bin Laden's organization slowly blossomed. Pakistani intelligence sources believe bin Laden's senior officers asked Yousef to travel to the Philippines – a country he had visited before the World Trade Center bombing – to help Abu Sayyaf, a vicious local Muslim terrorist group already patronized by bin Laden and known to Yousef. Yousef bade farewell to his wife and friends and flew from Pakistan to Malaysia, then travelled by boat to the city of Zamboanga in the southern Philippines, and took a ferry for the 90-minute crossing to Abu Sayyaf's secret base on the small island of Basilan in the Sulu sea, 550 miles south of Manila.[3]

Basilan and Zamboanga are part of the southern Philippines region of Mindanao and the Sulu archipelago, which in turn comprises more than one third of the country's 7,000 islands' total land mass. In a largely Catholic country the inhabitants of this region have followed Islam since the 14th century, well before the Spanish conquest of the islands or the arrival of Christian Jesuit missionaries in 1872. Despite their pre-colonial indigenousness, Muslims have always been an oppressed minority confined to the south of the country, while Christians dominate the government and parliament in Manila and the north. Osama bin Laden believed that an armed insurrection in the south by Abu Sayyaf and thousands of Islamic militants could lead to the creation of a separate independent Muslim state, and through his lieutenants he was funding Abu Sayyaf and encouraging the group's expansion.

Bin Laden asked Yousef to train men from Abu Sayyaf in the use of sophisticated high explosives. He spent several weeks on Basilan, travelling into the remote, hilly interior of the island to witness small-arms training, and taught his extraordinary bomb-making skills to more than 20 Abu Sayyaf terrorists in safehouses in and around Isabela, the provincial capital.[4] 'He was the imported foreign talent,' said a senior American investigator, who notes that Abu Sayyaf was nothing more than a collection of amateur guerrillas until bin Laden's money (and Yousef's expertise) made them a more efficient fighting force.[5]

Yousef seems to have found life on Basilan somewhat sedate. Less than 50 miles wide, the island has a population of under 250,000. Isabela itself is a small coastal town with a humble cathedral, several Muslim teahouses and a market; the ferry from Zamboanga sails gently into the wharf down a channel lined with tiny villages, mangroves and houses suspended on stilts. Despite its natural beauty, the island would never be able to hold the interest of a committed international terrorist who was earning something of a reputation as a playboy. Yousef soon decided to move north to Manila, the capital, to sample its cosmopolitan delights and prepare another terrorist 'spectacular'.

Although he was working far from his home and family, Yousef was never alone in the Philippines or a stranger in the country. He had visited the south, and possibly Manila, several years before the WTC bombing, and he also had friends in the city, men who appeared in the country after the twin towers attack in 1993.

One of the first to arrive was an enigmatic member of the Yousef clan, a young Islamic militant who used the name Adel Annon. Several intelligence sources believe Annon to be one of Ramzi's brothers, and their investigations suggest he was a committed militant who had fought with the mujaheddin during the Afghan war.[6] Soon after he first appeared in the Philippines Annon bought the Mindanao Meat Shop, a small store selling Arabic food and halal meat on M.H. del Pilar Street in Ermita, a run-down former red-light and tourist area of Manila. Just a few doors away another young militant called Mustafa Abu Zainab bought the Al-Tanor restaurant and settled into the local community. Outwardly, the two men were respectable local businessmen: hard-working and religious, but always ready to stop for a quick chat with other traders.[7]

Filipino intelligence sources, however, claim that Annon and Abu Zainab, while building their legitimate businesses, were also establishing a terrorist cell in the city for a group called Hezbul Dawah Al Islamiah (the 'Islamic Preaching Group', sometimes known as the 'Ali Movement'). The group propagates the teachings of Ali Radiallahu, one of the pious four caliphs of Islam, and had cells in the United Kingdom, Pakistan, Australia, New Zealand, Iraq and the Lebanon. Abu Zainab, it is alleged, was the leader of the Hezbul Dawah in the Philippines, while Annon was thought to be his loyal lieutenant.[8]

By the summer of 1993, Yousef's friends in the Philippines had successfully established themselves as respectable members of society. One of them, Javed Rana, an 'associate' of Yousef, even married a cousin of former Filipino President Ferdinand Marcos.[9] Using the cover provided by their ownership of a host of restaurants, travel agencies, recruitment agencies and small hotels, the members of the Hezbul Dawah cell began plotting an assassination campaign against the ambassadors to the Philippines of the United Kingdom, Australia, New Zealand and Spain. They were strange countries to target, particularly New Zealand, and the plot never really left the planning stage, but the militants wanted to do something, *anything*. They just needed to focus on a target. Then Ramzi Yousef, terrorist legend, the man who had attacked the pillars of American imperialism, appeared in Manila from Basilan. Only a hand-grenade could have made more of an impact.

Yousef had left Basilan sometime in September 1994, taking a ferry from Isabela to Zamboanga and flying north to Manila using the name 'Adam Ali Qasim'.[10] The capital of the Philippines is a bustling city with thousands of Muslim immigrants, and Yousef had several friends in Manila who could shelter and feed him. He tracked down Hedi Yousef Alghoul, a distant cousin who was living and working with a group of friends, most of whom could be characterized as Islamic militants. They worshipped at the militant Golden Mosque in Quiapo, Manila, and lionized Yousef because of his attack on the US; even Alghoul's wife was taken to meet the famous terrorist.[11]

Yousef spent a few days in Manila making contacts, and then flew back to Islamabad to visit Abu Hashim and their mutual student friend Ishtiaque Parker. Hashim had visited Parker at the end of September to rekindle their friendship and given him a boxed laptop computer to look after for a few weeks. When Yousef arrived back in the city he met Hashim and they both went to see Parker and ate a light meal together in his apartment.[12] As they relaxed Yousef 'took out the computer from the box and fed information about South Africa [into it] and then displayed it for [Parker] on the computer'.[13]

Yousef was in a mood to brag, and he told Parker the computer – an expensive model with a colour screen – was worth $7,000–$8,000, and he was feeding information into the machine 'so that law enforcement authorities could never retrieve the information if they came to possess the computer'.[14] Parker later claimed that at this point Yousef still had not divulged his real 'career'. With hindsight it is clear Yousef was gradually recruiting Parker into his gang.

After this Yousef flew back to Manila to reel in more young militants for a future campaign of terror in the Philippines. Within the space of two months Yousef had gathered a group of supporters, including Adel Annon and Mustafa Abu Zainab, totalling about 23 men.[15] It was time for Ramzi Yousef to begin the next destructive phase of his career. He had decided he wanted to blow up passenger planes with a new type of tiny, undetectable bomb – the terrorist's

Holy Grail: a weapon that could be smuggled past airport security machines and on to jumbo jets.

Other terrorists have tried, and failed, to build these devices in the past, but few have had the same level of technical expertise as Ramzi Yousef. The bomb he used to wreak havoc in the World Trade Center had been used only once before in 73,000 explosions recorded by the FBI. Even the FBI admits that he is a master of explosives: 'He'll certainly be ranked right up there with the all-timers,' confirms Neil Herman.

To develop the new miniature bombs, Yousef studied hard, poring over textbooks he had stolen from libraries in Swansea five years before, and taught himself how to make a stable, liquid form of nitro-glycerine, the explosive component of TNT. His men bought an array of chemicals, including sulphuric acid, nitric acid, acetone, silver azide and the key ingredient, nitrobenzene, and fashioned them into sophisticated devices completely undetectable by any type of airport security device or X-ray machine. His trademark was converting a digital watch into a timing switch, hiding liquid nitro-glycerine in a contact lens case, with cotton wool as a stabilizer, and then using two nine-volt batteries to power light-bulb filaments and spark an explosion.

'The formula of nitro-glycerine would take five basic things,' one of Yousef's co-conspirators would later claim.[16] 'XX millilitres of glycerine, XX of nitrate, and XX of sulphuric acid, and when we, when we will mix nitro-glycerine, the density of the nitro-glycerine is about XX, which even you'll [sic] put it in the X-ray, you will never, nobody can . . . [tails off]'.

In a tiny space underneath the calculator on a Casio digital watch, Yousef installed electronic wiring attached to the watch alarm. Only a tiny plug was visible to indicate there had been any tampering, and the watch could be worn perfectly normally. The two batteries that formed the fuse were then wedged into the plug and attached to the contact lens case and light-bulb filament. 'Nobody in the world' can make bombs like these 'except us', bragged one of Yousef's gang.[17] For a while Yousef wondered how he could safely smuggle the two batteries, the only major metallic part of the bomb, through X-ray machines without anyone noticing. Then he realized that if he hid them in the hollowed-out heels of his shoes they would be below the range of almost every X-ray machine, and thus completely undetectable.[18]

It took Yousef weeks to develop the bomb, and when he was convinced it was ready he decided to try a simple test-run. By early

November 1994 Yousef was regularly travelling between Manila and Cebu City, a town of more than 700,000 people on the east coast of the Filipino island of Cebu, which is known as 'The Queen of the South' because of its friendly atmosphere. Yousef was apparently drawn to the city, the third largest in the Philippines, because he had friends from Mindanao and Basilan who were studying at its Southwest College. In November 1994 Yousef broke into the generator room of a shopping mall in Cebu City and left behind a small nitro-glycerine device. It exploded several hours later, causing only minor damage. More importantly, it showed that the device worked.

Yousef flew back to Manila to fine-tune his tiny bombs, and was met by emissaries sent by Osama bin Laden. They had travelled thousands of miles from Sudan with a message from their leader. If Yousef wondered why they had not simply contacted him by telephone, the reason was soon apparent. Osama bin Laden, who by late 1994 was already the most important independent financial sponsor of terrorism in the world, had decided to launch himself against the number one terrorist target in the world: US President William Jefferson Clinton.[19]

Bin Laden, his emissaries explained, wanted Yousef to assassinate President Clinton when he visited the Philippines on 12 November 1994, at the start of a five-day tour of Asia. Yousef appears to have been keen on the operation, relishing the prestige of his target, but he was also concerned that assassinating the most powerful man in the world would be no easy task – far harder than taking bombs into Iran or the World Trade Center.

Initially Yousef considered trying to kill Clinton with a missile or explosives placed along the route of the motorcade. He even queried whether American Stinger ground-to-air missiles could be used, either to shoot down the President's plane as it landed, or in a bizarre ground attack against his convoy.[20] Another option Yousef examined was the possibility of attacking him with phosgene gas, a chemical weapon – 20 times more powerful than chlorine gas – which caused an estimated 70 per cent of gas fatalities during the First World War, and kills by paralysing the lungs of the victim.

Killing President Clinton would have ensured Yousef's status as the pre-eminent world terrorist for decades to come, but – perhaps for the only time in his career – Yousef accepted his limitations. It would have been a difficult assignment for a suicide-bomber, let alone a young militant who valued his own skin. Yousef decided that security surrounding the President would be too tight and put the plan on hold. He then refocused on his original plot, which he code-named 'the Bojinka Plot' (Serbo-Croat for 'the explosion').

There were two main elements to the Bojinka Plot, both designed to spread panic and revulsion around the entire globe. The first was to use the tiny nitro-glycerine bombs to destroy several jumbo jets and massacre thousands of men, women and children. Yousef had no qualms about mass murder, indeed he wanted to be sure everyone on the planes would die, so after fine-tuning the device he had tested in Cebu, he decided it was time to test it again – underneath public seating to simulate the conditions aboard a passenger plane.

Yousef had brought his friend Wali Khan Amin Shah, a stocky terrorist with two fingers missing on his left hand, over from Pakistan to help with preparations for the bombing campaign. On 1 December 1994, at 4.26 p.m., Shah rang Yousef on a mobile phone he had rented to use during his time in the Philippines,[21] apparently to receive final instructions from Yousef on where he should place one of the small 'Mark II' bombs. Yousef gave his instructions and later that evening Shah allegedly left one of the bombs under a seat at the Greenbelt Theatre in Manila.

Thankfully, nobody sat in the seat, and when the bomb exploded at 10.30 p.m. there were only a few light injuries to an amorous couple sitting near by and several other locals. Twenty minutes after the explosion Shah rang Yousef again to brief him on what had happened. Yousef was pleased: the bomb had exploded precisely on time, and caused the level of destruction he had expected, but again he tinkered with the design increasing the bomb's destructive force still further. As he worked a small quantity of acid splashed on to his face, scarring his skin.[22] He promptly flew back to Pakistan, perhaps for medical help, perhaps just to meet members of his gang, but he stayed no more than a few days and then went back to Manila.

On 8 December he set in motion the second element of the Bojinka plot, appearing at the reception desk of the Dona Josefa Apartment Building, an anonymous six-storey, 60-room block at 711 President Quirino Boulevard, where he asked if a room was available at the front of the building.[23] Followed by a female member of staff, he climbed the stairs and cast an imperious eye over room 603, which was lying vacant. It was small, slightly dank, with just one bedroom and a little kitchenette in the corner. At first glance the room appeared to have little to offer a young terrorist growing used to a life of jetset travel and adventure.

Yousef sauntered over to the windows. The block is just a short distance from Manila Bay, and the cacophony of noise outside from the main road could wake the dead. The member of staff standing with him must have thought he would dislike the room, because she told him there were several other apartments available at the side of the block with spectacular views of the bay. Yousef just looked out of the window, gave one last glance around the room, and smiled. 'This is perfect,' he said. 'I'll take it.'

Downstairs he went through the paperwork with reception staff. 'My name is Naji Owaida Haddad,' he said, claiming to be a mechanical engineer from Morocco. 'I would like to take out a lease on the room for one month.' Yousef told the staff he was working in Manila for just a few weeks, and paid 11,880 Philippine pesos for the room (around £290 or $480). He gave the receptionist a Moroccan passport number, a home address in Rabat, Morocco, and a business address in Casablanca. The lease started that day, and Yousef retired to his room for a rest.

Yousef had something of a penchant for first-class travel, American Express Travellers' Cheques, and the luxuries of life: he was not staying at the humble Dona Josefa Apartment Building for the good of his health.[24] The young mastermind was planning an attack designed to provoke howls of outrage and anger in the Christian world, an act of terrorism that would reverberate around the world for decades to come, with his name as an echo. This was to be the second part of his plan. Deterred from his mission to kill President Clinton by the US leader's security precautions, Ramzi Yousef decided he would instead assassinate Pope John Paul II.

His nondescript apartment block would be crucial. The Pontiff was due to visit Manila in mid-January 1995 and the Dona Josefa Apartment Building sits on President Quirino Boulevard, a major road in Manila that the Pope would use regularly during his five-day visit. The block is also roughly 500ft from Taft Avenue and the Manila home of the Vatican's Ambassador to the Philippines, which would be the Pope's official residence during his stay in the country. But Yousef still needed to do one more test to ensure the first part of the Bojinka Plot would work.

On 9 December, the day after moving into the Dona Josefa Apartment Building, Yousef walked into a travel agency at the

Century Park Hotel in the Malate district of Manila. Using an Italian passport identifying him as Armaldo Forlani, Yousef bought a one-way ticket for a Philippines Airline flight to Cebu. He was, he told the travel agent with a sweep of his hand, an Italian member of parliament visiting the country.[25] The man certainly could not be accused of lacking gall.

Two days later Yousef walked through the X-ray machines at Manila airport, a nine-volt battery hidden in each of his shoes, boarded flight 434 to Cebu and sat near the back in seat 35F. The flight took off and Yousef asked a stewardess if he could move forward to seat 26K in the economy-class section of the Boeing 747-200. 'Do you mind?' he asked. 'I can have a better view from up there.'

Air stewardess Maria Delacruz, glancing at each passenger as she made her way down the aisles, noticed the solitary Arab. His prominent nose stuck in her mind.[26] Halfway through the short flight Yousef disappeared into the toilet, took off his shoes and assembled a bomb in a few minutes. Yousef returned to his seat, sat down and waited until Delacruz was serving snacks to the passengers. Then he leant forward and quickly tucked the tiny bomb into the life-vest under his seat. The plane flew on to Mactan Airport, Cebu, where Yousef disembarked before the final onward leg of the flight to Narita airport, Tokyo. Haruki Ikegami, a gentle 24-year-old engineer returning home to Japan from Cebu, where he had been adjusting industrial machinery for his employers, took Yousef's former seat on the right side of the fuselage, near the third door from the front.

Two hours later, after the plane had climbed to 10,000 metres and was flying over Minami Daito Island in Okinawa Prefecture, a flight attendant showing passengers a selection of duty-free goods spotted small traces of smoke rising from under Ikegami's seat. A fraction of a second later, at precisely 11.43 a.m. local time, Ramzi Yousef's tiny device exploded, mutilating the bottom half of Ikegami's body and nearly tearing him in two. The blast blew a small hole in the floor and severed the aileron cables that controlled the plane's flaps.

In the seat behind Ikegami another Japanese passenger called Yukihiko Usui had been asleep when the bomb went off. At first Usui thought the plane had blown apart or crashed, but in the split second as his eyes opened he glanced out of the window and saw clouds.[27] Usui's oxygen mask dangled down in front of him, burnt and useless. 'I looked at the person in front of me . . . the person was trying to ask for help,' said Usui.[28] Ikegami raised a solitary index finger in an agonizing last movement, then slumped back in his seat. Usui tried to move and reach Ikegami, but his legs were suddenly racked by excruciating pain. The bomb had burnt his legs and blasted small pieces of shrapnel into his lower body. It would take four months of hospital treatment and countless operations to repair Usui's damaged limbs.[29]

Nothing could be done to help Ikegami: the horrific nature of his wounds meant that Ikegami could never have survived – his pulse stopped in less than a minute. Ignoring the blood, torn flesh, smoke, and the screams of other passengers, PAL air steward Fernando Bayot bravely struggled to fasten an oxygen mask on to Ikegami's mouth and cover his body with a blanket, to make it look as if he was alive – 'so other passengers would not be scared'. He then went to brief Captain Ed Reyes on the chaos.[30] Four other Japanese passengers and a Korean man were also badly injured in the explosion. The jet's steering was crippled and Captain Reyes was unsure whether he could turn the plane.

'I'm going to force it,' Reyes told First Officer Jaime Herrera. 'Let's see if it will turn.'[31] The Captain dumped fuel over the sea and by brute force managed to put the plane into a wide turn. The plane limped on to make an emergency landing at Naha airport in Okinawa, on the southern tip of the Japanese archipelago, at 12.45 p.m. Only the skill of Reyes, Herrera and Flight Engineer Dexter Comendador prevented a greater disaster and the deaths of all 272 passengers and 20 crew.

With the plane safely on the ground Japanese investigators began scouring the passenger deck for clues. Initially they thought that firecrackers, which are popular in the Philippines during the Christmas and New Year holidays, were sneaked on board by a passenger and accidentally exploded during the flight. But then Ramzi Yousef, reluctant to miss out on notoriety, rang the Associated Press news agency in Manila anonymously and claimed responsibility for the explosion on behalf of the Abu Sayyaf group.

Superintendent Shigiro Yotoyama, a veteran Japanese police bomb expert, flew down to Naha from his office in Tokyo and met with other Japanese experts – Senior Superintendents Pateshi Iguchi and Jun Nakamura. They were joined by a small team of investigators from the Philippines, including Augustus Viso, PAL vice-president for operations, and Chief Inspector Edgar Gatumbato of the Philippine Aviation

Security Command (PASCOM), part of the Philippine National Police force. An investigator from Boeing also arrived from California, and the team began an inch-by-inch search of the plane.

From the force of the blast and the way it tore and twisted metal in the seats near Haruki Ikegami, Superintendent Yotoyama quickly concluded the explosion could only have been caused by a bomb. The problem, however, was finding proof, just as it had been for the FBI team working in the bowels of the World Trade Center.

The Japanese explosives team sealed off the section of the plane around the explosion to prevent contamination and cordoned off the plane in a hangar. Several detectives then began examining the area where Ikegami died for fragments of a device and took swabs for forensic analysis. The search went on for days, and yet the police found nothing but tiny traces of the bomb's fuse, battery, timing device and wiring. Superintendent Yotoyama concluded that to leave such minute traces the bomb had to be of an extremely high standard. It was the first bombing of a jetliner for five years.

The investigation went up a gear and more investigators were brought in. Superintendent Yotoyama eventually found chemical traces in the plane and deduced the bomb had consisted of liquid nitro-glycerine, virtually undetectable by airport security. The Japanese informed the US Federal Aviation Administration, which in turn issued a high-level security alert to all American air carriers travelling in Asia. Several months later police in Manila uncovered instructions detailing the inner workings of Yousef's Casio timer switches. They faxed a hand-drawn diagram to the Japanese police and Zenshin Taira, an explosives expert with the Okinawa police, painstakingly reconstructed fragments found on the plane. Taira rebuilt the watch like a tiny electronic jigsaw and finally confirmed the cause of the explosion.

Yousef was long gone by the time Superintendent Yotoyama had deduced that the PAL jet had been targeted by terrorists. His movements in the days immediately following the PAL bombing remain something of a mystery – several intelligence sources claim Yousef stayed in a safehouse in Cebu City with one of his militant student friends from Southwest College – but they are crucial because they may help to determine whether he was involved in the next great horror that stunned America. The massive bomb that ripped apart the Alfred P. Murrah federal building in Oklahoma on 19 April 1995 killed 168 people and injured another 600. Since the bombing there have been extraordinary claims that Yousef met and trained Terry L. Nichols, one of the two men charged with the atrocity. One of Yousef's friends has even claimed that Yousef's gang was responsible for the bombing.

The possible link was uncovered by Stephen Jones, the chief defence lawyer for Timothy J. McVeigh, who was sentenced to death for the Oklahoma bombing. Some FBI agents have dismissed Jones's claims as a legal manoeuvre to try and shift the burden of guilt from his one-time client to Nichols and create a wider conspiracy. 'He's just trying to portray McVeigh as the patsy,' said one FBI source.[32] Others believe the links are more than just mere coincidence.

The exact origins of the plot to attack the federal building in Oklahoma are still unclear, but in mid-November 1994 Terry Nichols left the US to spend Christmas with Marife, his Filipino 'mail-order' bride, and her family in Cebu. He had given his ex-wife Lana a package and told her to open it in 60 days if he had not returned safely. Lana, fearing Nichols was in trouble, opened it as soon as he had gone. She found instructions addressed to her and Timothy McVeigh, treasury bonds, Nichols's car keys, details of the location of a plastic bag stuffed with cash and more than $20,000 in gold and silver bars.

The instructions to McVeigh, in the event of Nichols not returning from the Philippines, read: 'Your [sic] on your own. Go for it!'[33] One obvious interpretation of Nichols's instructions and his visit to the Far East was that he knew he was going to meet highly dangerous characters and was unsure whether he would return. If he did not, McVeigh was to proceed with the plot to attack the Alfred P. Murrah federal building. The evidence is not conclusive, but even members of the Nichols jury believe a wider tale still waits to be told: Niki Deutchman, the forewoman of the jury that eventually convicted McVeigh, has said she and others on the panel believed McVeigh and Nichols had help.[34]

Stephen Jones investigated the possible Philippines link for months, and now believes that Ramzi Yousef's close friend and conspirator Wali Khan Amin Shah knew Marife Nichols and her sister through a mutual friend. Through his innocent wife it is alleged that Terry Nichols was introduced either to Muslim militants close to Ramzi Yousef or to a Filipino arms dealer who supplied and knew the militants. Either the militants or the arms dealer then arranged a meeting between the American and Ramzi Yousef.[35]

Details of one of these meetings were discussed during a video-taped interrogation of Edwin Angeles, one of the most senior members of the Abu Sayyaf terrorist gang, conducted at the Basilan Provincial Jail by Filipino investigators from the National Police and the National Bureau of Investigation. Angeles claimed he had met Yousef together with Nichols – whom he knew only as an American called 'The Farmer' – at meetings near the Del Monte labelling factory in Davao on Mindanao.[36] According to Stephen Jones, Angeles said that Yousef and Nichols met to discuss three specific topics: 'bombing activities; providing firearms and ammunition; training in making and handling bombs'.[37]

There are few terrorists in the world who could have given Nichols the advice Yousef could offer. In October 1994 McVeigh and Nichols tried to blow up a milk jug with a curious little ammonium nitrate bomb. Rather than exploding in a fiery ball, it simply fizzled. Six months later, after Nichols had spent time in the Philippines, his co-conspirator McVeigh was able to blow up the federal building in Oklahoma with a 5,600lb bomb made of ammonium nitrate and nitromethane.

There is no hard proof linking Yousef to the plot, but there is a wealth of circumstantial evidence. Abdul Hakim Murad, Yousef's terrorist deputy, heard of the April 1995 Oklahoma attack on the radio in his prison cell in New York, and was asked by a prison guard for his thoughts. Murad stated unequivocally that Yousef's 'Liberation Army' was responsible. A short time later Murad confirmed in writing that the Liberation Army was to blame.[38]

It is certainly possible that Yousef and Nichols *could* have met: both were in Cebu at the same time – November–December 1994. Many questions still surround Nichols's activities in the Philippines. Nobody has established the source of the money that Nichols used to buy numerous plane tickets on his regular trips to and from the Philippines. Some intelligence reports suggest a wealthy benefactor funded his trips. There are also questions surrounding the Southwest College in Cebu City, where a large number of Muslim students from the southern Filipino islands study, and where Yousef was known to have friends.

Marife Nichols went to live with many of them in a boarding house in Cebu after her husband Terry returned to America in January 1995. Between 31 January and 14 March 1995, Nichols made 78 phone-calls to the boarding house. Naturally, one assumes he was simply a devoted husband talking with his wife. Why then did he ring the boarding house another 12 times after his wife had left?

Stephen Jones believes the US government has since tried to hide evidence of foreign involvement. 'In the largest case of domestic terrorism in the United States, a crime of such violence that it would kill 168 people, 19 of whom are children under the age of six, and eight of whom are federal law enforcement agents, you can't say we didn't solve it. You have to solve it. You can't say, well, we caught two of them. What you say is, "We caught all of them." '[39]

Whether Yousef met Nichols in Cebu City or not, by mid-December he had certainly returned to his flat at the Dona Josefa Apartment Building in Manila and begun recruiting more terrorists. One of his first moves was to ring his old friend Abdul Hakim Murad in Pakistan and convince him to fly to Manila to help with the Bojinka Plot. 'Murad must have needed some persuading,' said an American intelligence source,[40] 'because we're pretty sure that Yousef flew back to Pakistan almost immediately to meet him.'

Yousef also went to see Ishtiaque Parker in Islamabad, and in a dramatic account of his crimes finally told the young South African about his terrorist career, his attack on the World Trade Center, the bombing of the shrine at Mashhad in Iran and the attack on the PAL plane. Then Yousef told Parker that he wanted him to take a parcel or bag overseas, probably to London.[41] He would pay Parker $10,000–$15,000 on his return, he told the quivering student, and would give him more instructions within the next few weeks.[42]

Secure in the belief he had recruited Parker, Yousef set about persuading Murad to travel with him to the Philippines. 'We're not sure what he said or did,' admits an American intelligence source, 'but he clearly had some sort of hold over [Murad]. I know there was some suggestion out of Pakistan that Yousef may even have threatened Murad, because eventually they fell out.'

Whatever ploy Yousef used, Murad was finally persuaded, and the two men arrived in Manila the day after Christmas and moved back into Yousef's small flat. Yousef, 'the Moroccan', told inquisitive staff the new arrival was a Pakistani called Said Ahmed. It was a rare unguarded moment: the two men were generally 'unfriendly' to staff and other residents. They even spurned the services of the daily maid service at the apartment block, allowing them in just a few times in December and January, and then only under close supervision. According to one maid, 'he would watch us – watch everything we do – very closely'. The maid remembers seeing some strange equipment in the room: timing devices, a soldering gun and bits of wire littering the kitchen table. 'I did not know what it was all for,' she said.[43]

Staff at the apartment had been suspicious of Yousef ever since he had arrived at the beginning of December, and by the time Murad arrived they were convinced the two men were up to no good. It was not just because they would come and go at all hours of the day and night – that was relatively normal for Arabs in the Philippines. 'He often went out late at night, but that is not surprising, since many Arabs come to the Philippines just for R and R – to go out to the bars at night,' one of Yousef's neighbours said later.[44] And it was certainly not because they behaved like Islamic fundamentalists, who were feared in Manila because of Abu Sayyaf bombings in the south of the country. The two men wore Western clothes, and Yousef had a girl-friend, a Filipino woman by the name of Carol Santiago who would regularly visit him in the hotel. Yousef was also gallivanting around Manila's bars, strip-joints and karaoke clubs, and flirting with women. 'It got to the point where he was almost flaunting himself around,' said Neil Herman, the supervisor of the FBI unit tracking him around the world.

Staff at Yousef's apartment block simply felt the two men 'did not quite fit in', according to a Filipino investigator.[45] 'Middle Eastern men kept coming by, bringing boxes and metal pipes,' said Julio Solis, a building attendant.[46] Another member of staff also claims to have kept an eye on Yousef: 'I was always suspicious of Yousef because he never would return my greeting,' he said. 'He was always looking down at the ground, like he was thinking of something, planning. People would see him, but nobody would ever talk to him. And he wore sunglasses, day and night.'[47]

If the staff could have seen inside his apartment, they would have found more than enough to justify their suspicions. Yousef was simul-taneously planning more plane bombings and buying the weapons and equipment he would need to assassinate the Pope. After analysing the effects of his bomb on the PAL plane, Yousef apparently concluded that he just needed to increase slightly the strength of the bomb to ensure it would down any jet.

The depth of Yousef's planning was extraordinary. Not content with simply placing his bombs at random on a plane, Yousef obtained Boeing 747 blueprints and calculated the most devastating location to place his devices: in a seat above the central fuel tank and adjacent to the wing.

The bomb alone would not destroy the plane, but it would detonate the fuel. His appalling dedication did not stop there: Yousef was also making more than a dozen false identification cards bearing his name and photograph – in each one he looks radically different. He created one card, for example, to use while buying chemicals in the Philippines to make bombs. Alongside a photo of his pursed lips and flapping ears, the card identified Yousef as 'Dr Adel Sabah, Chem [Chemical] specialist', an employee of the 'International Trading Corp' at 93 Sloane Gardens, London WC4N 2BW, and listed an address in Cairo.[48] Yousef added one final ironic touch to the card: an 'authorization date' of 26 February 1993, the date of the twin towers bombing.

Using his network of contacts he then bought cheap explosives and chemicals using the names Dr Adel Sabah and Dr Paul Vijay, a chemical company representative. He also rented a beach house near Manila where he could train his militant followers in preparation for a suicide attack. He sent them out to buy two Bibles, crucifixes, a large photograph of Pope John Paul II – apparently so they could recognize their target, several priests' garments, a map of the route the Pope would take in Manila, and a tobacco pipe – allegedly to hide a small quantity of plastic explosive. Yousef's research was meticulous. He even obtained confessional manuals and tunic buttons similar to those worn by Filipino cardinals.

But suicide attacks are not as foolproof as one might imagine. Bombers can sweat profusely and appear nervous, attracting the attention of security guards. Or they can detonate their bomb too early or too late, blasting themselves into martyrdom but failing to kill their target. Yousef knew the risks, and so he began considering other methods of killing the Pope. He seems to have let his imagination run wild.

In late December 1994 American investigators believe Yousef visited an airline charter company just outside Manila and inquired about hiring a small plane. His idea, apparently, was to get Murad – who had trained as a pilot at flight schools in San Antonio and Schenectady, New York, before graduating from an academy in North Carolina with a temporary commercial pilot's licence – to fly the plane along the route taken by the 'Popemobile' and drop bombs over the side.[49] Yousef eventually realized it was unlikely to work when he discovered the authorities were planning to enforce an air-exclusion zone over central Manila while the Pope was in residence. Yousef went back to the drawing board.

However, according to one American investigator there might have

The twin towers of the World Trade Center

Damage to the lower levels of the World Trade Center after Ramzi Yousef's bombing.

A crucial section of the Ryder Truck used by Ramzi Yousef to carry the World Trade Center bomb. This section was found by Joseph Hanlin of the ATF and Donald Sadowy of the NYPD's Bomb Squad in the remains of the World Trade Center within days of the explosion.

Neil E Herman, senior FBI Supervisory Special Agent in charge of the FBI-led Joint Terrorist Task Force during the World Trade Center investigation and the hunt for Ramzi Yousef. A veteran anti-terrorist investigator who was awarded the FBI Directors Award for his handling of the 'Tradebom' enquiry, Herman also supervized the TWA 800 investigation.

(PAUL SCHNECK PHOTOGRAPHY)

Rehman Malik, former Additional Director General of the Federal Investigation Agency (FIA), the Pakistani equivalent of the FBI. Malik, who was also the FIA Director (Immigration and Anti-Smuggling), was the senior Pakistani official investigating and tracking Ramzi Yousef.

(FEDERAL INVESTIGATION AGENCY, PAKISTAN)

Peter Probst, Pentagon terrorism expert who supervized the secret 'Terror 2000' report, which warns of a new age of terrorism, in an undated photograph taken during his previous career as an archaeologist.

(AUTHOR COLLECTION)

Battered and bloodied, a victim of the bombing at the holy shrine of Imam Reza in Mashhad, Iran, waits for hospital treatment. FBI and Pakistani investigators believe Ramzi Yousef was responsible for the attack on 20 June 1994, which they believe he undertook in association with the Iranian rebel MKO. The attack killed twenty-six pilgrims and injured another 200.

(ISLAMIC REPUBLIC NEWS AGENCY)

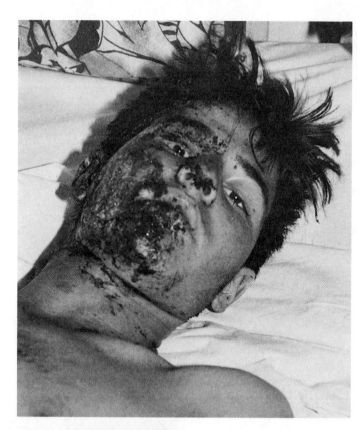

Victims injured by one of Ramzi Yousef's miniature bombs are removed from a passenger jet at Naha Airport in Okinawa, Japan, in December 1994.

(KYODO NEWS INTERNATIONAL)

A wealthy residential street in London, England. Yousef used 93 Sloane Gardens on one of his false identification cards, but the house does not exist.

(AUTHOR COLLECTION)

Oxford College of Further Education where British and American investigators believe Ramzi Yousef studied on a short course learning English as a Foreign Language.

(AUTHOR COLLECTION)

Swansea Institute, formerly West Glamorgan Institute of Higher Education (or 'Wiggy'), where the FBI and British investigators believe Yousef spent several years studying for a Higher National Diploma in computer-aided electrical engineering.
(AUTHOR COLLECTION)

The Uplands Tavern in Swansea, where several sources say they saw Ramzi Yousef.
(AUTHOR COLLECTION)

been another reason why Yousef chose to cancel the air attack. 'He may have wanted to save Murad for another bombing,' said the source.[50] While plotting to kill the Pope Yousef was also devising a special mission for his old friend that would inflict more devastation on 'the Great Satan'. 'The plan was for chemical weapons to be loaded on to a light aircraft and for Murad either to fly it – kamikaze-style – into the CIA headquarters in Langley, Virginia, or for Murad to fly overhead and spray the whole area with gas,' said the investigator.[51] According to a later Filipino police report, the attack was intended: 'to demonstrate to the whole world that a Muslim martyr is ready and determined to die for the glorification of Islam'.[52] 'It sounds extreme, but Yousef had the technical know-how,' adds the American investigator. 'Don't doubt the commitment of these men.'

Murad was the perfect accomplice for Yousef: an extremist he had known since childhood in Kuwait, undaunted by death or the prospect of causing massive civilian casualties. When he was later interviewed by Filipino investigators, Murad told them that 'killing Americans' was 'my [pause] best thing. I enjoy it. You can kill them by, eh, gas. You can kill them by gun. You can kill them by knife. You can kill them by explosion. There's many kinds.'[53]

Over the new year period Yousef's friend and co-conspirator Wali Khan Amin Shah travelled back to Pakistan from the Philippines for a short stay, and it was soon time for him to return to Manila and join up with Yousef. On 3 January Shah bought a single Casio watch from an airport discount shop in Singapore, then caught a flight to Kuala Lumpur, Malaysia, using a ticket issued to 'W. Khan'. According to US investigators, he was probably there to buy some of the raw materials needed for the Bojinka Plot. The next day, using the name 'Grabi Ibrahim Hahsen', Shah flew from Kuala Lumpur back to Singapore and then on to Manila to meet up with Yousef.[54]

By 6 January Yousef's preparations for a huge terrorist attack were well underway, and he was ready to start building more bombs. In their room at Dona Josefa Yousef and Murad worked late that night, heating and mixing chemicals in a cooking pot. It was a delicate stage of the operation: in their raw state the chemicals could explode, ignite, or release poisonous fumes. For all Yousef's bomb-making skill, something went drastically wrong, and just after 10.40 p.m. a small fire started in the room. Flames licked around the cooking area, driving the men back, and poisonous smoke began rising to the ceiling. A witches' brew of chemicals was on fire.

Yousef and Murad were lucky they were not immediately blown to pieces, but try as they might, they could not stop choking smoke billowing out of the cooking pot. Yousef opened the window, grabbed his mobile phone and the two men ran out into the corridor, slamming the door shut behind them. Inside the apartment smoke began slipping out of the open window towards the roof, while outside the door the two terrorists were desperately trying to fan the smoke out of the hallway with their arms and a coat.

On the roof of the block a male tenant was sitting with his girlfriend and enjoying the moonlit sky when a dark cloud of smoke curled over the side of the roof. The startled man, thinking the entire block was on fire, ran downstairs and alerted Roman Mariano, the Josefa Apartments' 27-year-old security guard. Mariano sprinted back up the stairs and discovered Yousef and Murad – whom he knew as Said Ahmed – trying to get rid of the smoke in the hallway. It was a farcical scene.

'I found the two men – the man who said he was Moroccan and the man who said he was Pakistani – outside the apartment door, trying to blow the smoke away,' said Mariano.[55] 'I asked to go into the apartment, but they said no. They said the smoke was from firecrackers and they kept saying, "Don't worry, we're just celebrating a late new year's." They didn't want me to call the police.'

The smoke was billowing out in acrid black clouds, and the young security guard ignored their protestations and shouted to Yousef that he was going inside. When Mariano entered the room the fire was already starting to die out, but smoke was still choking the air. 'The smoke hurt my eyes and was painful to the skin,' said Mariano. Even in the gloom Mariano could see lead pipes and wires, a laptop computer and bottles labelled 'grape juice'. He glanced at the kitchen area and could see the fire had started in the sink, leaving it coated with a thick layer of a strange substance that looked like salt.

Outside the room, the two men had disappeared. Mariano ran downstairs and as a fire-engine pulled up outside the block, he then saw Yousef calmly walking out of the building, talking intently into his mobile phone. As firefighters ran inside, Murad was also spotted making his escape by climbing into the back of a waiting taxi.

It took the firefighters just 10 minutes to extinguish the remaining few flames and begin venting smoke from the room. Local policemen then had a quick look around the room and saw enough to arouse their suspicions. Security in Manila had been tightened in preparation for the Pope's visit, and the officers called their headquarters and requested specialist back-up. A squad of senior police officers was soon on the way.

Yousef and Murad had arranged to meet in a small karaoke bar near their apartment after the fire, and together they walked slowly back down the road and stood in a doorway near the block to check the firemen had left. Yousef knew someone had to take a chance and get back into the room. His computer, manuals, and files would reveal his plans and many of his aliases. It would be a disaster if they were to fall into the hands of the police. But Yousef was no fool – he had no intention of risking his own neck. So instead he persuaded Murad to go back into the apartment block on the premise that he wanted to remove some of his luggage.

Murad dutifully made his way back into the hotel and carefully checked that the firemen and police had left. Then he crept up to the room and began packing Yousef's bags. Unfortunately for Murad, just as he was putting Yousef's laptop into a black carry-case a squad of senior officers arrived with a search warrant. They took one look around the room and arrested him on the spot.

Inside the dingy room the officers found an array of chemicals and disguises: several containers of sulphuric acid, bomb-making manuals, wire, timing devices, a soldering gun, Bibles, a large photograph of Pope John Paul II, priests' garments, and a map of the Pope's route. There was also the tobacco pipe, the Toshiba laptop computer and several floppy disks, and four small pipe-bombs.

Among the haul were the reference books stolen from Swansea library which showed how Yousef had been researching his plot to assassinate President Clinton. The collection of books included *How to Build Electronic Alarms* and the *Condensed Chemical Dictionary*, with passages on the manufacture of explosives highlighted. In the dictionary, under the entry for dichlorocarbane, which Yousef had highlighted with a marker pen, it read: 'Hazard: Explosive reaction with carbon, forms phosgene on reaction with oxygen.' The chemistry book stated that dichlorocarbane 'use' was only for 'research.' According to FBI investigators, however, Ramzi Yousef had been planning to use phosgene gas to murder the leader of the free world.

The police officers engaged in the search could scarcely believe their eyes. On the floor of the apartment, stains and burns marked spots where Yousef and his friend had spilt mysterious chemicals during their experiments. In a cabinet above the kitchen counter was a fragmentation bomb packed into a pipe that was already attached to a timer and detonator. 'The pipe, well, he told me it's, eh, for explosion. I mean, his new – new idea of, of an explosion,' Murad said later during questioning. But it was the Toshiba laptop that proved to be the most astonishing find.

Chief Inspector Taas of the Philippines National Police (PNP) had a quick look at the machine inside room 603, then took it back to his office, turned it on and had a browse through its directories. Then he contacted the PNP's Presidential Security Group, and sent it over to them in a police car for examination. A computer expert working for the PNP as a consultant and another technical investigator both examined the machine and began to find snippets of information that hinted at a massive terrorist attack.

In a file Yousef had created on his laptop under the heading 'Bojinka' he detailed how five of his men would plant bombs timed to explode simultaneously on 11 US airliners over the Pacific. If successful the operation would have caused the deaths of up to 4,000 people flying from Asia to the United States and almost certainly shut down the entire airline industry.[56] It was an astonishing plot hallmarked by Yousef's meticulous planning. Each of the five terrorists was given a code-name:

1. 'Mirqas' was to plant a bomb on a United Airlines flight from Manila to Seoul and leave the flight in South Korea. The plane would then continue towards San Francisco from Seoul and explode over the Pacific. Mirqas would also plant another bomb on a Delta flight from Seoul to Taipei. That would explode on the next leg of the flight to Bangkok, but Mirqas would have left the plane in Taipei and flown to Singapore, then home to Karachi.
2. 'Markoa' would place a bomb on a Northwest Airlines flight from Manila to Tokyo, then disembark. The plane would blow up en route to Chicago, by which time Markoa would have already boarded a Northwest flight from Tokyo to Hong Kong and planted a bomb timed to explode over the Pacific, as the plane was on its way to New York. Markoa would get off in Hong Kong, fly to Singapore and then on to Pakistan.
3. 'Obaid' was to plant a bomb on the United flight from Singapore to

Hong Kong: it would then detonate in the middle of the flight's continuation to Los Angeles. Obaid, meanwhile, would board the United flight from Hong Kong to Singapore, plant a bomb set to explode on the return leg to Hong Kong, and then fly directly from Singapore home to Pakistan.

4. 'Majbos' would fly from Taipei to Tokyo on United and leave a bomb set to go off as the jet headed on to Los Angeles. He would then fly from Tokyo to Hong Kong and place a bomb aboard another United flight set to go off as the jet flew from Tokyo to New York.

5. 'Zyed' would have the most difficult task: he was supposed to fly Northwest to Seoul, hide a bomb under his seat and get off. The bomb would then explode on the next leg of the flight to Los Angeles. Zyed, probably the code-name for Yousef, would by then have flown on to Taipei on United, left a bomb to explode on the Taipei–Honolulu leg of the flight and disembarked. He would then fly to Bangkok on United and leave the plane, having hidden a bomb under the seat timed to explode as the plane flew towards San Francisco, and leaving the terrorist plenty of time to fly to Karachi from Bangkok.

Investigators now believe that Yousef, Murad and Shah were three of the terrorists. Filipino officers and the FBI claim one of Yousef's brothers was to have been the fourth terrorist, and the fifth is alleged to have been a man called Khalid Al-Shaikh (*aka* Khalid Sheikh Mohammad) who Pakistani intelligence sources claim is Ramzi Yousef's other uncle. Mohammad allegedly arrived in Manila just before the apartment fire but then disappeared; he is now a fugitive, with a $5 million reward on his head. According to Pakistani intelligence sources he is now living in Qatar.

The plan was frighteningly close to fruition: 'Obaid', the code-name for Murad, was to have boarded the flight from Singapore to Hong Kong on 21 January, two weeks from the date of the fire. It would have been a campaign that eclipsed every other terrorist atrocity in history.

References

[1] Author interview with a Pakistani investigator.
[2] Ibid.
[3] Ibid.

4 Author interview with Filipino investigator.

5 Author interview.

6 Author interviews.

7 Author interview with a Filipino investigator.

8 Ibid. Annon was later arrested and charged, but he was acquitted in July 1996 and disappeared.

9 Author interview with senior Pakistani investigator. There is no suggestion Rana did anything wrong.

10 Author interview with Filipino investigator.

11 Ibid.

12 Interrogation of Parker by Pakistani investigators Rehman Malik and Sajjad Haider. Report obtained by author.

13 Ibid.

14 Ibid.

15 Author interview with Filipino investigator.

16 From the transcript of Murad's interrogation by unidentified Filipino police officers, dated 7 January 1995, and passed to the author. 'XX' substituted for precise quantities by the author.

17 Ibid.

18 Ibid.

19 Author interview with Filipino and American investigators.

20 Ibid.

21 United States District Court, Southern District of New York, USA v. Ramzi Ahmed Yousef et al., Indictment, S12 93 Cr. 180 (KTD), Count 12, subsections a, b and c.

22 Interrogation of Parker by Pakistani investigators.

23 Information for this section is taken from interviews by the author with Neil Herman, other investigators in America and the Philippines, court records, and Philip Shenon, 'Broad Terror Campaign Is Foiled By Fire In The Kitchen, Officials Say', *New York Times*, 12 February 1995.

24 Interrogation of Parker by Pakistani investigators. Report obtained by author.

25 Author interview with Filipino investigators.

26 Testimony of Maria Delacruz to the Manila Air bombing trial, 30 May 1996.

27 Testimony of Yukihiko Usui to the Manila Air bombing trial, 3 June 1996.

28 Ibid.

29 Ibid.

30 Testimony of Fernando Bayot to the Manila Air bombing trial, 3 June 1996.

31 Testimony of Captain Ed Reyes to the Manila Air bombing trial, 3 June 1996.

32 Author interview.

33 Stephen Jones, *Others Unknown*.

34 Richard A. Serrano, 'National Perspective', *Los Angeles Times*, 20 January 1998.

35 Author interview with Stephen Jones. Also: Petition for Writ of Mandamus of Petitioner-Defendant Timothy McVeigh, in the US Court of Appeals, Case No. 96-CR-68-M, 25 March 1997.

36 Further investigation is now difficult, as Angeles was murdered on 15 January 1999.
37 Jones, op. cit.
38 Writ of Mandamus, op. cit.
39 Author interview with Stephen Jones.
40 Author interview.
41 Interrogation of Parker by Pakistani investigators.
42 Ibid.
43 Shenon, op. cit.
44 Ibid.
45 Author interview.
46 Anon, 'Fire led to NY bomb suspect', *Toronto Star*, 13 February 1995.
47 Shenon, op. cit.
48 The London postcode does not exist, and the houses in Sloane Gardens, a wealthy residential street, stop at no. 59.
49 Author interview with American investigators.
50 Author interview.
51 Ibid.
52 Author interview with Filipino investigator. The police report was written in March 1995.
53 Murad interrogation, op. cit.
54 USA v. Yousef, Indictment, op. cit. Count 12, subsection k.
55 Shenon, op. cit.
56 Author interview with Neil Herman.

FIVE

The Long Arm of the Law

WHEN FILIPINO officers first searched the Manila apartment, nobody immediately suspected Yousef was involved in the fire. However when the PNP discovered the stash of chemicals they informed their counterparts in Washington as a matter of routine, just as they informed Interpol, Scotland Yard, and intelligence agencies in neighbouring countries. The FBI took more interest than most, because they were extremely concerned at the technical sophistication of the PAL bombing a month previously. When the PNP made contact and said their technicians had found a partial fingerprint in the flat, and matched it to prints of Yousef stored on Interpol computers, the FBI went into high gear.

'We had information connecting Yousef to Manila,' confirms Neil Herman. 'And we'd been there before on the investigation.' When the fire started FBI agents had left Manila and moved to other Asian cities in pursuit of Yousef: 'but as soon as [the fingerprints were found] we were notified almost immediately and despatched a team of agents.' A squad of investigators was airborne within a day.

Apart from confirming that Yousef was still active and alive, the apartment also gave the police and FBI clues to the other conspirators. Murad had been arrested on the spot, and then on the morning of 11 January 1995, Wali Khan Amin Shah walked out of his apartment block on Singalong Street in Manila and was immediately surrounded by three armed Filipino detectives. Shah was taken back up the stairs into his flat and the detectives opened the small black bag he had been carrying. Inside were four passports: Pakistani, Saudi Arabian, Afghan and Norwegian. Three of them contained Shah's photograph. Four days later Shah managed to escape from police custody, in circumstances that have still not been explained adequately. He made his way to Malaysia, where he was re-arrested by alert police officers and extradited to the US.

Despite an 'intensive manhunt' by the Philippines police, who claim they issued Yousef's description to all their officers in Manila and thousands more in the south of the country, Yousef again managed to avoid capture.[1] In the early hours of 7 January he paid $848 in cash for a first-class flight from Manila to Hong Kong and flew on from there to Singapore. From there he jumped on to a flight to Pakistan and disappeared.

The FBI, meanwhile, were taking a healthy interest in the contents of Yousef's laptop. Mary Horvath, an FBI computer expert, flew to Manila and made three back-up copies of the computer's hard-drive. Initially the FBI had problems with the machine, and there were bizarre rumours the CIA had got hold of the laptop and wiped files that implicated their agents in Yousef's campaign of terror. The truth was less exciting: 'there were some problems decoding the computer ... some of the people that tried to decode it could not,' said Herman.

So in New York Dietrich Snell, an Assistant United States Attorney involved in building a case against Yousef, contacted a corporate lawyer at the giant Microsoft computer corporation and asked if the company had an expert who could examine a copy of Yousef's hard-drive. Snell then flew across the US to meet David Swartzendruber, a forensic investigator working for Microsoft who had spent 23 years in law enforcement, and gave him a 'mirror image' of the hard-drive stored on a 4mm DAT tape.[2] Swartzendruber downloaded the 4mm DAT on to a 'control computer', which was used solely for the investigation, and began his examinations. 'After restoration I always conduct a virus check, make sure the drive specifications are in sync and there are not any hidden partitions, [then] conduct a text search in the slack, hidden areas, and the various directories on the hard drive,' said Swartzendruber, who previously worked as a financial investigator and forensic computer specialist for the San Diego Drug Enforcement Narcotic Task Force.[3]

Swartzendruber then began looking for any hidden or encrypted data, as well as 'unusual, bad, or lost clusters'. 'I then activate the computer and run the programs as the original user would,' he said. The investigator found and bypassed several encryption programmes running on the computer, and found numerous temporary files in the

Windows directory. 'Whoever used the computer failed to create a temporary directory, and because of this oversight all of the temporary files were written to the Windows directory,' said Swartzendruber. 'To elaborate, whoever caused a file to be written to the computer would unknowingly write a temporary file to the Windows directory. You could then erase the original file, however the temporary file would remain and provide a time and date stamp of the original file, and in some cases the contents or partial contents of the original file.'

Swartzendruber began recovering deleted files, which were still stored on the computer's hard-disk waiting to be overwritten by new data, and the laptop files produced a wealth of information. There were flight schedules, projected detonation times, chemical formulae, and, bizarrely, a sound file containing a recording of a telephone conversation between Yousef and an Asian-sounding woman. 'Don't forget that I love you,' she coos to him sweetly. 'Shut up, you bitch,' Yousef responds.

There was also a letter in which the 'Fifth Battalion of the Liberation Army under the leadership of Lieutenant General Abu Baker Almaki' threatened more attacks on American targets 'in response to the financial, political and military assistance given to the Jewish State in the occupied land of Palestine by the American Government'.[4] There was even a file on the computer containing a 'business card' identifying Yousef as an 'International Terrorist'. 'I almost fell over when I saw it,' said one US investigator.[5]

Herman remembers: 'There was a lot of material on the computer, a lot of which was coded. It was a diary, a history, a strategy of what they were planning to do. Once the disk on the computer was looked at we discovered the project he was working on. We were able to connect the Fifth Liberation Army to our case. We knew it was the same people. Once the materials in the apartment were analysed we knew he was our man.' The concern for Neil Herman and his Joint Terrorist Task Force was what Yousef might do next. 'He was also looking at other acts he was planning, including [assassinating] the President, when he was travelling out there. We knew he was a timebomb.'

The pressure on Yousef was intensifying. He knew the Philippines police had his laptop, and he realized they would pass it on to the FBI. What he did not foresee was the speed with which the Feds would discover his bombing plans, because he thought he had successfully deleted the most incriminating files from his computer. His main concern, it seems, was the liberty of his old friend Abdul Hakim Murad.

Yousef knew he would need Murad in any future air attack on the CIA headquarters; he wanted his friend released. So Yousef wrote a draft letter in which he, as the 'Chief of Staff' of 'The Liberation Army' demanded the immediate release of Murad, threatening 'the strongest actions' against 'all Filipino interests', including passenger planes and the assassination of the president of the Philippines if his demand was not met. Perhaps Yousef was just too busy plotting other bombings to mail the letter, but he also wrote another, headlined 'WE DEMAND HIS RELEASE', written on behalf of the 'Liberation Army', and claiming the 'ability to make and use chemicals and poisonous gas ... for use against vital institutions and residential populations and the sources of drinking water and others'.[6]

Sources differ on Yousef's location during the days after the Manila fire. One senior Pakistani intelligence officer says Yousef stayed in Islamabad, the Pakistani capital, while an American investigator believes Yousef hid in a safehouse in Karachi provided by his friends in the Sipah-e-Sahaba terrorist gang. Whatever hole Yousef crawled into, he did not go to ground for long.

On 23 January 1995, Yousef contacted his friend Ishtiaque Parker and asked if they could meet at the Pearl Guest House in Islamabad's Sector F-7/4.[7] Parker has since claimed that he was terrified Yousef would kill him if he did not obey, so he dutifully appeared at the Guest House, where Yousef told him they would both be going to Bangkok.[8] He was still furious at the arrest of Murad in the Philippines, and vowed to have him freed. Yousef told Parker 'that he and his friends wanted to kidnap [the] Philippines ambassador in order to pressurize the Philippines government to set his friend free'. Yousef also told Parker that his friends were monitoring the ambassador's daily routine so they could work out the best time to kidnap him.[9]

When Parker arrived Yousef already had two large suitcases and a black nylon bag in his room, and he had bought smart clothes and 'many new suits' for both men 'worth hundreds of dollars'.[10] Yousef packed the bags and suitcases with clothes and the tools of his trade: 'apart from other things, the bag contained incendiary cotton ... Yousef had shown him [Parker] the cotton and burned it as a test to show him. Parker further stated that Yousef had treated the cotton with chemicals in order to make it highly flammable. He was also shown two toy cars which were wrapped with the cotton.'

Yousef's brain was working overtime, plotting and scheming more bombings and ways of evading capture by American and Asian investigators. He gave Parker $7,000 to pay for hotel rooms and buy suitcases, watches and clothes in Thailand, and then stuffed the toy cars into the cotton, apparently to make the cotton look less suspicious, and placed one in Parker's bag and another in his own. Then he packed Parker's bag with two Casio 'Databank' watches, batteries, more incendiary cotton, several capsules of a mysterious white powder (thought to be TNT)[11] and liquid nitro-glycerine stored in contact lens bottles.[12]

On 30 January 1995 Parker walked slowly through the departures hall at Islamabad airport past unsuspecting security officers, pausing only to buy a copy of *Newsweek* magazine containing an article on the World Trade Center bombing and a photograph of Yousef, and then he boarded a plane for the short flight to Bangkok. On arrival he took a taxi to Bangkok's Grace Hotel, and rang Yousef to tell him he had arrived safely. Yousef had wanted Parker to take the route first in case security officers were stopping people from carrying liquids through customs. He had even chosen the hotel specifically because it was one of the largest in the city and was popular with other visitors from Pakistan and the Middle East. Parker told him there had been no problems en route, and so Yousef ordered Parker to be at Bangkok airport to meet him the next day.[13]

Parker rose early the next morning to meet his friend on the five o'clock flight from Pakistan, and the two men travelled back into Bangkok and locked themselves in Parker's room at the Grace Hotel. Given that the massed forces of Neil Herman's Joint Terrorist Task Force, the CIA, Pakistani intelligence, Interpol and Iranian security police – as well as most of Asia's police and law enforcement officers – were now doggedly on Yousef's trail, his behaviour in the teeming Thai capital is nothing short of astounding. His arrogant belief in his own brilliance was rapidly consuming any instinct for self-preservation.

Parker had bought several soft-shelled suitcases, but the terrorist mastermind was not happy. He wanted hard, expensive ones – suitcases he thought security officers would not bother to check as they passed through an airport. While Parker went out and bought more suitcases and clothes to fill them, Yousef quickly assembled several more bombs from the components Parker had smuggled through customs. When Parker returned with the new suitcases Yousef then told him they were going to pack his bombs into the cases and put one on a Delta Airlines flight and another on United Airlines. 'Parker further stated that Yousef made a number of phone-calls to various cargo agencies in Bangkok to ascertain whether they handle cargo for American airlines or not. The cargo agencies had instructed Yousef to deal directly with the airlines and then Yousef called both the airlines for their flight schedules.'[14]

By now Parker was getting scared: he knew that Yousef was using him, letting him take the risks.[15] Yousef may even have told Parker that his wife and young child would be harmed if he did not co-operate. He certainly seems to have made few attempts to reassure his young friend, and instead simply told him to take the cases packed with explosives to the airport for shipment to the USA. 'Yousef wanted the bombs to explode over a populated area of the United States,' Parker later told Pakistani interrogators Rehman Malik, the Additional Director General of the Federal Investigation Agency (FIA), and Sajjad Haider, the FIA Assistant Director, during a ten-hour interview.[16]

Ishtiaque dutifully left for the airport with the luggage, but he then started to get cold feet. He feared Yousef, but he was also scared of the consequences of his actions; after all, he had a wife and young son, and little desire to blow aircraft out of the sky. Fortunately for Parker and passengers on flights out of Bangkok that day, Yousef had given him a get-out clause by telling him to return to their hotel room if the airlines asked for his passport or fingerprints. Parker spent most of the day loitering around at the airport, too scared to approach the airlines with his bags, and too scared to go back and tell Yousef he could not go through with the plan.

Eventually he telephoned Yousef and lied, saying that staff in the airline cargo sections were asking for passports and taking fingerprints even from Americans who wanted to ship goods home. 'Yousef then instructed him to come back [to the hotel] but he was really disappointed. However Yousef had told him that if [t]he [sic] bombing of Delta or United Airlines in Bangkok was not a successful operation, he would attack Air France due to the French support of the Algerian government.'[17]

By the time Parker returned to the hotel room a few hours later, Yousef was already planning another attack, one that may reveal a crucial source of Yousef's support: he told Parker he had sought the help of a friend of his in the wealthy Gulf state of Qatar. He then claimed he had rung the friend and persuaded him to take the bags to London and fly them from there directly to the United States on a jumbo jet, where they would explode and destroy the plane.

After they later interrogated Parker, Pakistani intelligence officials Rehman Malik and Sajjad Haider wrote in a report that Parker said Yousef had told him that his friend's father was a very senior politician and leading member of the establishment in Qatar.[18] Intelligence sources believe Yousef was planning to use his friend's diplomatic immunity to ensure safe passage for the bags containing the bombs. For legal reasons, the name of the friend and his father's position in Qatar have been withheld.[19]

Whoever Yousef's friend was, there were apparently problems with his involvement in the plot, and the plan could not be put into operation. Yousef opened the contact lens bottles containing the nitro-glycerine and 'emptied the bottles into the sink'.[20] The attack had fallen to pieces, and it was time for the two men to return to Pakistan. Parker flew back to Islamabad on 2 February 1995, while Yousef took a more circuitous route and returned via Lahore.

Still there was no halt to Yousef's campaign. He ordered Parker to buy batteries and toy cars, which he was then going to pack with incendiary cotton wool and use in another bomb attack in Iran, this time to pressurize the Iranian government to release his father, who had been arrested after the attack at Mashhad.

Within hours of landing Yousef also sent Parker to the Singapore Airlines office in Islamabad to collect flight schedules, and was simultaneously planning to give his small coterie of followers in Islamabad their first major test. Yousef decided to give them a mission in Asia, an attack that would hurt his enemies, but one from which the chosen recruits could easily escape and return to Pakistan. According to Pakistani investigators, he planned to send two of his Pakistani supporters and a young Thai militant, a man he had met in Bangkok, on missions against the Israeli consulate in Bombay and the Israeli embassy in New Delhi.

With the target decided, Yousef just had to prepare the explosives and ensure there could be no direct link back to his activities in Pakistan. His supporters were expendable; he was not. From a safehouse in Islamabad, Yousef dictated more letters threatening to attack Filipino targets if Murad was not released and then began listing the chemicals and wiring he would need to build more bombs. He also told Parker to find a bungalow in a wealthy part of Islamabad where

Yousef could kidnap and hold the Philippines ambassador to Pakistan, or a senior member of his staff, and ransom them in exchange for Murad.

It was all too much for Ishtiaque Parker. After they had returned from Bangkok Yousef confessed that the Filipino police had found his laptop computer, and that Parker's name was one of few stored on the machine without encryption – it was just a matter of time before the FBI tracked him down. Parker must have been terrified, particularly when Yousef asked him to take a mysterious parcel to a mosque in the Shiite sector of Islamabad the next day. 'This made me suspicious,' said Parker later.[21] 'I did not like the fact that he was compelling me to do something I didn't want to. When I refused, he told me I had to do it because I was part of his organization and I was involved in subversive activities in the world.'

It was a foolish attempt at blackmail, and it proved to be Yousef's undoing. Parker knew that his friend was one of the most wanted men in the world, and he seems to have been genuinely scared that his life was in danger.

Yousef's time was now running out. On 3 February 1995, at about 10.45 a.m., Parker telephoned the US embassy in Islamabad, and told the switchboard operator he had important information about a terrorist. The call was routed through to Jeff Riner, an agent with the State Department's Diplomatic Security Service (DSS), and Parker nervously babbled out his story. He knew Ramzi Yousef, he said. The most wanted man in the world, the man who blew up the World Trade Center. He knew where he was; he knew there was a $2 million reward for Yousef's capture; he had read it all in *Newsweek* magazine.

From their unique positions at American embassies around the world, DSS agents are often in the front line against terrorism. They have more personal experience of bombings and other terrorist acts than any other US government agents. They have been blown up, taken hostage, ambushed and shot at by snipers with guns and anti-tank weapons. Experience teaches them to be wary.

Riner and Bill Miller, another DSS agent in the embassy, were intrigued by the phone-call and wanted to believe Parker was telling the truth, but they knew the huge reward money offered for Yousef was attracting con-artists and crazies. Art Maurel, the Regional Security Officer in charge of all security and counter-terrorism issues at the embassy, contacted his superiors in Washington and requested guidance. The response came back promptly: 'Check him out, but be careful.'[22]

Riner and Miller arranged to meet Parker near the embassy, in a safe spot away from prying eyes, and jumped into an embassy car to make the short journey. They found a slightly built, nervous little man, but they were not disappointed by what he had to say. 'The more I questioned him,' said Riner, 'the more excited I got.'[23] Once both agents were convinced that Parker had credible information they disguised their new informant and smuggled him back into the embassy for another four hours of questioning. Soon everyone was sure he was telling the truth. Parker just knew too much about Yousef's personality, his career and past crimes to be making it up. Events took on a more urgent tone, and Maurel contacted the State Department in Washington, who in turn rang the FBI's headquarters in the city.

From the Counterterrorism Section at FBI headquarters, senior FBI agent John Lipka rang Neil Herman on a secure telephone line at his home just outside New York. A man called Parker had come forward, he told Herman: the breakthrough had been made. It was still early in the morning in New York, but Herman immediately ordered the opening of the FBI command centre at 26 Federal Plaza and drove into Manhattan to help arrange a rendition plan in the event of Yousef's arrest. 'DSS did the right thing. They were instrumental in working with us to make sure it was done right. There weren't too many bureaucrats who got involved,' said Herman.

Agents from the FBI and DSS were rushed to Islamabad. FBI Legal Attaché Ralph Paul Horton arrived the next day, 4 February, from his base in the US embassy in Bangkok, and automatically became the most senior FBI official in the region, responsible for all FBI personnel entering Pakistan. 'I don't think we would have been as successful without him,' said Herman.

Parker's information was dynamite. He told the agents Yousef was almost certainly still in Islamabad, but he was unsure where. The US agents would have to wait until their prey emerged from the shadows.

For Neil Herman and his JTTF agents it was a tense time. They had spent two years investigating the World Trade Center bombing and tracking Yousef around the world. He had slipped through their fingers before: in Thailand, the Philippines, New York – where he escaped just hours after the bombing, and Pakistan, where US and Pakistani forces had raided his house in Quetta a day after he had left. Now he was within arm's reach, and this time they had to catch him.

For the next few days Parker became one of the US government's most important double agents, working undercover around Islamabad hunting for Yousef. Finally, on 6 February, Parker called Agent Miller to tell him Yousef had been spotted in the city, but he was about to leave on a bus to Peshawar in north-western Pakistan. Peshawar is bandit country, a lawless city where tribal fighters walk around openly with AK47 assault rifles. It is also the gateway to Afghanistan, and some intelligence sources believe Yousef was planning to make his way from Peshawar through the Khyber Pass into Afghanistan, and then on into Iran to lead another murderous attack. If Yousef slipped across the border it could be two or three weeks before he resurfaced. By that time news of Parker's betrayal could have leaked out, and Yousef would have known that his friends and safehouses in Islamabad were being watched. He might have disappeared for good.

There was no time to wait for reinforcements or the FBI's élite Hostage Rescue Team. A small team of US agents was cobbled together from the DSS and the embassy's Drug Enforcement Agency (DEA) office, and agents were disguised, issued with Yousef's photograph and sent to watch for him at the Islamabad bus terminal. Art Maurel, meanwhile, was busy ringing his contacts within the Pakistan government, persuading them to co-operate and agree to an extradition if Yousef was arrested. It was a difficult task because the American agents were far from home, in a country with no formal extradition agreement with America, and there were many powerful groups in Pakistan who were explicitly anti-American and anti-Western.

However Benazir Bhutto, who was Prime Minister of Pakistan at the time, now says she had few doubts about co-operating with the US to capture Yousef: 'I thought the Islamists in Pakistan were a danger to Pakistan and to the larger Muslim world,' said Bhutto.[24] 'I felt that what was at stake was not the prosperity of Pakistan but the prosperity of the larger Muslim world, and I feel that very strongly. I think Ramzi Yousef was an important terrorist, but he was a soldier in a larger group. We could not allow fringe groups to dictate the agenda.' Pakistan 'bent over backwards' according to one agent involved in the case, and even agreed to let US forces be involved in any operation to capture Yousef.

The Americans were not the only ones making plans. Yousef still had a few issues to resolve before he could leave for Peshawar, and he had decided to stay one more night in Islamabad. At around 4.30 p.m.

on the afternoon of 6 February he arrived at the shabby two-storey Su-Casa guesthouse in Islamabad's Sector F7/2 carrying two small suit-cases bearing Bangkok flight stickers and sporting a day's growth of stubble. He chatted with the desk clerk, who thought Yousef looked weary and courteously asked him if he had travelled a long distance.

'From Karachi,' Yousef replied with a wan smile.

The clerk passed Yousef a pink registration form, and was in turn shown Yousef's Pakistani identity card bearing the name Ali Mohammad. Yousef entered his false name in the ledger and paid around £20 ($33) for a small room on the second floor. Despite his apparent fatigue, Yousef politely spurned the clerk's offer of a porter to carry his bags: he could manage, he told the clerk.[25]

Yousef stayed in his room for the next five hours, making two tele-phone-calls to Peshawar and several more within Islamabad via the hotel switchboard. At 8.30 p.m. an Arab friend of Yousef's arrived at the hotel and went upstairs. A few minutes later the two men emerged together, walked back downstairs and across the road to the hustle of the local Rana food market. Yousef's friend apparently had a flat near the hotel and was well known in the area: local stallholders remem-bered the two men walking through the market at around 8.35 p.m.[26] For the next hour, Yousef and his friend disappeared. Whatever the two men were up to, it did not take long, because Yousef returned to his hotel at 9.30 p.m. and went straight to his room. And there he stayed until the morning.

While Yousef slept, in Washington Louis Freeh, Director of the FBI, was personally giving the task of arresting the FBI's most wanted fugi-tive to Bill Gavin, the head of the FBI's New York office. A team of 20 FBI agents was assembled in preparation for take-off in an unmarked US government jet at 2 a.m. New York time. But events in Islamabad moved too quickly.

Agents were staking out the tidy white Su-Casa guesthouse from 7 a.m. on 7 February just in case Yousef was planning to leave town early. They were given explicit orders that if the suspect left the hotel, they were to use all reasonable force to effect an arrest. Bradley J. Garrett, a sharp FBI Special Agent with a doctorate degree in crimi-nology, arrived in the city early the same morning, and with Parker and reinforcements from the US embassy he pulled up near the guest-house in the back of a van at around 9.15 a.m. It was time for the infor-mant to earn his share of the reward money. The plan was for Parker to go into the guesthouse and check that Yousef, who still thought Parker a willing accomplice, was actually inside.

Parker went inside and upstairs and had a short conversation with Yousef. At 9.30 a.m. he trotted downstairs, left the guesthouse, crossed the road, took off his hat and ran his fingers through his hair. This was the pre-arranged signal to tell the agents that Yousef was inside: the critical moment had come.[27] Accompanied by a team of seven heavily armed Pakistani special forces, Jeff Riner, Art Maurel, Bill Miller, Bradley Garrett, and a DEA agent ran across the road into the hotel. Two men swerved around to the back of the hotel and took up positions from where they could stop Yousef if he fled. The rest of the group ran in through the front door.

'Where is Room 16?' said the leading Pakistani soldier to the desk clerk.

'On the second floor,' replied the bewildered man.

The team swarmed quietly up the stairs, removing the safety catches on their submachine guns and drawing pistols from hip and thigh holsters. They paused in the darkened corridor outside Yousef's door. As one of the soldiers tapped officiously on the painted door, the men shot nervous glances at each other, not knowing what to expect.

Yousef, who had been sitting barefoot on one of the room's two single beds, stood up and walked over to the door. He was barely awake and sleep was still misting his eyes. He swung the door open, framing his silhouette, and the posse pushed him through into the room, two men bundling Yousef face-down on to the floor and pushing his hands behind his back.

'STAY WHERE YOU ARE!! DON'T MOVE!! DON'T MOVE!!' screamed the rest of the team as they crowded into the room, their guns trained on Yousef's head and torso. One of the Pakistani officers slipped handcuffs on to Yousef's forearms, picked him up and shoved him up against a wall of the room.

'Is this the man you want?' the officer asked Riner.

Riner pulled Yousef's mugshot from his pocket and held it next to the captive's flattened face. Riner studied the man's piercing eyes, his lips, his ears; then he checked Yousef's scarred fingers and the burn-marks around his eyes. There was no doubt. They had their man.

'It's him,' said Riner. 'Take him away please.'

The team bound Yousef's feet, put a black hood over his head, and proceeded to drag him unceremoniously down the stairs and through the white marble entrance hall.

'It was like a hurricane, a big panic,' said Khalid Sheikh, a businessman from Karachi who was staying in a room on the ground floor at the time of the arrest.[28] Even under pressure, Yousef resisted vociferously. 'He was blindfolded, barefoot and had his hands and legs bound, and was shouting, "I'm innocent, where are you taking me?" and "Show me your arrest warrant!"'

The arrest team bundled their quarry into the back of a waiting car and sped off, leaving four Pakistani police officers to guard the room and its contents. The entire operation was such a secret that several hours after the arrest an agent from the Pakistani Intelligence Bureau arrived at the guesthouse to investigate reports from neighbours that a foreign student had been kidnapped from the hotel. It was left to the staff to tell the IB agents who had been staying in room 16.

'For us he was just another guest,' said one member of staff who asked to remain anonymous.[29] 'We did not have a clue who he was. If we knew . . . we would have put our lives at stake to get him arrested since the reward of two million dollars was on the line!'

Later that day, as dusk fell across Islamabad, an American DSS agent from the embassy and officers from the city's bomb squad arrived to check through Yousef's belongings. They found flight schedules for Delta and United Airline flights from Asia to the US. On the floor, partially hidden under a couple of plastic bags, lay two children's remote-control cars. Yousef was packing them with plastic explosives for yet another atrocity.

Ishtiaque Parker became a rich man for helping to capture Yousef. In August 1996, after Neil Herman had fought a long battle with federal bureaucrats on Parker's behalf,[30] Mike Posillico and Jeff Riner of the DSS were given plane tickets to a secret destination and a cheque for $2 million bearing Parker's name.[31] They found their man and then moved him, along with his wife Fehmida and baby son Mohammad, in conditions of utmost secrecy back to the United States.[32]

Parker rejected an offer to enter the Witness Protection Program, instead choosing to go it alone under a false name. He still calls Neil Herman occasionally for a chat, and has no regrets about his actions.[33] According to a senior FBI agent closely involved with the case, his motivation for coming forward was based in part on his understanding of his religion: 'He didn't want innocent women and children hurt. He didn't do this solely for money.'[34] Several death threats have been issued against his life, but Parker says his conscience is clear: 'I don't feel guilty because I believe that I have not committed any wrong. I don't see the killing of innocent people as an act of jihad.'[35]

It was night-time in New York when John Lipka rang Neil Herman to tell him Yousef had been arrested. 'I was surprised,' admits Herman. 'On the one hand I was surprised it had taken two years to catch him, and on the other hand after so many negative leads that proved fruitless I was perhaps a little jaded.'

Stifling his excitement, Herman rang Bill Gavin and drove back into Manhattan to the FBI's command centre to implement the rendition plan. Several key people were woken in their beds and called into the office, including Lewis D. Schiliro, who would go on to head up FBI investigations into Osama bin Laden.

The original rendition flight had been cancelled because of the speed of events in Pakistan, but over the next 24 hours another small team of agents assembled near Washington, including medical staff and members of the élite FBI Hostage Rescue Team; legal papers for the US ambassador in Pakistan were signed and sealed, and later that weekend a military USAF 707 jet left the United States for Islamabad.

'We despatched a rendition team from New York, led by Bill Gavin,' said Herman, who also sent Chuck Stern from the FBI and Brian Parr from the Secret Service, both of whom had tracked Yousef while on the JTTF. Herman guided the rendition from FBI headquarters in New York. 'It was a very secret operation,' he said. 'It was a once in a lifetime type of operation.'

The USAF jet landed in Islamabad and taxied to a quiet area of the airport to await its precious cargo. Yousef was driven out to the airport and bundled on to the jet. FBI agent Frank Pelligrino, who had devoted the last two years of his life to catching and prosecuting Yousef, had been travelling in Asia hunting for leads on the case when Yousef was captured. Ironically, he flew into Islamabad to try and catch the USAF flight, but just missed the plane.[36] His colleagues from the JTTF were left to look after Yousef.

The flight back to America from Pakistan with Yousef proved lucrative for the US investigators. Parr and Stern, as the two agents who knew most about the case, went and sat down near Yousef and tentatively asked if he would be prepared to talk to them without an attorney. Unable to avoid bragging about his exploits Yousef agreed to talk on the strict condition the two agents did not take notes or try to record any part of the conversation. Stern and Parr agreed, and spent the following six hours alternately chatting away with Yousef, then secretly reconstructing the conversation and making notes in another part of the plane. 'He thought that anything he said wouldn't be admissible in court without notes,' said an American investigator.[37]

Yousef's brazen attitude to his attacks was astonishing. When Stern and Parr quizzed him about the WTC bombing he told the men that he had wanted to topple the tower into the other, causing perhaps 250,000 fatalities, and had deliberately built the bomb to try and shear the support columns holding up the tower. He had also considered a poison-gas attack on the complex, but claimed he had ruled it out because it would have been 'too expensive'.

At one point Yousef used a notepad to make a sketch of the World Trade Center, the underground parking complex, and the route the van had taken before it was parked. One of the agents took the pad back and left it beside him on the seat. 'You told me no notes,' said Yousef indignantly. Parr ripped out the page and gave it back to Yousef, who promptly 'tore a piece of the diagram out, bent over and threw it in his mouth and he ate it', according to Parr.

'But what about funding for the operation?' asked the JTTF agents. Yousef told the men he had been given money by friends and members of his family, but when pressed for more information he refused to elaborate. If he had been given more money, he would have made 'a more efficient bomb', he said.

Yousef may have been guaranteeing himself a place in prison with his boastful valedictory, but he was not completely stupid. He refused to tell the agents exactly what the World Trade Center bomb was made of, on the grounds that he did not want the US government banning the sale of some of the chemicals and preventing other terrorist attacks on American soil.

So why did he not attack an Israeli target? wondered the US agents. Yousef replied that Israeli targets were too well defended, and if you could not attack your enemy, 'you should attack the friend of your enemy'. It was a chilling confession, but one aspect of the case still fascinated Brian Parr: 'I asked him why Mr Salameh ever went back to retrieve that $400 deposit,' said Parr.[38] Yousef looked up at him, grinned, shook his head slightly, and said simply: 'Stupid.'

Even though Yousef was on board a USAF flight heading back to New York the logistical problems were not over for Neil Herman and his team. For legal reasons the 707 could not stop during its flight from

East to West. 'Yousef had to be brought back into the jurisdiction of the US Attorney's office in New York without landing anywhere, so he had to be flown back non-stop and the plane had to be refuelled several times in the air,' said Herman.[39] 'There were all kinds of issues because we weren't allowed to fly over several countries and their airspace and then ultimately the plane had to land within the jurisdiction of [New York-based US Attorney] Mary Jo White. If it hadn't then there would have been all sorts of legal problems.'

Even storms and strong weather conspired against the FBI, threatening to force the plane down. 'We had real problems with the weather on the plane and even at the end we were worried we would have to land it,' said Herman. The stubborn crew soldiered on, eventually landing at Stewart Airport in Newburgh, New York, just after 8.30 p.m., and taxiing to a remote corner to be greeted by a phalanx of heavily armed FBI and Secret Service agents. Yousef was hustled down the stairs and on to the tarmac. He was back in America, one year, eleven months and three weeks since he bombed the World Trade Center; time he had used to bomb his way around the Philippines, Pakistan, Iran and Thailand. The agents checked his handcuffs and led him to a waiting Port Authority Sikorsky S-76A helicopter for the flight into Manhattan.

There were eight seats in the back, and Yousef was carefully strapped in between two federal agents. The chopper took off at 8.55 p.m., circled the field and then headed off towards Manhattan. Bill Gavin, the head of the FBI in New York, sat opposite Yousef, watching his blindfolded young charge. The Sikorsky followed the Hudson River towards the southern tip of Manhattan, and rounded the proud towers of the World Trade Center at a height of 600ft. Gavin leant forward and eased Yousef's blindfold away from his eyes. 'Look down there,' he said to Yousef, gesturing towards the twin towers. 'They're still standing.' Yousef squinted and looked out of the window. 'They wouldn't be, if I had had enough money and explosives,' he replied defiantly.[40]

Yousef settled back in his seat, and the helicopter landed at a private helipad occasionally used by the FBI in southern Manhattan. Then he was transferred to the back of a waiting car for the final leg of his journey, and a small convoy ploughed its way through the streets of southern Manhattan towards the FBI headquarters at 26 Federal Plaza.

Neil Herman remembers the scene well: 'He was motorcaded with special services right into our offices and then Bill Gavin and the team returned. And then there was a little bit of euphoria, because then we actually had him back. He was brought in, processed, and we "major cased" him – took detailed fingerprints and his palm prints and photographs.' Herman vividly recalls watching Yousef as he was being fingerprinted and photographed: 'I remember thinking as I observed him, you know, I would have loved to have sat down and got inside his head. I remember thinking that he was two years of my life. But he really did look like his photographs. It really was him.'

References

[1] Author interview with Filipino investigator.
[2] Author interview with David Swartzendruber.
[3] Ibid.
[4] United States District Court, Southern District of New York, USA v. Ramzi Ahmed Yousef et al., Indictment, S12 93 Cr. 180 (KTD), Count 12, subsection g.
[5] Author interview.
[6] USA v. Yousef, Indictment, op. cit. Count 12, subsection o.
[7] Interrogation of Parker by Pakistani investigators Rehman Malik and Sajjad Haider. Report obtained by author.
[8] Author interview with an American investigator.
[9] Interrogation of Parker by Pakistani investigators. Report obtained by author.
[10] Ibid.
[11] Author interview with senior Pakistani investigator.
[12] Interrogation of Parker by Pakistani investigators. Report obtained by author.
[13] Ibid.
[14] Ibid.
[15] Author interview with American investigators.
[16] Interrogation of Parker by Pakistani investigators. Report obtained by author.
[17] Ibid.
[18] Ibid.
[19] The name of Yousef's friend and his father's senior position in Qatar are both known to the author, but cannot be published for legal reasons.
[20] Ibid.
[21] 'US Trade Center Bombing Informer Hides in Johannesburg', *The Sowetan*, 24 November 1995.
[22] Author interview with American investigator.
[23] Louis R. Mizell Jr, *Target USA: The Inside Story of the New Terrorist War.*
[24] Author interview with Benazir Bhutto.
[25] Yousef's arrest based on author interviews with Neil Herman, Pakistani

and US investigators, and Christopher John Farley, 'The Man Who Wasn't There', *Time*, 20 February 1995.

[26] According to an author interview with an American investigator.

[27] Ibid.

[28] Farley, op. cit.

[29] 'Witnesses Recount Arrest', *The Nation*, 10 February 1995.

[30] Author interview with Neil Herman.

[31] Mizell, op. cit.

[32] Names from interrogation of Parker by Pakistani investigators. Report obtained by author.

[33] Author interview with Neil Herman.

[34] Author interview.

[35] *The Sowetan*, op. cit.

[36] Author interview with Neil Herman.

[37] Author interview.

[38] Testimony of Brian J. Parr to the second World Trade Center bombing trial.

[39] Author interview with Neil Herman.

[40] Gavin is adamant this happened; Yousef unequivocally denies it.

SIX

The Origins of Terror

RAMZI YOUSEF is not the real name of the man Neil Herman watched being fingerprinted in 26 Federal Plaza. Nor is he Adam Adel Ali, Adam Khan Baloch, Dr Richard Smith, Adam Ali, Yousas, Dr Paul Vijay, Alex Hume, Dr Adel Sabah or any of his other 40-odd aliases. The man the world has come to know as Ramzi Yousef was born with the name Abdul Basit Mahmoud Abdul Karim on 27 April 1968. Although Yousef is not his real name, it is the name he gave on entry to the US, the name he has adopted, and thus the name the United States chose to use when hunting and prosecuting him.

Much of his life remains clouded in secrecy. 'He's a riddle wrapped in a mystery,' said an American investigator, paraphrasing Winston Churchill.[1] However, investigators now believe Yousef was born in a working-class suburb of Kuwait City, the son of Muhammad Abdul Karim, a tribesman from the wild Baluchistan region of Pakistan, who moved to Kuwait during the boom years of the oil trade and worked as an engineer for Kuwaiti Airlines.

Karim had met and married a local Kuwaiti woman whose family was originally from Palestine. Then together they raised Ramzi and their brood in Fuhayhil, an area vibrant with immigrant life. Moderate and radical Palestinians – who comprised about 40 per cent of the town's population – would argue the toss and debate politics in street-side cafés. There were communists from Iraq, members of Egypt's Muslim Brotherhood, Pakistanis and Indians, all thrown together in an oil-rich kingdom still grappling with the 20th century.

Karim does not appear to have been an overtly religious or political man while Ramzi was a child but as Ramzi entered his early teenage years, his father began to openly espouse the cause of Baluchi nationalism and grew to despise members of the Muslim Shiite sect.[2] Karim became involved with mullahs from the puritanical Wahhabi school of Sunni Islam, whose doctrines are the official form of Islam in several Gulf states, and appears to have become friends with several members of an extreme fundamentalist group who called themselves the Salafis.

There can be little doubt that his father's transformation into a radical Islamist would have deeply affected Ramzi. The Salafis were no mere proselytizers: they believed that Sunni Muslims were the true believers and that Shiites were an abhorrence. The schism between the two broad camps of Islam springs from the death of the Prophet Mohammad in AD 632, and beliefs as to his true successors. Sunnis (the larger of the two main sects) accept the legitimacy of the first three caliphs (or 'deputies'), whereas Shiites (who are dominant in Iran) believe that Mohammad's cousin and son-in-law Ali, the fourth caliph, was the only true successor of Mohammad.

Over the generations the split deteriorated into virtual war between the two groups, and in most Arab nations Sunnis and Shiites still have a tense relationship. Salafi members have an extreme view, believing that 'purification' is the only option available to Shiites, and that they should be killed to rinse the earth of their heathen beliefs. At breakfast and at the evening dinner table, young Ramzi Yousef had these views rammed into his head, along with romantic tales of his father's tribal homeland, intoxicating Yousef and his brothers, Abu Sahman, Abdul Muneem and possibly another – known as Adel Annon, who some intelligence sources believe to be Yousef's twin.[3]

Yet despite the extreme nature of their father's beliefs, Yousef and his brothers had a relatively stable Muslim upbringing, albeit one that never quite reached the status of middle class. 'Ramzi's family were of pretty humble means,' said Neil Herman. Yousef's mother taught him Arabic, which he now speaks with a Palestinian accent, and his father taught him Urdu, the main language of Pakistan; teachers at his local Kuwaiti school taught him English, which he speaks fluently, but with a hint of an Arab accent.

As a child young Ramzi did well at school, where he was a popular, above average student, particularly in English, and positively shone at mathematics, physics and chemistry, receiving glowing praise from his teachers.[4] Even as a teenager Yousef enjoyed playing with chemicals. But developing an aptitude for science was not the only benefit of Yousef's schooling in Kuwait. His friends from that period became some of his most important conspirators in later life, including Abdul Hakim Murad, whose father was working in the country as an engineer for the Kuwaiti Petroleum Company. Another of his latter-day colleagues, Eyad Ismoil, who drove the Ryder truck containing Ramzi's massive bomb into the World Trade Center, grew up near him in Fuhayhil and kept in touch with him after leaving the area.

'His friends [from Kuwait] told me he had lots of friends at school and near his home, but he was very domineering, always wanting to be the leader, always getting angry if things didn't go his way,' said a senior Pakistani investigator.[5] Strangely though, 'he doesn't seem to have got into many fights. He had a menacing air which discouraged others [from picking on him].'

In October 1984, when Yousef was 16, his family obtained his first passport from the Pakistani consulate in Kuwait. It was not needed, it appears, for any urgent foreign trip, it was requested just because his family had never felt secure in Kuwait and decided it was sensible to have one ready. It was the action of a restless, transient family that felt it had to be prepared to travel at any moment. Foreign workers were treated like serfs in Kuwait, and discontent was spreading through Fuhayhil. Muhammad Abdul Karim wanted to return to his homeland in Baluchistan. 'They [the guest-workers] were treated like dogs in Kuwait at the time. They were second-class people,' said the Pakistani investigator.[6] 'Is it any wonder so many became militant?'

Two years later Abdul Karim had his way, and the family packed their belongings for the long trek back to western Pakistan. The contrast between Kuwait City and Baluchistan could hardly be greater. Kuwait was a country packed with wealth and employment, while Baluchistan was, and is, a dry and barren region in the remote south-west of Pakistan. Even today most of its nomadic people still survive by spending winter in solid huts on the flat plains, and spring and summer in tents and small mobile huts in the hills with their sheep, camels, donkeys and cattle. It is a rugged way of life amid inhospitable terrain, and over centuries the inhabitants of Baluchistan have evolved into some of the toughest people on the planet.

Ethnically and culturally, Baluchistan extends many miles into Afghanistan and south-eastern Iran, and the Baluchi people, ferociously independent, show little respect for governments or national boundaries; no border stops their travels. By the time Karim began moving his family back to the region war was raging in Afghanistan between the mujaheddin and Soviet troops. Baluchi tribesmen were roaming unhindered between Afghanistan and Pakistan, smuggling drugs and weapons, occasionally attacking Russian forces alongside the mujaheddin, or striking into Iranian Shiite territory and destroying trains and power plants.

Yousef's family settled in the area around the small Baluchi town of Turbat, a particularly wild and lawless area roughly 350km from Afghanistan, 50km from the Iranian border and a similar distance from the Arabian Sea. Turbat itself is a town of 100,000 people with the nominal distinction of having shops selling 300 different varieties of dates. It is a small claim for a town with few links to the modern world. There is a dusty and badly kept road which runs through the town to Awaran and Bela in the east, and Mand in the west, and another running south to Pasni and Jiwani on the coast. Flights arrive at a local airport almost daily from Quetta and Karachi, but it is remote and otherworldly, and an important transit centre for the Pakistani heroin trade.

When the journalist Mary Anne Weaver visited the town in 1989, just after Yousef's family had settled in the region, she found some 4,000 Iranian Baluch encamped in the hills around the town, fully armed and supporting Iraq.[7] The Baluch, it seems, were running cross-border operations deep into Iran, and intelligence sources believe most of the male members of Yousef's family joined one or another of the factions battling for supremacy in Afghanistan, and have been involved in the persistent internecine fighting in the country ever since.

Yousef, however, was still a young man intent on education, and while his family were moving to Baluchistan he was preparing to study overseas in Britain. Using his passport, which bore Yousef's real name and a permanent address in Karachi, his family obtained a British visa for their son from the British vice-consul in Kuwait on 16 November 1986, and he flew out of the city and arrived at London's Heathrow Airport the next day.

Britain may have been a strange destination for young Ramzi, but some Pakistani investigators believe his family had friends or relatives in the country who agreed to keep an eye on him. 'He may have had some family or friends in Britain,' confirms a senior American investigator, 'but we were never sure.'

Yousef travelled first to the city of Oxford, and appears to have spent several months studying at the local Oxford College of Further Education. Some sources claim that he studied for several A-levels, in order to qualify for a place at university, but what seems more likely, given his short period of study, is that he studied English as a Foreign Language (EFL), a 12-week course run regularly at the college.[8]

Yousef's attendance at the college is now difficult to confirm, however, as records at the college go back only as far as 1988. Former staff state there were more than 13,000 full and part-time students at the college in the late 1980s, and senior officials had been engaged in a drive to attract more foreign students, particularly from the Gulf states. The college paid to advertise in guidebooks and leaflets promoting English tuition in Great Britain that were distributed throughout the Gulf.[9] It seems likely that one of Yousef's family, perhaps even Ramzi himself, spotted one of the adverts for the college and decided it would be a good place for him to improve his English.

Bureaucracy conspires to prevent further investigation: the education authority which used to set the majority of EFL exams taken at Oxford College has been incorporated into Cambridge University, and officials at Cambridge refuse to divulge whether a Ramzi Yousef or Abdul Basit Karim obtained a qualification, citing the British Data Protection Act.[10] Only Yousef himself could authorize the release of details.

Only slightly less mystery surrounds the rest of his education. After finishing his studies in Oxford, Yousef flew home to his family for the summer holidays, and then returned to the UK on 10 August 1987, arriving back at Heathrow and travelling west to the Welsh city of Swansea. 'We were never really clear on why he actually went to Wales,' said Neil Herman.

But just like Oxford College, West Glamorgan Institute of Higher Education, known as 'Wiggy' to its students (and now called the Swansea Institute), had been aggressively targeting foreign students and encouraging them to study in Wales. Indeed, several years later one senior member of staff resigned amid complaints that he had made 33 trips abroad – spending 38 weeks away from the college over a four-year period – drumming up business from foreign students. The British National Audit Office spent six months investigating the college, and in January 1997 concluded that the college's management of its overseas courses was 'seriously flawed'.[11] There were even allegations that degree certificates had been printed abroad and sold to wealthy foreigners.

Wiggy's drive to recruit more foreign students brought dozens of perfectly innocent teenagers to south Wales, young men and women who have gone on to become teachers and engineers. But among the intake in late 1987 was Ramzi Yousef, whom the college does not like to mention as one of its alumni. His course, studying for a Higher National Diploma in computer-aided electrical engineering, sounds innocent enough. His major project was applying computer design to geometric Islamic patterns, but he also studied a course in micro-electronics, which the FBI believe almost certainly helped him to build his miniature nitro-glycerine bombs later in life.[12]

Yousef made little impression on his tutors. 'He was hard-working, conscientious and kept himself to himself,' said his computer graphics instructor, who asked to remain anonymous for fear of reprisals.[13] 'That about sums him up over the two years he was here. There were other older Arabic students at the time, but to the best of my knowledge he didn't socialize with them. He was hard-working and very capable.' Staff at the institute are anxious to dispel any suggestion they might have trained the master terrorist. 'His project was quite innocuous,' said one of his former tutors. 'Nothing that might be useful for a bomb-maker.'[14] Staff do recall that specialist electronics magazines arrived at the college for Yousef long after he left, and two tutors claim he left a package behind with a member of staff after he finished his studies.[15] Mysteriously, however, nobody can recall who the member of staff was, or what was in the package.[16]

Former students at the college remember Yousef with more clarity. He was based, they say, near the centre of Swansea, on Wiggy's Mount Pleasant campus – a collection of new buildings built around an imposing old technical college – and lived in several student bedsits in Uplands, a residential area of the city with detached houses and carefully kept gardens. Wiggy's Townhill campus is near Uplands, and former students remember seeing Yousef in the 'Townhill library', the witty name for the student bar. Down the hill from Townhill, past Taffy's Barbers, a launderette and a smattering of shops, Yousef was also seen in Swansea's Uplands Tavern, a pub frequented by Dylan Thomas that still has a corner dedicated to the legendary Welsh poet.

Students who remember Yousef recall an intense young man, but one who clearly enjoyed his time in Swansea and mixed freely with locals and students. This appears to create a paradox, for while Yousef clearly enjoyed the 'sinful' pleasures of 'the West' in Wales, America and the Philippines, he also loved blowing them up. But in this apparently contradictory behaviour he is not alone: many Islamic militants profess admiration and even love of Western culture.

Osama bin Laden also embraced decadent Western values during his late teens and early twenties. Even Fat'hi ash-Shiqaqi, the de facto head of Islamic Jihad, the extreme terrorist group responsible for the murder of dozens of Israelis, was known to be particularly fond of European literature, including Sartre, Eliot, Chekhov, Dostoevsky and Shakespeare, until he was assassinated in Malta in the spring of 1997. Shiqaqi, a Palestinian, read Sophocles' *Oedipus Rex* at least ten times in English translation and claimed to have wept 'bitterly' each time.[17]

While Yousef certainly had fun in Wales, investigators believe it was also the period of his life that saw his politicization and set him on the path towards mass murder. Senior investigators believe that while Yousef was in Swansea he became friendly with members of the Egyptian-based militant group the Muslim Brotherhood, the oldest and largest Islamic group in the Arab world, which is banned in Egypt but has bases around Europe and America, and small cells on hundreds of university and college campuses.[18] Hard-liners criticize it for being too liberal, while moderates and secular states such as Egypt criticize it for supporting terrorism.

According to investigations by British detectives a small cell was operating in Swansea at that time, the same cell who were later involved in organizing anti-Israeli demonstrations in Swansea during the Gulf War.[19] 'There was a culture of anti-Semitism in Swansea at that time [during the Gulf War],' adds Julie Cohen, a Jewish former student at the university.[20] 'There was graffiti, intimidation, and there was tension between Jews and the large numbers of Muslim and Middle Eastern students. The atmosphere wasn't pleasant.'

According to a British intelligence source the Muslim Brotherhood cell 'concentrated its activity on Swansea University rather than [Wiggy]'. However, 'we believe Yousef came into contact with its members and became an enthusiastic supporter'.[21] In more recent years Yousef has admitted he was a member of the Brotherhood, but says he left the group in the early 1990s after deciding they were not adequately committed to the revolutionary Islamic cause. 'I was with them for a number of years until I knew them closely. Then God enlightened me to what is better than them,' he said. Yousef eventually accused the Brotherhood of 'currying favour with the [sic] governments' and of misinterpreting Islamic law. 'All their concerns with Muslim issues don't keep them away from soccer matches or ... weekly programs of merrymaking', he later wrote.[22]

Until Yousef arrived in Swansea he was an empty vessel, a politically naïve young man with limited experience of life and the world.[23] His father had installed a sense of passion and pride in young Ramzi, but it was events in Asia and the influence of his friends in the Muslim Brotherhood that would turn Yousef into a committed terrorist.

The central issue in the late 1980s for Muslim militants, even those in Swansea, was the war against Soviet aggression in Afghanistan. Across the globe the Muslim Brotherhood was actively seeking young Muslim recruits for the mujaheddin. Yousef viewed the war as a struggle against oppression, and from the relative comfort of south Wales he must have felt he was missing out: his family in western Pakistan was sending regular updates by post and telephone. The war was going well, they said, the Soviets were on the run. Yousef must have felt that the war was finishing before he had had a chance to play his part.

During the summer of 1988, with his studies at Wiggy on hold for the holidays, and while most of his fellow students lazed around on beaches, Yousef decided to return to Asia and join the war.[24] Flying from London's Heathrow airport to Islamabad, and travelling by bus to Peshawar, Yousef trod a well-worn path. For thousands of young Muslims the war in Afghanistan was a watershed event. Outraged at the invasion of an Islamic nation by the Soviet Union in December 1979, more than 25,000 foreign 'jihadis' from more than 35 countries – many seeking adventure or a sense of purpose in life – flew to Pakistan and then made the long trek into Afghanistan to fight with their Muslim brothers.[25]

Yousef entered the region at one of the most crucial periods of the entire war. Approximately half the estimated 115,000 Soviet army troops in Afghanistan had already been withdrawn by their humiliated leaders in Moscow, and the rest were due to pull out by the middle of February 1989. Afghan troops supporting the hated pro-Soviet government in Kabul were supposed to fill the gaps left by the retreating Red Army, and many mujaheddin leaders felt they could not wait for the government troops to re-establish themselves. It was time for the rebels to make a final push and claim the country.[26]

In early August 1988 the mujaheddin captured the northern provincial capital of Kunduz, only 40 miles from the Soviet Union's

River Oxus frontier, while the next week a force of up to 17,000 ferocious Afghan rebels launched a major offensive against the strategic
southern city of Kandahar, just across the border from Quetta, the
capital of Baluchistan. Within months the mujaheddin would defeat
the massed forces of the Soviet Union, after a decade-long struggle
that ultimately led to the collapse and fragmentation of the great
communist empire. For the warriors of the holy war, it was an exciting
time, none more so than for a young student from Wales.

FBI and Pakistani investigators believe Yousef travelled to
Peshawar, just 13 miles from the legendary Khyber Pass. Peshawar is
the capital of the North-West Frontier province and the most lawless
city in Pakistan. Riddled with intrigue, American, Soviet, British and
Pakistani spies during the war, it is best characterized by its huge
'Smugglers' Bazaar' where contraband televisions and satellite dishes
are sold alongside lamb kebabs and AK-47 assault rifles. Mud huts are
the main dwellings in the region and four-wheel-drive vehicles are the
only real transport.

It might have seemed like an alien environment compared to cold
Swansea, but Yousef did have friends and relatives to make him feel
at home, including his beloved Uncle Zahid Al-Shaikh (*aka* Zahid Al-
Sheikh), the brother of Yousef's mother, who was living in the city and
working as a senior figure within Mercy International, a Saudi-funded
charity providing aid and assistance to Afghan veterans and refugees.
Originally born in Kuwait, Al-Shaikh seems to have been an important
figure in the region. Western agents investigating the World Trade
Center bombing were surprised to discover that Pakistani President
Farooq Ahmad Khan Leghari attended the opening ceremony for
an orphanage in Peshawar funded by Mercy International on
28 February 1993, two days after the WTC bombing. Ramzi Yousef's
uncle had delivered a speech of welcome for the President, and the
two men were later seen talking earnestly together.[27]

FBI and Pakistani investigators do not believe Yousef actually
fought in Afghanistan during 1988, something he confirmed during an
interview while in prison in New York.[28] Instead he appears to have
spent several months in Peshawar in training camps funded by
Osama bin Laden learning bomb-making skills and teaching electronics (a skill American investigators believe he learnt in Swansea) to
other fighters. Crucially, he also met and befriended Mahmud
Abouhalima, one of the group later convicted of the WTC bombing,
who had somehow survived several military 'tours' in Afghanistan.

One can well imagine how the battle-hardened fighter and the young technical firebrand were drawn together by their mutual hatred of the West. 'We know he was in Afghanistan at the same time as Abouhalima,' said Neil Herman. 'They were probably both influenced by what was going on there. The likelihood is that they were comrades. We believe Yousef was involved in several training camps, giving and receiving training in explosives.'[29]

Despite the excitement of his time in Afghanistan, by the end of the summer Yousef had to return to his rather more mundane life and studies in Wales. On 6 September 1988, Yousef arrived back at Heathrow and returned to Swansea to finish his studies.[30]

By the following spring Yousef had obtained his Higher National Diploma (an academic qualification below a Degree) in computer-aided electrical engineering, and left Swansea to travel to Kuwait. He still had relatives in the Emirate, and some sources claim he obtained a job in the Planning Ministry.

Intelligence sources believe it is 'likely' Yousef was in Kuwait when Saddam Hussein's Iraqi forces invaded the Emirate in August 1990.[31] Angry at the corrupt and racist Kuwaiti government, which treated guest-workers as second-class citizens, Yousef – like many Palestinians in the country – is believed to have aided the Iraqi invaders. Official Kuwaiti records were thrown into chaos by the invasion, but Sheikh Ali al Sabah al Salim al Sabah, the Kuwaiti Interior Minister, has since suggested that Yousef was a 'collaborator' with the Iraqi forces, but the Kuwaiti Government now refuses to provide more details.

By early 1991 Yousef had disappeared. Even the FBI seems unclear of his movements during this period, but the consensus of opinion among Pakistani and American investigators is that he travelled in the Gulf, Pakistan and possibly even to Britain using a false passport. Some sources also suggest that Yousef travelled to America, making a series of visits – previously unknown even to many in the intelligence world – prior to his arrival at New York's JFK airport in September 1992 to plan the World Trade Center attack (which the FBI has always believed was the first time he set foot on US soil). These sources also claim the visits connect him to a mysterious businessman called Ihsan Barbouti, a notorious international fixer who helped Libya and Iraq establish their chemical weapons programmes, and is believed to have been the architect of the Libyan Rabta chemical weapons plant. Some intelligence sources believe that Barbouti, an overweight, goateed

Iraqi, was involved in the bombing of Pan Am flight 103, so it is hardly surprising that he then reputedly faked his own death in July 1990 – on his 63rd birthday – apparently to avoid prosecution in the German courts for his involvement with Iraq and Libya, or assassination by agents of the Israeli Mossad.

Barbouti had been friends with Loizos Lysandrou, a Greek businessman who was himself something of an international 'fixer'. 'Loizos knew how to fix things on a person-to-person level. How do you get your goods by customs? Who do you talk to at the port? You need a warehouse near by? All that kind of stuff,' said one source.[32] Despite being business partners, Barbouti and Lysandrou fell out over an extraordinary deal to ship C-130 aircraft parts and Chinook helicopter parts to Libya in breach of American sanctions against the country.

Lysandrou and another businessman called Nomikos Phillipos approached William Ploss, a Miami-based lawyer, and asked him to represent them in a court case they were involved in with Barbouti. It became, in the words of one lawyer, 'a piss fight'.[33] 'There was a draft for $3 million in New York, and there was a draft for about $800,000 in Florida,' said Ploss.[34] 'Barbouti claimed non-delivery [of the parts to Libya] to stop payment on the drafts. Lysandrou and Phillipos came to me here in Miami because Lysandrou had flown from Brazil to Florida to deposit the money.'

It was only just before Ploss was due to represent his new clients in court that he finally discovered what the men were arguing about. 'There was an agreement purportedly for the delivery of some C-130 parts and some Chinook helicopter parts. The evidence showed the delivery of the goods was to have taken place in Brazil for transshipment to Libya,' said Ploss.[35] When the judge discovered the case involved an illegal transaction the US Customs Service was called in. On 7 October 1994, Stanley Marcus, a district judge in the Southern District of Florida, issued a 33-page order in a forfeiture case involving the $800,000 claimed by the estate of Ihsan Barbouti but held by Barnett Bank in South Florida in the name of Loizos Lysandrou.[36]

On page 21 of the court's order there are details of one of 17 depositions given by Loizos Lysandrou during his various court battles with Barbouti, this particular one during the summer of 1991.[37] Lysandrou was being questioned about a letter he had received from Alexander Von Ludinghausen, one of his lawyers, dated 4 January 1991, and enclosing a copy of a telex to Von Ludinghausen, dated

22 November 1990, from someone called Mustafa El Mahmudi who was working for a Libyan company known only as 'Cement'.

Lysandrou was being asked whether he had received the fax, which might have indicated whether the C-130 and Chinook parts actually arrived in Libya, and he replied: 'I don't know that company [the Libyan "Cement" firm]. Neither do I know who that person who signs as Mustafa El Mahmudi – neither do I know him. I communicated with somebody who co-operates with Libya, and the name is Yousef, and I asked him to check and see if, between July and – July to October, if any containers [containing the C-130 and Chinook parts] had arrived in Libya, from July to October. He, himself [Yousef], communicated with Libya. I don't know with whom.'

In an interview Lysandrou later clarified his deposition: the full name of 'Yousef' was 'Ramzi Yousef', he said.[38] This is further confirmed by William Ploss, who said: 'I knew it [the name "Ramzi Yousef"] before the World Trade Center case. The name "Yousef" stuck in my mind. Lysandrou called me; I can't remember where from, maybe Cyprus, Greece, or London; and I remember writing "Ramzi". For me it's a weird name. It was definitely before the World Trade Center. It was at least a couple of years before the World Trade Center bombing. I figured it had to be the same guy.'[39]

Further investigations have raised the possibility that the 'Ramzi Yousef' mentioned by Lysandrou was actually working for Barbouti and acting as an intermediary between Lysandrou and Libya. According to two reports allegedly passed to Mark W. Caldwell, a senior agent of the US State Department's Diplomatic Security Service, on 13 January and 13 March 1995,[40] Lysandrou was quoted as claiming that the 'Ramzi Yousef' he knew had previously worked for the government of Iraq, specifically the Iraqi National Oil Company (INOC), prior to working with Barbouti, and had flown in and out of Houston several times with an individual extremely close to Barbouti. Indeed, Yousef 'may have lived for a time in Houston', said the report.[41]

Ahmed Mohammad Ajaj – who arrived with Yousef in the US in September 1992 on the same plane, and who was later convicted of involvement in the World Trade Center bombing – lived in Houston (the heart of Barbouti's empire) and allegedly worked for Edwards Pipeline Testing and Technical Welding Laboratories, whose boss is said by some intelligence agents to have been a close associate of Barbouti's.[42] The connections, however, are still not clear.

A senior US intelligence source was reluctant to discuss the case, but did claim that his agency had investigated the links, and said another foreign intelligence agency – thought to be Mossad – had monitored Lysandrou's telephone conversations.[43] The conclusion of the source, based on the phone taps and his agency's investigations, was that the 'Ramzi Yousef' who knew Barbouti was Ramzi Yousef the terrorist. Another separate British source also said Lysandrou has claimed that he met 'Ramzi Yousef' at Ihsan Barbouti's office in London, near the famous Harrods department store, prior to the 1993 attack on the World Trade Center.[44]

Mark Caldwell of the DSS certainly appears to have taken the reports seriously. He is understood to have flown to Washington after receiving the second copy, and hand-delivered it to his superiors at the State Department. For unknown reasons the US authorities appear to have ignored the information. Two months later Caldwell was transferred to Greece and the report was handed to a senior agent in another American government agency. While he was actually talking on the telephone to the author of the report, the senior agent consigned it to his 'File 13' – the rubbish bin.[45] The DSS now denies ever receiving the reports.[46]

However if Yousef was working with Barbouti he would have been in his early twenties – very young to be representing secretive organizations such as INOC. Neil Herman, the FBI Supervisory Special Agent responsible for the Tradebom investigation and the hunt for Ramzi Yousef, was never shown the report, but he does not automatically dispute any possible link between Yousef and Barbouti. 'I was not aware of any connection between Yousef and Barbouti. That's something new that you're telling me now,' he said.[47] Herman remains sceptical, but added: 'It's possible Yousef could have been in the US before September 1992 if he had a false passport that we never found out about. If you have 30 aliases you have to assume there's 40. If you have five false passports you can assume there's ten.'

The two men able to shed light on the mystery are surely Ihsan Barbouti and Loizos Lysandrou. Although Barbouti is supposed to be dead several sources believe he faked his death, something he managed twice before – once escaping from Baghdad in a coffin. Barbouti's body was supposedly buried in Brookwood Cemetery, Surrey, under two feet of reinforced steel mesh and concrete topped off with four tonnes of marble – allegedly to prevent anyone checking the corpse.[48]

Despite rumours that Lysandrou, who by 1999 was in his mid-sixties, was living in the United States or Cyprus, he has now been traced to London, where he suffered a bout of illness during Christmas 1998 and is said to have had his stomach removed.[49] Lysandrou was last heard of living in a small flat on a council-housing estate in Hackney, a depressed area of north-east London.[50] He refused to respond to requests for an interview, but through an intermediary he has denied that the 'Ramzi Yousef' he knew is the World Trade Center bomber, while flatly refusing to discuss further details.[51]

An American intelligence source familiar with the links wonders whether the truth will ever be known. 'These people are shadows,' he said.[52]

Many reporters and analysts have applied the blanket label of 'Islamic fundamentalist' to Ramzi Yousef, suggesting – largely on the basis that he claims to be a Muslim – that his motivation is religious ideology and a wish to fight a holy war against the Christian West. It is a false assumption: there is scant evidence to support any description of Yousef as a religious warrior. 'He's not someone you would ever describe, in any shape or form, as being religious,' said Neil Herman. 'He hid behind a cloak of Islam.'

Despite the best efforts of some politicians and elements of the Western media to portray Islam as something akin to religious Communism, as a virulent and contagious disease threatening good Christian families, Islam is not and has never been a religion that espouses violence, the murder of children or the indiscriminate killing of innocent men and women. Islam is a creed of peace and veneration, but one that has in recent decades become inextricably linked with a struggle between the Western, broadly Christian democracies of Europe and North America, and the Muslim nations of the Middle East and their battle against the perceived oppressive policies of the state of Israel. Obscene crimes have certainly been committed in the name of Islam, but centuries of evil have been perpetuated by zealous Christians massacring, enslaving, torturing and destroying civilizations and races they arrogantly deemed heathen and ungodly. Identifying Yousef simply as an Islamic terrorist is not only inaccurate, it also does an injustice to one of the world's great religions.

Yousef may claim to be a religious man and a good Muslim,[53] but while he was a student in Wales, when he was a wanted terrorist on the run in the Philippines, and even when he was on trial in New York, many aspects of his behaviour would have been frowned upon even by liberal Islamic leaders.

Good pious Muslims, for example, do not beat their young defence-less wives, as Yousef did (one of his relatives even complained about his marital violence during an interview with Pakistani investigators).[54]

Good Muslims also do not flirt with married women or view them-selves as international playboys. During a brief lull in proceedings several weeks into one of Yousef's trials his attorney approached Christine Cornell, the blonde, attractive 42-year-old married courtroom sketch artist, and told her Yousef would like to go on a date with her if he was acquitted. Was she interested, he wondered? Cornell had already realized she was becoming a target for Yousef's affections when he had turned to her during a pre-trial hearing and gave her what she later described as 'one of those up-and-under smiles'. Cornell might have liked sketching Yousef, apparently because of his 'intense eyes', but she sensibly declined his offer with a gracious 'thank you'.

After his arrest Yousef gave just one serious interview before strin-gent restrictions were imposed on his communications with the media: to Raghida Dergham, a senior correspondent from the London-based *Al-Hayat* newspaper, which is circulated widely within the Middle East. When asked whether he considers himself an Islamic fundamentalist, Yousef himself merely answered with another ques-tion: 'First, Israel itself was established on an extremist fundamental-ist thinking, why is this not mentioned about Israel while it is said about the Muslims in every case they are accused of?'[55]

Unlike most fundamentalist terrorists, Yousef raised no objections to being interviewed by a woman – indeed he actually tried to flirt with Dergham.[56] He also failed to fast during the Muslim holy month of Ramadan while in jail, an event observed with pride by millions of liberal Muslims living in the West.

So Yousef did not start his bombing campaign because of simple Muslim zealotry. Although he is certainly a complex character, the prevailing view of intelligence agents and investigators who have stud-ied Yousef closely is that he cannot be labelled simply as an 'Islamic fundamentalist'. Investigators have considered other more direct politi-cal motivations for his crimes which can be found elsewhere in his back-ground and upbringing.

Ramzi Yousef, the investigators and agents conclude, is the first of a new breed of terrorist, one with no clear or definable political goals. His motivation was not wholly religious or wholly political, but a combination of the two which manifested itself in a desire to inflict pain and suffering on his enemies, mainly the West for its political arrogance and support for Israel, but also on those Shiite Muslims who oppose his own Sunni Muslim views.

In his eyes it is guilt by association: the West supports Israel, and the Israelis oppress the Palestinians. So the West must suffer for its crimes. Raghida Dergham from *Al-Hayat* recalls that when Yousef arrived for their interview in New York's Metropolitan Correctional Center he brought with him a whole stack of papers to prove his claim that the Israeli occupation of Arab lands was illegal.

Dergham does not believe Yousef is particularly religious. 'In fact, he did not come across as a fundamentalist as such,' she said.[57] 'He would fit more as a freedom fighter for the liberation of Palestine than the description of an Islamic fundamentalist driven by religion. He is very convinced there is something unjust in the actions of Israel and there has to be a way to bring attention to it. By that he justifies "terror for terror".'

Although he has a Pakistani father and was born in Kuwait, Yousef identifies with two cultural groups: the Baluchi people of his father's homeland, and the Palestinians. He describes himself as 'Pakistani by birth, Palestinian by choice'.[58] The genesis of Yousef's aggression against the West is two central beliefs. The first is that Israel is an illegitimate state,[59] and its existence 'is void morally and legally'. The second is an almost natural conclusion of his first: because of their suffering the Palestinians have the right to attack Israeli targets and any other organization or country that interferes in support of Israel.

Yousef invokes the law of collective responsibility to justify acts that kill and maim innocent civilians. The Israelis were the first to 'kill the civilians', he says, and Israel 'has invented its own way of collective punishment'. What the Israeli authorities do when a Palestinian is suspected of a terrorist act, according to Yousef, 'is they would go inside the house, would take the whole family out and they would blow up the house. They would punish the whole members of the family because one person was charged with [terrorism]. It was only last year when more than 200 houses were blown up ... to get a so-called terrorist.'[60]

In his mind Yousef then makes a direct connection between the actions of the Israeli military, which have indeed been criticized by dozens of international human rights groups, and individual American taxpayers, who, he says, 'have been supporting Israel throughout all the years in killing and torturing peoples'.[61]

'Anyone that commits a killing crime or helps the killer with money or weapon[s], legally he is considered a participant in the crime and in the punishment,' said Yousef, who believes that terrorist attacks that kill civilians are a result of the 'collective punishment' inflicted on Iraq and Libya, where 'the United States punishes the entire population for the mistakes of the government'.

Thus, according to his logic, Americans and Israelis are equally responsible for crimes committed in Palestine. America 'finances these crimes [in Israel]' and supports Israel with weapons, he says. 'These funds are taken from the taxes which the Americans pay,'[62] so this makes the American people, 'logically and legally', 'responsible for all the killing crimes and the settlements and the torture and the imprisonment which the Palestinian people are exposed to. And it doesn't help them that they do not know the area where the money from their taxes which they pay to the government goes.'

Yousef claims he is an avenging warrior, but despite his hatred of Americans and the Israeli state, he does not appear to have an all-consuming hatred of Jews *per se*. One Jew who has met and talked with Yousef is Avraham Moskowitz, a court-appointed New York lawyer initially picked at random to represent him after his arrest in Pakistan. Moskowitz, then 38-years-old, is an Orthodox Jew who wears a yarmulke almost everywhere. 'My Jewishness is obvious from my name and from the minute you meet me,' said Moskowitz, a partner at the law firm of Anderson Kill Olick & Oshinsky.[63] 'People tell me that it's something that I can't and I don't hide.'

With Yousef, however, a man portrayed by elements of the media as the world's most dangerous Islamic fundamentalist, Moskowitz's religion, and his 'obvious Jewishness' was not an issue. 'He didn't say, "No, I don't want you, you're a Jewish lawyer." Nor did he ever question the validity of the advice or the motivation behind what I was telling him because of the fact that I was Jewish,' said Moskowitz. 'To his credit, the issue of my being Jewish did not affect his ability to take advice from me or to relate to me.' Moskowitz admits that he was 'mildly surprised' Yousef had no objections to having a Jewish lawyer. 'There was reason to suspect that I was the last person he would want to represent him,' he said.

It is Yousef's anger at the interminable suffering of the Palestinian people that has been the central anger driving him to terrorism, and he will happily produce evidence to back his claim that crimes have been committed against 'his people'. 'The numbers of Palestinians in 1917 according to United Nations publications was about 1.1 million,' he said. 'And now after more than 80 years there are less than 700,000 and the rest of them were either killed, deported, or living now in temporary shelters and camps in overseas countries as foreigners, and you [America] have been supporting all of this killing and deportation throughout the 80 years.'

There is a distinction, says Yousef, between Israel, which he believes is fighting to expand its borders, and the Palestinians, who 'are not fighting to steal a land which does not belong to them or to confiscate properties or to steal properties which don't belong to them'. What they are fighting for, says Yousef, 'is to get their lands and confiscated properties and historic properties back while those who are killing and stealing and torturing, you are supporting them'.

Ramzi Yousef is the archetypal angry young man. Like an incandescent student radical from the 1960s, his anger crosses continents as he rails at the world's inequities. He rants against Israeli kibbutzim to which only Jews have access, and claims that such practices in America would be called racism. But America supports Israel because the US 'was based on racism and founded on racism on the slavery of black people and confiscation of land and properties of indigenous people, Indians in this country'.

In Northern Ireland, Yousef is furious that Sinn Fein, the political wing of the IRA, has engaged in talks with the British and Irish governments without guarantees that would 'bring those responsible for the occupation of Northern Ireland before a War Crimes Court'.[64] Even China has not escaped his attention.[65] He expresses outrage at the apparent hypocrisy of the West, which keeps talking 'about human rights in China and the Chinese prisoners' when, according to him, the only reason the West is concerned is because Chinese prison inmates are forced to work for free making products that are flooding the West.[66]

The West, says Yousef, was the first to kill innocent people and introduce terrorism into human history when America dropped an atomic bomb 'which killed tens of thousands of women and children in Japan and when you killed over 100,000 people, most of them civilians, in Tokyo with fire bombings', he said. Civilians in Vietnam, he adds, were massacred with chemicals such as Agent Orange. 'You went to wars more than any other country in this century and then you have the nerve to talk about killing innocent people. And then you have invented new ways to kill innocent people. You have [the] so-called economic embargo which kills nobody other than children and elderly people, and which other than Iraq you have been placing the economic embargo on Cuba and other countries for over 35 years.'[67]

According to Yousef he has simply used the same tactics against America. 'Since this is the way you invented and since this is the means you have been using against other people which you continue until this day to use in killing innocent people, innocent people just to force countries to change their policies, it was necessary to use the same means against you because this is the only language which you understand. This is the only language which ... someone can deal with you and talk with you.'[68]

So does Yousef consider himself to be a terrorist? 'If the terrorist means to retrieve my land and to fight everyone who has attacked me and my relatives, I have no objection to being called a terrorist,' said Yousef, 'it is the right of all the Muslims, in addition to the Palestinians, to fight the Zionists'. If Jews were exposed to oppression at the hands of the Nazis, says Yousef, 'why do the Palestinians pay the price for this? And also the Blacks were exposed to slavery and oppression in [the United States], so why are they not given a state such as the Jews?'

Yousef is too arrogant to apologize for the appalling crimes he has committed, but he offers a pathetic justification. 'Although it is very painful to innocent people and very painful for anyone to lose a close relative or a friend, but it was necessary. This is what it takes to make you feel the pain which you are causing to other people and this is what it takes to make you understand what you are causing and doing to other people and the pain which you are causing.'[69]

Although Ramzi Yousef likes to portray himself as a sophisticated polyglot, most of his knowledge is second-hand, passed on by his father, friends, family, and taken from books and pamphlets. His hatred has been imbued rather than learnt from bitter personal experience. Ramzi Yousef has never been shot at or tear-gassed by Israeli soldiers on the West Bank: he has never even visited Palestine.[70] Yet the battle for the creation of an independent Palestinian state became a powerful romantic lure for the young radical. Born and brought up in Kuwait, Yousef does not consider himself a Kuwaiti.[71] Despite a Pakistani father and a Pakistani passport; despite a secure upbringing, and several years of education in the West, Yousef chose to affiliate himself with the Palestinians and launch a devastating terrorist war against America on their behalf – one that could have led to terrible repercussions against the Palestinian people. Only an arrogant man could have such total belief in his own righteousness, but arrogance is a personality flaw that Yousef enjoys to excess.

When a questioner asked Yousef if he considers himself to be a genius, he thought for a brief moment, then smiled shyly and answered with conviction: 'Yes.'[72] When he was asked to describe the type of personality that he most admires, Yousef could well have been talking about himself when he replied: 'The personality of the messenger on whom God has prayed and greeted.'[73] Yousef sees himself as an emissary, one sent by a higher power to deliver unpalatable news to the world. His message, put simply, is that those responsible for the ill-treatment of the Palestinians, a people whose suffering he has adopted as his own, must face the wrath of God, administered by God's self-appointed representative: Ramzi Yousef.

Such is the importance of Yousef's 'mission' against the West that even his own death is little more than an occupational hazard. 'If it was true that I made the bomb which was used in the [bombing of the] World Trade Center, if this was true, then the person who manufactures the explosives, and transfers them and uses them, accepts all the risks which result from this ...' he said.[74]

Within this answer perhaps lies evidence of the psychological strength necessary to survive the intense mental pressure of spending two years on the run from the determined agents of the only surviving superpower. Vanity and belief in his 'mission' has blocked any innate sense of self-preservation – even the lives of his two young daughters are expendable in pursuit of his wider objectives: 'If the case is more important than my own self, no doubt it will be more important than any other thing, we [he uses the plural to identify with the Palestinian people] haven't chosen this path voluntarily but we were forced to go through it as a result of the killing and the occupation which we are living through. He who accepts the work of manufacturing explosives accepts what is less than that of dangers ... And if God wills they [his daughters] are in safety.'

Perhaps this supreme self-confidence makes Yousef a more seductive character. Physically, he has large flapping ears, a bulbous nose, a wiry, lean shape, dark hair and brown eyes. He also bears the scars of his trade. One of his eyes is unstable, roaming around slightly out of sync with the other. There are faint burn marks on his face, and several of his nails are cracked and broken right up to the flesh of his fingers. Yet he still retains rugged good looks which have helped to attract a wife and several girlfriends. His radical beliefs, meanwhile, won him a gang of followers in the United States, Pakistan and the Philippines, all within the space of a few years.

Yousef specialized in recruiting simpletons to act as his expendable soldiers. Several of his supporters, including Mohammad Salameh and Eyad Ismoil, are of below average intelligence. However Yousef also persuaded intelligent university graduates such as Nidal Ayyad, a conspirator in the World Trade Center bombing, to risk his life and comfortable career in grand terrorist plots, while Abdul Hakim Murad seems to have been willing to take his own life in one of Yousef's plans for a suicide attack. His talent for manipulating those around him, and his strength of personality, was even noted by the judge who presided over his later trials. 'I watched you closely during two long trials,' Judge Kevin Duffy told Yousef. 'I have observed you during your many appearances in court. You tried to charm the jury, and, I will admit, you are not without charm. So I can well understand how you were successful in charming others to join in your cause.' And, Judge Duffy added: 'You are smart.'

A senior Pakistani intelligence officer gives a similar summary: 'Everywhere Yousef went he was able to convert religious young men to his terrorist cause. His power was based partly on fear and partly on persuasion – he convinced some of these youngsters that what they were doing was in the name of Allah. He knew exactly what to say and what to do to win them over. Ramzi Yousef is an evil genius.'[75]

References

[1] Author interview. Radio broadcast by Churchill regarding the likely actions of Russia, 1 October 1939.
[2] Author interviews with Neil Herman, other American investigators and intelligence sources, Pakistani investigators, and Mary Anne Weaver, 'Children of the Jihad', *The New Yorker*, 12 June 1995.
[3] Annon was arrested in Manila in December 1995 amid police claims he was plotting terrorist attacks. He was later released without charge.
[4] Author interview with Pakistani investigator and Weaver, op. cit.
[5] Author interview.
[6] Author interview.
[7] Weaver, op. cit.

8 Author interviews with retired college officials.

9 Ibid.

10 Author interviews with Janet Kazeem and Richard Hall of the University of Cambridge Results Department, Historical Records.

11 Author interviews with college officials, and David Charter 'College lax with overseas courses', *The Times*; Simon Targett, 'Audit office calls for university ombudsman', *Financial Times*; Lucy Ward, 'Institute slated for overseas course', *Independent*, all 31 January 1997; and Barry Hugill and Michael Prestage, 'UK colleges face inquiry into foreign marketing', *Observer*, 30 June 1996, and 'The troubled international joint ventures', *The Times*, 23 October 1998.

12 Author interviews with investigators.

13 James Bone and Alan Road, in 'Terror by degree', *The Times*, 18 October 1997.

14 Ibid.

15 Author interviews with serving and former members of staff.

16 Ibid.

17 Anecdote related by Western terrorist analyst to the author.

18 Author interview with a British investigator.

19 Ibid.

20 Author interview with Julie Cohen. Cohen studied at Swansea University from October 1989 until June 1992.

21 Author interview.

22 Letter from Yousef published in the January 1997 issue of *Politics and the World*, Jersey City, New Jersey.

23 Based on author interviews with Neil Herman and investigators from America, Pakistan and Britain.

24 Author interview with American investigator.

25 Ibid.

26 Author interview with retired CIA official.

27 Author interview with Pakistani intelligence source. There is no suggestion the President knew that Yousef was involved in the bombing.

28 Interview with Yousef by Raghida Dergham of the *Al-Hayat* newspaper. Yousef stated plainly: 'I did not participate in the fighting in Afghanistan.'

29 Author interview with Neil Herman.

30 Based on a stamp in his passport.

31 Author interview with US intelligence source.

32 Author interview with confidential source.

33 Author interview.

34 Author interview with William Ploss.

35 Ibid.

36 Order of Transfer, US District Court, Southern District of Florida, Case number 90-2367-CIV-Marcus. Order obtained by the author from the US Federal Records Center, Atlanta, Georgia.

37 Lysandrou deposition, p.683–8.

38 Based on author interview with a confidential source. There is no suggestion Lysandrou has been involved in terrorism.

[39] Author interview with William Ploss.

[40] According to an author interview with the author of the reports.

[41] Author interview with anonymous source.

[42] There is no suggestion that anyone connected with Edwards, or any living member of the Barbouti family, has done anything wrong.

[43] There is no suggestion Lysandrou had done anything wrong.

[44] Author interview.

[45] Author interview with anonymous source. Caldwell later became the Regional Security Officer at the US Embassy in Kinshasa and then left the DSS.

[46] Author interview with Andy Laine, DSS official.

[47] Author interview with Neil Herman.

[48] Author interview with British intelligence source.

[49] Author interviews with several people close to Lysandrou.

[50] Ibid.

[51] Author wrote to him directly and via members of his family.

[52] Author interview.

[53] Based on his interview with Raghida Dergham of *Al-Hayat* in April 1995.

[54] Author interview with senior Pakistani investigator.

[55] Yousef's interview with Raghida Dergham of *Al-Hayat* in April 1995.

[56] Author interview with Dr Laurie Mylroie, an American expert on terrorism and Iraq.

[57] James Bone and Alan Road, in 'Terror by degree', *The Times*, 18 October 1997.

[58] Interview with Raghida Dergham of *Al-Hayat* in April 1995.

[59] Dergham, op. cit. Since his conviction he has not been allowed to speak to any member of the media, including the author.

[60] Ramzi Yousef, speaking in court on 8 January 1998, before he was sentenced by Judge Kevin Duffy, S12 93 CR 180 (KTD).

[61] Ibid.

[62] Dergham, op. cit.

[63] Jon Kalish, 'A Case of Conscience', *The Jewish Week*, 17 February 1995.

[64] In a seven-page statement Yousef issued through his lawyer Roy Kulcsar on 25 March 1995.

[65] Ramzi Yousef, speaking in court. Op. cit.

[66] Ibid.

[67] Ibid.

[68] Ibid.

[69] Ibid.

[70] During an interview with Raghida Dergham of *Al-Hayat*, Yousef said he was not permitted to visit such places.

[71] Dergham, op. cit.

[72] Ibid.

[73] Ibid.

[74] Ibid.

[75] Author interview.

SEVEN

Coming to America

BY THE middle of 1991 Ramzi Yousef was a well-travelled young man who had tasted life in Europe, the Middle East, Asia, and possibly even America.[1] The summer of that year, however, found him living back in Pakistan, forging alliances with other militants and seeking his role in the fight against the West and Shiite Muslims. He was following the example of his father, Muhammad Abdul Karim, who had by then fully embraced the militant cause and joined the Sipah-e-Sahaba group of Sunni Muslim extremists that believed eradicating Shiites was its holy duty.[2]

Yousef spent days sitting on buses in stifling heat, shuttling between meetings and gatherings in the sprawling city of Karachi, the remote Baluchi town of Turbat, and the bustling 'Wild West' town of Peshawar, where, during the final weeks of the summer, serious romance entered Yousef's life. American and Pakistani investigators are unsure how he came to meet his partner, but it seems to have been a family affair. Yousef and one of his brothers are understood to have married the sisters of Abu Hashim, a Pakistani militant and former student of Islamabad's Islamic University.[3] Yousef's bride was a quiet, pretty Baluchi girl in her early twenties, and he bought a house in Quetta, the capital of Baluchistan, where his wife lived during his subsequent travels. Within 15 months of marriage Yousef's wife gave birth to their first child, a baby daughter. Another baby girl was born early in 1994, while Yousef was still on the run from the FBI.

The summer of 1991 was important in Yousef's life not only because of his wedding: it was also a turning point in his development as a terrorist. 'It was the moment his terrorist career really began,' according to one American investigator.[4] Yousef began appearing again at several of Osama bin Laden's terrorist training camps, honing his already broad knowledge of electronics and explosives, and receiving further indoctrination from veterans of the Afghan war in the righteousness of the militant cause.

Amid this terrorist milieu surrounding the frontier town of Peshawar, at parties, meetings and teaching camps, Yousef is believed to have met and befriended Abdurajak Abubakar Janjalani, a militant Muslim born on the island of Basilan in the southern Philippines, and the two young men became friends. An Islamic missionary had encouraged Janjalani to study Islamic jurisprudence in Saudi Arabia during the early 1980s, and he eventually appeared in Afghanistan and spent several years fighting against the Soviets with 200 other Filipinos.

When the Red Army fled Afghanistan Janjalani began travelling back and forth between his home on Basilan, where he was fostering a new spirit of Muslim militancy, and the area around Peshawar, staying in veterans' guesthouses and hunting for supporters.[5] Janjalani was the founder and leader of Abu Sayyaf (Janjalani's Afghan fighting name), the principal hard-line Islamic terrorist gang in the Philippines, and Osama bin Laden, either directly or indirectly, offered him financial backing for his attempts to create an independent Islamic state in the southern Philippines. Yousef's relatives in Peshawar had close links with Osama bin Laden and his charitable organizations in the city, and Yousef – either on his own initiative, or at the behest of bin Laden or encouragement of Janjalani – decided to travel to the Philippines with Janjalani to ferment dissent.

Edwin Angeles, who became Janjalani's deputy in Abu Sayyaf, later confirmed in interviews with the Philippines' National Police that Yousef first briefly appeared in the country with Janjalani in the summer of 1991, and then, after a spell in Pakistan, returned in December 1991. Angeles knew Yousef as 'The Chemist' because of his abilities with explosives, and claims that Yousef, Abdul Hakim Murad and Wali Khan Amin Shah trained Abu Sayyaf terrorists in the southern Philippines and stayed for roughly three months.

The timing fits with Pakistani investigations into Yousef's movements during this period. Agents believe that he spent several months in the Philippines from December 1991, and then arrived back in Pakistan on 15 May 1992, to spend a few months in a secret location with his wife. One question, however, is how Yousef gained entry to the country: he apparently used an Iraqi passport bearing a visa issued by the Pakistani embassy in Baghdad. However, on the day the visa was supposed to have been issued none were processed, the round seal on the visa does not correspond with the seal in use at the embassy at that time, and the actual signature of visa officer Muzaffar Illahi Malik does not correspond with the signature in Yousef's passport.[6] It all remains something of a mystery, until one considers the opinion of a senior American intelligence official involved in the case: 'Yousef was developing high-level contacts in Pakistani intelligence through his links with bin Laden, mainly in the ISI [Inter Services Intelligence]. It's a dirty mess. They facilitated much of his travel. Getting airport officials to turn a blind eye to his entry would have been nothing.'

Just as Yousef was returning to Pakistan from training terrorists in the Philippines, the lure of Islamic militancy was calling another young firebrand named Ahmed Mohammad Ajaj, a scrawny former Domino's Pizza delivery-man from Houston, Texas. Yousef and Ajaj may have known each other before spring 1992, if Yousef was involved with Ihsan Barbouti and the Iraqi National Oil Company, but within a few months of Yousef's return to Pakistan there can be little doubt that they were close conspirators.

On 24 April 1992, Ajaj told his landlord he was leaving his home in Houston and going to live and work in New York. He bought a cheap long-haul flight to Pakistan and travelled to the North-West Frontier province, to a sprawling camp roughly 30 miles east of Peshawar: the University of Dawa and Jihad, one of the most infamous terrorist training camps in the whole of Pakistan. Through his contacts among Islamic militants in Texas, Ajaj had learnt details of the camp curriculum, which included hand-to-hand combat, weapons training, and preparation and detonation of explosives. It was perfect for Ajaj – he wanted to build bombs – big bombs.

At first glance the Texan-based radical would appear to have the archetypal life history of a militant Palestinian. In a petition he later filed in America as part of a political asylum request,[7] Ajaj claimed the first time he could remember being tear-gassed by Israeli forces was when he was six years old. His arm was broken a couple of years later by an Israeli soldier who discovered a crude drawing of the Palestinian flag in his school text-book, and he spent his first night in prison when he was 17, during a 'round-up' of Muslims praying in Jerusalem's Old City. As he poured out his tale to contacts in Peshawar, it must have sounded impressive, but the suspicious men behind the 'university' feared the American infidels were trying to plant spies in their midst. They had reservations, they told Ajaj; he would have to get a letter of introduction from someone they could trust.

On 16 May 1992, Ajaj obediently flew from Pakistan to the United Arab Emirates in the Gulf, and then travelled on to Saudi Arabia. He appears to have won the trust of individuals close to the camp, possibly even meeting with one of its Saudi funders, because he procured a letter, dated 21 May, requesting that the bearer be trained in the use of weapons and explosives.[8] Ajaj left his new friends in the Saudi kingdom and flew out of the Middle East on a flight from the United Arab Emirates on 13 June, arriving in Pakistan the next day.

His instructors at the University of Dawa and Jihad did not disappoint. One instructor at the camp was particularly enlightening; a young man with a passion for chemicals and electronics considered by his peers to be something of a genius bomb-maker: Ramzi Yousef.[9] In dusty fields surrounding a large bungalow, the University of Dawa and Jihad's main building, Yousef explained to his students how to build bombs to destroy large buildings – such as American embassies – or blow up aeroplanes. He lectured, advised and guided, according to a Pakistani investigator, imitating Yousef with a wave of his hands: 'These clocks can be used as timers, these [remote controls] are good for wireless detonation. Snip the wires here. This explosive is good for this attack, this for another.' The camp was packed with battle-hardened fighters and training was rigorous: men were often injured by shrapnel from exploding shells and bombs. Yousef himself stood with the students and listened attentively as groups were taught to use automatic weapons and drilled in unarmed combat.[10]

The moment when Yousef began planning the World Trade Center bombing may never be known, but investigators believe the origins of the February 1993 atrocity can be traced back to June or July 1992, when Yousef and Ajaj met at the University of Dawa and Jihad.

This was a difficult period for Yousef and militant Islamists. War against the Soviets in Afghanistan had degenerated into internecine battles between rival Afghan warlords, while the Palestinians, Yousef's chosen cause, were in disarray. The Palestine Liberation Organization (PLO) was running low on money because Saudi Arabia had cancelled £59 million ($100 million) worth of support in retaliation for PLO backing for Iraq during the Gulf War; morale within the Palestinian movement was at rock bottom. Ahmed Abdulrahman, the PLO's Director of

Information, was even quoted as saying the PLO did not even have enough money 'to produce a single poster'.[11] Israel was dominating the emerging Middle East peace process like a petulant child, with the US government obediently agreeing with the Israeli government when they refused to allow PLO participation in the process.

It was in this atmosphere that Ramzi Yousef began plotting an attack on the United States. American and Pakistani sources differ over who might have been behind him: some suggest it was a senior agent from Iraqi intelligence; another claims Iraq used the anti-Shiite and anti-Iranian MKO terror group as the conduit for proposing the attack; another senior American source claims Yousef himself proposed the attack after his old friend Mahmud Abouhalima made contact with him from New York, and mentioned plans for a pipe-bombing campaign in the city. Whoever was the originator, the World Trade Center would not have entered discussions at this stage: the crucial objective was to hurt America.

By the middle of July 1992 Ajaj finished his terrorist training and was deemed ready to accompany Yousef on his mission to the US. First, however, the two men had to get into the country. Ajaj travelled to the American embassy in Islamabad and asked politely if he could return to his home in Houston. He told Karen Stanton, a US immigration official at the embassy, that he had a five-year American visa but had left it at home. Stanton, who had heard just about every story, tale and excuse possible during her time at the embassy, refused to believe Ajaj, and told him bluntly that she could be of no further help.[12] Looking dejected, Ajaj left the embassy and travelled back to Peshawar to meet with Yousef. The two men would have to find another way of entering the USA. It did not take them long.

On 31 August 1992, Yousef and Ajaj left Peshawar for Karachi on flight PK-339. They stayed overnight in a cheap hotel near the airport, and then left Karachi for New York on flight PK-703 early the next day. In Pakistan, just as in most countries, problems with visas, passports, and international regulations were miraculously overcome by money. Yousef bribed an official with $2,700, and the two men were given boarding passes and allowed on to the flight.[13] He might even have had more direct assistance from senior Pakistani intelligence officials: several are alleged to have helped in Yousef's attempts to enter the United States, and then later to avoid capture, and their names have been given to the Pakistani government by the FBI.[14]

The consequence of this collusion with terrorism could be seen at New York's JFK airport on the morning of 1 September 1992, when a tall, lean young man carrying an airline ticket bearing the name 'Azan Muhammad' stepped from the first-class cabin of Pakistan International Airlines, and strode confidently through the throng of passengers towards the arrivals hall. Dressed in harem pants, a puffy-sleeved shirt, a vest and jacket in orange, brown and olive-green Afghan silk, the man presented himself at the desk of Martha Morales, an agent of the Immigration and Naturalisation Service (INS), and politely requested political and religious asylum.[15] It is a routine played out dozens of times every day.

'What is your full true name?' asked Morales, as the man handed her an identification card from the Houston-based Islamic Information Centre. The bearded man lent down, and in soft, faintly accented English, carefully replied, 'Ramzi Ahmed Yousef'. He had been persecuted by Iraqi soldiers, he said. Then he raised one hand, solemnly swore he would be oppressed if he was not allowed entry to the United States, and presented an Iraqi passport bearing another name.

Thirty feet away at a second INS desk, Ajaj was going through the same ritual. Travelling under the name Khurram Khan, he was the 'mule' carrying Yousef's bomb-building manuals to protect his genius friend from arrest. Ajaj handed a Swedish passport to INS agent Cathy Bethom and requested asylum. It was an astonishing performance.

Bethom looked at the Swedish passport and held it up to eye-level in disbelief. She could clearly see that the photograph of Ajaj was stuck over a picture of the real owner. As she peeled off the photo with her long fingernails, Ajaj began shouting. 'My mother was Swedish! If you don't believe me check your computer.'

Ajaj was 'loud and belligerent', according to Mark Cozine, an INS inspector, and was taken to a back office for questioning.[16] At the other INS desk, Yousef was a picture of innocence. While Ajaj shouted and swore, Yousef smiled sweetly and politely asked to be admitted to America. He was taken to an interview booth and subjected to a standard list of questions; he was even asked if he had ever been involved in terrorism (he said no). Martha Morales was not convinced, but her suggestion that Yousef be detained was overruled by superiors – the 100 spaces in the INS Detention Center were all taken. Yousef was told to appear before a judge for an asylum hearing on 8 December, and released on his own recognizance. He quietly gathered up his bags, thanked Morales profusely, and walked out of the terminal towards a waiting line of taxis.

Ajaj, meanwhile, was being questioned. 'What is your real name?' asked Cozine. 'Why are you carrying a false passport?' Ajaj gave reasonable answers, and the interview was almost routine until Cozine opened Ajaj's leather hand-luggage. Inside were Jordanian, British and Saudi Arabian passports, all bearing different names. 'He had multiple pieces of identification,' said Cozine.[17] 'He had several passports from various countries, several photographic IDs . . . lots of books and videotapes and papers and maps, and all kinds of pictures of weapons, showing assembly [and] disassembly, bombs, rocket launchers . . . aerial pictographs, strategy like you would see in almost a military manual.' The INS agents who began a thorough search of Ajaj's luggage could hardly believe their eyes.

Cozine flicked through books containing detailed instructions on the manufacture of huge, improvised bombs. There was a videotape of a suicide bombing, purportedly of an American embassy, which also provided instruction on the manufacture of explosives; handbooks describing how to make explosives and improvised weapons; a videotape showing a chemistry lesson on how to manufacture explosives; and manuals on catalysts, detonators and the ingredients needed for large bombs. Ajaj was also carrying a 'cheat sheet' containing 'all the questions that would be asked by an inspector during the normal course of inspection', according to Cozine, and another document urging violence and terrorist acts against the enemies of Islam, bearing the title, 'Facing the enemies of God terrorism is a religious duty and force is necessary'.

There was another booklet entitled 'Rapid Destruction and Demolition' that described in precise detail the best methods for destroying buildings, and gave the chemical formulas necessary for making bombs capable of the task. On page 28 of one of Ajaj's pale-blue bombing manuals was a series of Arabic instructions for making a pipe-bomb, and hand-drawn pictures of beakers: one labelled nitric acid, another filtered urine. Ajaj was hustled off to the cells to await a court hearing.

Refugees from the Middle East are no strangers to New York, the great melting pot of North America. Immigrants from Egypt, Lebanon, Syria, Jordan and across the Arab world have sat in cafés and restaurants on Atlantic Avenue in Brooklyn since the 1930s, eating and arguing about politics. The Al Kifah 'refugee centre' on the road even supplied fighters for the holy war in Afghanistan against Soviet invaders during the 1980s.

For decades Muslims and Jews lived in New York in relative peace, despite the tinderbox situation in the Middle East. Racial hatred between the two groups erupted occasionally, but it was not until 1990 that the embers were fanned into roaring flames by the murder of a crazed Zionist Rabbi called Meir Kahane.

Kahane was, by any judgement, a racist, murderous, religious zealot for whom Arabs were 'jackals', and African-Americans were 'savages' and 'animals'. A former CIA 'asset', Kahane was recruited to subvert Jewish-American opposition to the Vietnam War, and then established his own militant groups and shook the pockets of wealthy Jewish benefactors for money, much of which he spent picking up women and conducting adulterous affairs.

On the evening of 5 November 1990, Kahane was speaking to around a hundred of his followers in the ballroom of the Marriott Hotel on the corner of 49th Street and Lexington Avenue. A lone young Arab called El Sayyid Nosair sat at the back, a yarmulke on his head to disguise him as a dark-skinned Sephardic Jew. The Rabbi finished his speech and stepped down from the podium into a small crowd. Nosair rose and walked to the front, drew a gun and shot Kahane once in the neck.

The room erupted in chaos. With a grin plastered across his face the Arab sprinted outside pursued by some of Kahane's younger followers. Nosair jumped into the back of a yellow cab waiting outside, and banged on the dividing partition to tell his friend to race away. But the driver was a Hispanic from the Bronx, not his friend Mahmud Abouhalima, the giant redheaded Egyptian, who – investigators allege – had been supposed to act as the getaway driver, but had been moved on from outside the door by hotel security. The young Arab panicked, jumped out of the cab and ran down the road. Nosair careered towards Carlos Acosta, an armed postal police officer standing three blocks from the hotel, raised his gun and shot Acosta in the chest. But the officer managed to draw his own .357 Magnum and fired once, hitting Nosair in the chin and putting him in hospital.

It was, thought the investigating detectives, a classic open-and-shut case. There were a hundred witnesses, there was a motive, and not only was there a smoking gun, but it had been found in the hand of the arrested suspect and bullets in his pocket matched the one that killed Kahane.

Occasionally, however, juries make horrible, inexplicable mistakes. The 12 men and women who heard the case – one of whom sold home-made food outside the courthouse during lunch breaks – were evidently baffled by the astonishing defence constructed by Nosair's lawyer William Kunstler, a brilliant sophist who expounded more conspiracy theories than now surround the assassination of President Kennedy. In December 1991 they acquitted Nosair of murder.

'Nosair was caught right at the scene, with a gun. It was incredible. Very strange decision. Very hard to understand,' said Neil Herman, who had been having dinner just four blocks from the Marriott Hotel on the night of the murder. The judge was equally shocked: he said the verdict 'defied reason' and sentenced Nosair to the maximum possible 17–25 years on firearms charges. Outside the court it mattered little that Nosair would be imprisoned on the gun charges. Abouhalima hoisted Kunstler on to his shoulders and several dozen Muslim militants began to celebrate.

Ramzi Yousef had met Abouhalima during the war in Afghanistan in 1988, when the older man had searched for mines with a thin stick of wood and somehow survived. After avoiding detention by the INS at JFK airport and climbing into the back of a cab, Yousef immediately directed the driver to the offices of the Al Kifah refugee centre on Atlantic Avenue, where he was due to meet his old friend. The bearded giant, who was working as a chauffeur for the militant religious leader Sheikh Omar Abdel Rahman, was thrilled to see Yousef, and quickly took him to meet the Sheikh. 'This is Ramzi Yousef,' Abouhalima told the blind fundamentalist cleric. 'He is a friend from Afghanistan, a guy who will do anything.'[18]

Yousef is believed to have slept on the floor of Abouhalima's apartment for his first night in New York, but within two days he was introduced to a friend of Abouhalima's called Mohammad Salameh, a slight young Jordanian with a bushy black beard. Born in Biddya in the district of Nablus on 1 September 1967, Salameh had left Jordan for the US in 1987 with a five-year entry visa. Like the majority of his countrymen, he was of Palestinian origin – on his father's side – and like Yousef he felt a strong affinity for the Palestinian cause. Salameh was a simple, impressionable young man; El Sayyid Nosair had been something of a mentor to him before his arrest. Yousef immediately filled those shoes and began preparing to move in with Salameh at Apartment 4, 34 Kensington Avenue, Jersey City, in an area known locally as 'Little Cairo' because of the large number of Arab immigrants.

Salameh's apartment was tiny. As Yousef walked into the flat he saw a small kitchen off to the right, a small living room to the left, one bedroom at the back and a small adjoining bathroom.[19] There was a common hallway, which meant other residents could see them coming and going. Yousef might have been the imported expert but there was no time for him to be choosy. The accommodation was spartan, with furnishing consisting of nothing more than single mattresses, but at least they were among other young Muslims.

The flats had been rented in 1991 by Mohamud F. Mohamud, a former waiter and city taxi driver, and had become something of a safe haven for impoverished young men from the Middle East. Upstairs from no. 4 was Apartment 8: by the time Yousef arrived there were up to twenty men living in the two flats, communicating up and down the stairs via an intercom system, holding meetings and prayers together, and eating large communal meals.

Abouhalima became Yousef's guide during his first few days in New York. They walked along Atlantic Avenue together and Yousef introduced himself to Abouhalima's friends as an Iraqi called 'Rashid'. Few believed him: it was an area rife with inter-communal intrigue. The Egyptians suspected every newcomer of being an agent from Cairo, the Lebanese suspected everyone of being an Israeli spy, and the resident Iraqis suspected everyone of everything. Yousef was not helped in his disguise by the Palestinian accent with which he spoke Arabic, and a Pakistani accent when he spoke Urdu and English. He knew nothing about Baghdad, not even the famous fish markets along the Euphrates river, and many of those he met found him instantly suspicious.[20] His landlady during his time in America even searched his room looking for his passport, such was her conviction that he was lying about his nationality.[21]

As Yousef settled in during the second half of September 1992, the small militant milieu he entered had a shock. The FBI had been watching them since the murder of Rabbi Kahane and even had a double agent, Emad Salem, working in their midst. Just over a month before Yousef's arrival the Feds had fallen out with Salem, accusing him of being unreliable and inventing intelligence information, but in late September they heard rumours of a plot to assassinate Hosni Mubarak, the Egyptian President, and hauled more than twenty militants in to 26 Federal Plaza for fingerprinting and questioning.

The session was supposed to intimidate the men into spurning terrorism. Some of their photographs were deliberately left on the wall as proof of the FBI's interest. Apart from warning the men they were under investigation, it had little effect: many of the militants had been through torture, had been shot at, tear-gassed. Abouhalima had walked through minefields in Afghanistan; the law enforcement agents of the free world could do little to frighten them. One of the men questioned but not involved in the bomb plots, a New York postal worker, allegedly even stopped listening to his questioner at one point and started reading his Koran.[22] The others waited in the hallway, tutting loudly and complaining.

Neither did the attention of the FBI scare off Ramzi Yousef. Within weeks of arriving in the US he began his preparations for the World Trade Center bombing. But Yousef could never have worked in the apartment on Kensington Avenue; there was simply not enough space or privacy with twenty other men roaming around. In October 1992 Salameh heard that Ashraf Moneeb, a genial young Egyptian student, was looking for someone to share his apartment in a redbrick building at 251 Virginia Avenue, less than a mile from Kensington Avenue. It was cramped but cheap, and Yousef and Salameh moved in.

At first the arrangement worked well. Moneeb lived and studied in the living room, and Yousef and Salameh shared the bedroom. Moneeb saw Abouhalima visiting them on several occasions, and each time Yousef and Salameh would retreat into the bedroom with their friend, closing the door in a vain attempt to give their flatmate some privacy. The two terrorists would also talk loudly for hours in their room,[23] shouting down their bedroom telephone line to contacts in the Middle East, Pakistan, Turkey and even Yugoslavia.

By October 1992 the outline of the plot was becoming clearer. It was time for Yousef to take control, to turn a rag-tag group of Islamic militants centred around Sheikh Omar Abdel Rahman into a group of conspirators capable of attacking the pillars of American power. As Abouhalima later confirmed to a cellmate in jail, the group's plans for jihad were basic until Yousef arrived in New York: 'the planned act was not as big as what subsequently occurred . . . Yousef showed up on the scene and escalated the original plot . . . Yousef used [the group, including Abouhalima] as pawns and then immediately after the blast left the country.'[24]

Nidal Ayyad, a tall, skinny chemical engineer with a degree from Rutgers University and a good job with a firm called Allied Signal, entered the plot. An old friend of Salameh's – both men were from Jordanian families – Ayyad grew up in Kuwait, and might even have known Yousef as a child. On 14 October 1992, Salameh and Ayyad opened a joint bank account together and immediately deposited $8,567 in cash. Eight days later they withdrew $8,560 in cash from the account – in an apparent attempt to hide the source of the money – and Salameh deposited it in a separate account registered in his own name.

Salameh, Yousef's obedient little helper, then bought a dark green Chevrolet car and began scouting around Jersey City for a place where the bomb-making equipment could be stored. He found the perfect spot within half a mile of the Virginia Avenue apartment, and on 30 November Salameh cashed a cheque for $3,400, took some of the money to Space Station Storage at 60 Mallory Avenue, gave the name 'Kamal Ibraham' and rented locker 4344, a 10ft-by-10ft room on the second floor of the fourth building, for $90 a month.

That same day, Yousef, also using the name 'Kamal Ibraham', one of 11 aliases he used during his six months in the US, began ordering chemicals from a local firm called City Chemical, including 1,000lbs (454kg) of urea, 105 gallons of nitric acid, and 60 gallons of sulphuric acid. Yousef told City Chemical's salesman he knew exactly what he wanted: the nitrogen content of the urea crystals had to be 46.65 per cent and the sulphuric acid had to be 93 per cent pure. Yousef paid $3,615 in cash and arranged for the chemicals to be delivered to the storage shed.

The ease with which Yousef was able to acquire the chemicals for his bomb may have encouraged him to consider using other even more potent materials. According to Oliver 'Buck' Revell, the former Deputy Director of the FBI – who was involved in the investigation into Yousef and has been privy to some of the most secretive discoveries the Bureau has made in the last few decades – during investigations into the World Trade Center case intelligence agents uncovered evidence that Yousef and his conspirators 'were looking for radioactive isotopes and radioactive waste to add to their explosive device, not for any atomic device, but for contamination'.[25]

Using an atomic bomb in the attack would have been beyond Yousef's resources and limited time.[26] However, Revell and other investigative and intelligence sources claim Yousef did try to obtain radioactive material to create a less potent 'radiological bomb'.[27] Such a device typically consists of high explosive surrounded by incendiary material and radioactive isotopes. In one possible scenario, the bomb would have been placed outside the World Trade

Center and detonated; a fierce fire would have resulted and radioactivity would have risen into the atmosphere to be scattered downwind as fallout, rendering the affected area uninhabitable until completely decontaminated.

Virtually nothing has been spoken publicly about this element of Yousef's plan since the WTC bombing, but the effect on the US if he had been successful would have been unprecedented. Depending on the level of radiation present in his bomb, a large tract of southern Manhattan could have been rendered uninhabitable. New York would have been paralysed and mass panic would undoubtedly have caused the evacuation of the entire city, while the government in Washington would have come under pressure to respond against the likely perpetrators using overwhelming force.

According to an American intelligence source, while Yousef was beginning his preparations for the World Trade Center he was in regular contact with another, unnamed conspirator back in Pakistan. It is unclear whether contact was made directly, or via a third party. The conspirator in Pakistan, who the intelligence source alleges was close to Osama bin Laden, apparently tried to obtain radioactive material for the WTC bomb from contacts in the former Soviet Union. For several years Western intelligence agencies have publicly warned of the dangers of radioactive material being smuggled out of Russia, and in this case the Pakistani conspirator is believed to have focused his attention on obtaining strontium-90 or caesium-137. Both would have been extremely difficult to render safe if used by Yousef: strontium has a half-life of 28.8 years and when ingested by humans in even tiny quantities can cause cancer; caesium has a half-life of 30.2 years and 'sticks' to surfaces.

Although Yousef's anonymous Pakistani conspirator was unable to provide the radioactive material, possibly because of a lack of time, few of those who investigated the case believe Yousef would have hesitated to use them. 'To be honest, it's not something we like to think about, let alone talk about,' admitted one intelligence source.[28]

While his conspirator in Pakistan concentrated on trying to develop the potency of the bomb, Yousef was troubled by more conventional problems in New Jersey. By the time all the chemicals for the bomb had been safely loaded into the locker at Space Station Storage, Ashraf Moneeb had been driven to near distraction by the constant chatter from his companions in the Virginia Avenue flat. He could hardly hear himself think, let alone study, and he told Yousef and Salameh it was time for them to move. Salameh went looking for another apartment, this time one where they could actually build the bomb, while Yousef plotted and planned.

Ahmed Ajaj, meanwhile, who had helped Yousef into the US, was keeping in close contact with his friend from jail, where he was serving eight months for immigration fraud. He offered tips and advice about maximizing the bomb's impact, but would never contact Yousef directly, instead telephoning his friend Mohammad Abukhdeir in a fast-food restaurant called Big Five Hamburgers, in Mesquite, Texas. Abukhdeir would then either relay a message or set up a three-way telephone conversation.[29]

Ajaj knew all the payphones in the prison were monitored by the authorities, but he thought this ruse would prevent them hearing details of the plot. They also used codes to discourage monitoring, referring to Yousef as 'Rashid', the bomb plot as the 'study' and the terrorist materials as 'university papers'.[30]

On 29 December 1992, Ajaj rang Abukhdeir in Texas and told his friend to patch Yousef into a three-way chat. Ajaj was excited: the United States district court for the Eastern District of New York had ordered the US government to return Ajaj's belongings to the amateur terrorist, including all his bomb manuals. Ajaj could barely contain himself.[31] Yousef was also delighted, and wanted the manuals sent directly to his address in Jersey City. Ajaj initially agreed, but then cautioned against it, saying its shipment to Yousef might jeopardize Yousef's 'business', 'which would be a pity'![32]

Instead Ajaj said it would be 'preferable that you send someone else to get them'. Yousef thought for a few seconds, his impatience battling with his knowledge that he could be followed by the government if he went to collect the manuals personally, and then he agreed. He would 'send someone else than me' and would give Ajaj, through their mutual friend Abukhdeir, the 'address of someone here' – one of Yousef's friends. That pleased Ajaj.[33] He felt he was still involved in the plot against the Great Satan, and the manuals could be passed to Yousef without trace.[34]

While Yousef talked with Ajaj, Salameh was finding the two men somewhere to live. On New Year's Day 1993, Yousef and Salameh moved again, this time to an apartment at 40 Pamrapo Avenue in Jersey City that would become known as 'the bomb factory'. Salameh told the owner of the flat he was a Turk, gave the name 'Alaa Mahrous', paid $1,100 in cash for a month's rent and deposit, and told the owner he would need the flat for one year.

The small apartment comprised two bedrooms, one living room, a bathroom and a small kitchen, all on the ground floor of a quiet residential street. For Ramzi Yousef, it was the perfect base for an urban terrorist campaign. He wanted to follow his terrorist manuals to the letter, and one of his favourite books recommended that a terrorist base should always be established on the ground floor of a block, so a gang would have an easy escape in the event of a police raid or an emergency.[35] The flat did lack a refrigerator, which Yousef needed to stabilize nitro-glycerine, a highly volatile explosive. He explained the problem to Abouhalima, and the bearded giant trotted off to a local store.

The plan was slowly coming together. From the beginning of January Yousef and Salameh worked quietly late into the night, mixing chemicals, including urea nitrate and nitro-glycerine, in their apartment at Pamrapo Avenue. The preparation took commitment: the chemical fumes from the mixture were horrendous, choking Yousef's lungs when he removed his respirator, staining the walls with a bluish tint and rusting the inside doorknob and the hinges of the back bedroom door.[36] But the potency of the concoction still needed to be checked, and on four or five occasions Yousef drove out of New York to test small-scale versions of his chosen bomb.[37] It is perhaps ironic that Yousef's desire for perfection, manifested in his continual testing of the bomb, nearly conspired to scupper the entire operation.

The night of 23 January 1993 was freezing cold in the Woodbridge township in central New Jersey, and Fred Weimann, a veteran police officer with the New Jersey police, was cruising empty streets. He wasn't bothered. Woodbridge nestles next to interconnecting highways that criss-cross the state. 'If you have to go any place in Jersey, north, east, south or west, you have to come through our town,' said Weimann.[38] Anything could happen. Variety was one reason Weimann had stayed in the force for 13 years.

Just after 1.00 a.m. Weimann and his partner received reports of an accident at the junction of Leesville Avenue and Woodbind Avenue in Avenel, a small town that forms part of the Woodbridge township. The two officers sped to the scene, lights flashing, siren screaming, and found a car resting on the lawn of an apartment complex. 'It was a one-car accident,' said Weimann.[39]

The car had driven over the high kerb on to the lawn, wrecking the entire undercarriage and injuring the driver and passenger. The driver, Mohammad Salameh, was walking around in a daze and sat down next to the vehicle as Weimann pulled up. The young man in the passenger seat did not move. Fred Weimann called for an ambulance and gently placed a blanket over the man sitting on the ground to ward off the cold and prevent him going into shock. An ambulance was called at 1.45 a.m.

Marianne Coyle was one of three paramedics and a driver from the Iselin First Aid Squad, based near Avenel, who responded to Weimann's call. As her ambulance pulled up at the kerb Coyle spotted the two injured men and ran over to the man in the car.

'What's your name?' she asked.

'Ramzi Yousef,' whispered the man.

Coyle pulled a back board and a collar brace out of the ambulance, slid the board gently underneath Yousef and put the collar around his neck. Yousef, however, appeared to care little about his injuries.

'Where is the car going?' he kept asking in faintly accented English. 'What happened to the car?!'[40]

Coyle tried to keep him quiet, fearing he might be slipping into shock. Her team gingerly slid Yousef into the back of their ambulance, and made the three-minute dash to the local hospital. Yousef spent approximately 10 hours flat on his back in the Rahway Hospital emergency room before he was taken upstairs to 3E, the orthopaedic unit. Mary Ellen Kuch, the registered nurse running 3E, recalls a tall, thin young man with dark hair and dark features. With the help of an assistant, Kuch wheeled Yousef on a trolley up to room 335, a small room with two beds, and helped him off his stretcher and into the second bed by the window. Yousef, who was conscious and coherent, told Kuch he was from Jersey City.

'I remember seeing that his address was pretty far, like he was quite a distance from home,' said Kuch.[41] 'I saw he was from Jersey City, which is, you know, little bit of a ways. Usually we get like neighbouring people, and I remember feeling a little sorry for him because he was so far from home. I thought maybe he was at a nightclub or something. It was a Saturday night, and he was in a car accident, and he said he was visiting friends and they were in a car accident.'

Even though he was in pain from a back injury, Yousef noticed there was a phone in the room and began scheming.

'Can I make a phone-call from here using my calling card?' he asked Kuch.

The nurse replied that she didn't think so. 'So we got on the subject of calling cards, and then we got back to the issue of the phone, you know, and at that time, it wasn't hooked up,' said Kuch.

But Yousef kept asking staff if the phone could be connected, and eventually he charmed the nurses and got his way. Within hours of his accident he was calling the other members of his terrorist cell. Even though he was in hospital, Yousef was still in charge. First he wanted to check what had happened to the chemicals that had been in the back of the car. He need not have worried. His car was safe and his equipment was intact: the police never checked the boot, and Salameh reclaimed the car the day after the accident.

By early February Yousef's plot was close to execution. Yousef and Salameh told their landlord they had both found jobs in Brooklyn, and would move out by the end of the month. On 15 February Nidal Ayyad, the skinny chemist, rented a red Oldsmobile sedan from the National Car Rental company in Newark, New Jersey. One week later Ayyad and Salameh appeared at the offices of a Ryder van hire office on Kennedy Boulevard, Jersey City, and arranged to hire a large Econoline van with the Alabama licence-plate number XA70668. The deal was simple, manager Patrick J. Galasso told them: $220 a week or $59 a day, with the first 100 miles free and 25 cents a mile thereafter. Salameh checked the van fitted the dimensions Yousef had given him, and slapped down four $100 bills.

But who would drive the van? Perhaps remembering that Salameh had failed his driving test four times, and he was still an appalling driver, Yousef had already decided he needed more help. At around 1.00 a.m. on the morning of 9 February, Yousef plodded out to a call-box on Pamrapo Avenue and rang Eyad Ismoil – a former computer student at Kansas University whom Yousef knew from childhood in Kuwait – at the Casa View Grocery in Dallas, Texas.[42] Only they can know what was said, but the point of the discussion is easily deduced: Yousef told Ismoil, a Jordanian, that he needed his help. Perhaps he told him what was planned; perhaps he did not. He certainly made Ismoil realize it was urgent, because later the same day Ismoil went to a travel agency in Dallas and bought a plane ticket that took him to New York 12 days later.

Events moved quickly. Ayyad and Salameh drove into Manhattan and scouted at least one target, driving down into the World Trade Center car park and sketching the route they would take in and out. Yousef, meanwhile, was making final adjustments to his bomb, and he

151

decided to add tanks of compressed hydrogen to the mixture waiting in the bomb factory. On 25 February Nidal Ayyad rang a supplier of compressed gases from his office at work and arranged for several tanks to be delivered immediately to the storage centre. Yousef and Salameh dutifully made their way to the Space Station to await delivery, and just before noon the two men were seen standing outside, rubbing their hands and stamping their feet to ward off the cold. One of the staff asked if they wanted to wait inside, and Yousef and Salameh sat down opposite the counter.

'When most people come into the facility and they are waiting, whether they are waiting for a taxicab or something, we engage in conversation, because it's kind of odd to just stand behind the counter and they are sitting out there and you are doing the work. And they are just staring,' said David Robinson, the assistant manager of the centre.[43] 'We generally talk to make them feel at ease. It's part of our customer service orientation.'

Robinson chatted with the two men. 'We were just curious,' he said later.

'So what do you do?' Robinson asked Yousef.

'We work in manufacturing,' replied the terrorist. 'We have a factory.'

Robinson, relieved that his opening conversational gambit had been accepted, then asked the men where they were from.

'I am from Israel,' said Yousef.

'You were born in Israel?' queried Robinson.

'Yes,' said Yousef.

The two Arabs then began talking to each other in Arabic, and Robinson continued listening and smiling.

'We got to the point of languages,' Robinson remembered. 'And the other one said that he spoke Arabic and Hebrew, [and another language] but I don't recall what he said.'

'What do you guys manufacture?' said Robinson, who wanted to battle on with the conversation regardless of the language barriers. Salameh turned to Yousef, unsure how to respond to this inquisitive American. They could hardly tell Robinson they were making bombs, so what could they say?

Yousef just smiled wanly and said to Robinson: 'I don't know how you would say it in English.'

Any further potential embarrassment was saved by the arrival of the tanks of compressed hydrogen. Yousef and Salameh walked outside to help Dennis Walsh, the driver, unload three 4ft-long cylinders, but Robinson was not happy: 'We can't have gas in here,' he said, remonstrating with Walsh and the two foreigners. Yousef and Salameh pleaded and then bargained. They will only be here for 20 minutes, they said; a friend would be coming to collect them. Robinson relented, and Yousef and Salameh waited awkwardly for a while until the Ryder hire van arrived to move the cylinders back to the bomb factory.

The final touches were in place. All that remained was for Salameh to report the Ryder van stolen, so no loose ends would be left for the FBI to investigate. After all, Yousef must have reasoned, when the bomb brought down the twin towers the van would never be found. And so on the eve of the World Trade Center bombing Mohammad Salameh calmly rang the police from near the Pathmark supermarket at the Route 440 shopping plaza in Jersey City and told them his Ryder van had been stolen from the plaza car park.

Officer Ron Badiak and his partner responded to the call at about 10.00 p.m. and arrived at the supermarket 10 minutes later. Salameh sauntered over to greet them and explained what had happened – or, at least, give them his version of events. Badiak listened and nodded, then told Salameh he would take him in the police car back to the West District police station and file a report. Calm, polite, and without displaying any nerves, Salameh sat with the officers in the car while Badiak entered some of the details into the police computer during the five-minute journey back to the station.[44] Salameh showed the officer his driving licence, and even a receipt for groceries. It was a clever touch that Salameh could never have dreamt up on his own.

Yousef would probably have suggested the plan: the van would be blown to pieces inside the World Trade Center, the infidels would never find a trace of it, and the rental company would never get suspicious about their missing van and inform the police because Salameh had told them it had been stolen. The only worry for Yousef and the conspirators must have been how to prevent the van being stopped by the police as it made its final journey. So Salameh gave the police the wrong licence-plate number.

Salameh waved goodbye to the police officers and made his way back to the bomb factory. Yousef and his gang were all inside, preparing to load the bomb into the back of their Ryder van, which was resting, slightly hidden, at the end of a driveway next to the apartment at

153

Pamrapo Avenue. Just after midnight the men started loading their bomb.

Four large cardboard boxes were stacked into the back of the van, each containing an obscenely ingenious mixture of paper bags, newspapers, urea and nitric acid. Next to them were placed the three red metal cylinders of compressed hydrogen, which Yousef was hoping would provide an additional 'kick' to the bomb which would shear support columns and topple one of the twin towers. Finally, four large containers of nitro-glycerine were loaded into the centre of the van and Atlas Rockmaster blasting caps were connected to each in turn. The gang attached four 20ft-long fuses to the blasting caps. There would be no mistakes: three out of four of the fuses could go out and the bomb would still detonate. There would be no failure.

The judge at Yousef's trial would later claim that he included cyanide gas in the bomb, but that it burnt up in the explosion; Neil Herman disagrees – he doesn't think cyanide was included.[45] Nobody, however, disputes the size of the bomb: the FBI eventually concluded it was the 'largest by weight and by damage of any improvised explosive device that we've seen since the inception of forensic explosive identification – and that's since 1925'.[46]

With Yousef and Salameh sitting in the driving cabin the van pulled out of the driveway next to the bomb factory and turned on to the streets of Jersey City. Within 12 hours Yousef had launched the most devastating international terrorist attack on American soil in the nation's history. Jihad was beginning.

References

[1] If reports passed to the Diplomatic Security Service are correct.
[2] Author interview with Pakistani investigator.
[3] Ibid.
[4] Author interview.
[5] Ibid.
[6] Author interview with Pakistani investigator.
[7] After his arrival in New York with Yousef in 1993.
[8] Author interview with American investigator.
[9] Author interviews with American and Pakistani investigators.
[10] Author interview with Pakistani investigator who has interviewed alumni.
[11] Christopher Walker, 'Tunis Notebook', *The Times*, 24 March 1992.
[12] Author interview with American investigator.
[13] Ibid.
[14] Ibid.

15 Testimony of Martha Morales to the first World Trade Center bombing trial on 15 November 1993.
16 Testimony of Mark Cozine to the first World Trade Center bombing trial on 9 October 1993.
17 Ibid.
18 Author interview with American investigator.
19 Based on FBI agent James Kyle's testimony at the first World Trade Center bombing trial.
20 Author interview with American investigator, and Mary Anne Weaver, 'Children of the Jihad', *New Yorker*, 12 June 1995.
21 Ibid.
22 Ibid.
23 Testimony of Ashraf Moneeb at the first World Trade Center trial.
24 Abouhalima to Mohammad Abdul Haggag, who later turned state's evidence.
25 Author interview with Oliver Revell.
26 Author interview with a US intelligence officer.
27 Ibid.; also author interviews with other senior American investigators and several US intelligence sources.
28 Author interview.
29 US v. Salameh, US Court of Appeals for the Second Circuit, August Term, 1997.
30 Ibid.
31 Ibid.
32 Ibid.
33 Ibid.
34 Ibid.
35 Ibid.
36 Author interviews with US investigators and US v. Salameh, op. cit.
37 According to conversations between Yousef and Brian Parr and Charles Stern during his flight back to the US.
38 Testimony delivered at the first World Trade Center bombing trial.
39 Ibid.
40 Testimony of Marianne Coyle at the World Trade Center bombing trial.
41 Testimony of Mary Ellen Kuch at the World Trade Center bombing trial.
42 According to an American investigator and Ismoil's mother, Najla, in an interview by Radio Monte Carlo, 3 August 1995.
43 Testimony of David Robinson to the first World Trade Center bombing trial.
44 Testimony of Officer Ron Badiak to the World Trade Center bombing trial.
45 Author interview with Neil Herman.
46 Jim Dwyer, David Kocieniewski, Deirdre Murphy, and Peg Tyre, *Two Seconds Under the World*.

EIGHT

The Eminence Grise

WITH RAMZI Yousef safely in custody, Western and Asian intelligence agencies began turning their attention to those who supported him during his terrorist career. Investigators knew that lurking in the background of several of Yousef's attacks was the shadowy figure of Osama bin Laden, a Saudi-born businessman who was the most significant individual sponsor of international terrorism during the 1990s. 'Look at the campaign [Yousef] waged, and how close he was to committing murder on such a vast scale,' said an American intelligence source. 'What's most worrying is that he was just one guy. How many more could bin Laden or someone like him send against us?'[1]

According to Pakistani investigators the first significant link between Yousef and bin Laden dates back to when Yousef met Abdurajak Abubakar Janjalani, founder of the Filipino Abu Sayyaf terrorist group, in Peshawar in the summer of 1991. It was a time when Osama bin Laden was eagerly funding militant Islamic groups around the world, Janjalani was looking for financial support and terrorist expertise, and Yousef was looking for a quest. 'It all came together in Peshawar,' according to the US source.[2]

During this period bin Laden was flitting between Saudi Arabia, Pakistan, London and Sudan. 'He had hundreds of Afghan Arab fighters to worry about . . . he probably never met Yousef before the Trade Center [bombing],' added the American.[3] Indeed, American and Pakistani intelligence agents remain unsure whether Yousef and bin Laden ever actually met face to face.

There is however hard evidence to suggest strong, direct connections between Yousef and bin Laden, maintained by bin Laden's close supporters and acquaintances of the two men – most notably their mutual friends Wali Khan Amin Shah and Muhammad Jamal Khalifa. Shah, who was staying near Peshawar in the summer of 1991, had fought alongside bin Laden during the war, and trained and worked with Yousef on several of his bombing campaigns. 'Wali Khan is a Muslim youth,' said bin Laden. 'In Afghanistan, he was nicknamed "The Lion". He is one of the best. We were good friends. We fought in the same trenches against the Russians.'[4]

Khalifa, another Afghan fighter, a tall, slender and bearded man occasionally mistaken for bin Laden, is the husband of one of bin Laden's older sisters. American investigators allege that he was sent to the Philippines by bin Laden in 1988 to recruit fighters for the ongoing war in Afghanistan from among the 6 million Filipino Muslims. Khalifa quickly established a rattan furniture-making business as well as various Islamic organizations and charities; most notably the Daw'l Imam Al-Shafee Center (*aka* the Imam Shafie Institute) in Patikul, a little fishing village in the remote southern Sulu archipelago, where pirates still roam the seas and more than 90 per cent of the population is Muslim. He then married a Filipino and helped to recruit dozens of young Muslims from the island province of Basilan, and the nearby areas of Cotabato, Maguindanao, Souo, and Tawi-Tawi, also in the Sulu archipelago, and arranged their passage to bin Laden's training camps in Pakistan and just inside the Afghan border.[5]

Around this time Muslim rebels from the Moro National Liberation Front, who were fighting for a separate Muslim state in the southern Philippines, had been debating whether to compromise and make peace with the government in Manila. Osama bin Laden, however, who was watching the struggle closely, 'was fundamentally opposed to the idea', according to an American intelligence source.[6] 'He wanted an independent Islamic state from where he could lead a global Islamic revolution.' Bin Laden pumped money into Filipino terrorist gangs and fostered a new wave of Muslim extremism that swept through the region in the early 1990s. Filipino veterans of the Afghan war then returned home to join Janjalani's Abu Sayyaf ('Bearer of the Sword').

Pakistani and Filipino investigators believe Khalifa was in Peshawar during the summer of 1991, and they claim that he, under instructions from bin Laden, offered Janjalani funding to develop Abu Sayyaf, and then persuaded Yousef and Shah to visit the Philippines and train Janjalani's fighters. Khalifa denies that he ever did anything wrong.

According to Filipino police interviews of Edwin Angeles – a senior member of Abu Sayyaf, when Yousef arrived in the Philippines in the summer of 1991 – he introduced himself as an emissary of Osama bin Laden. It was the start of a direct relationship between bin Laden and international terrorists that would continue throughout the 1990s.

Osama bin Laden is a tall, lanky man with a high-pitched voice, and a thin, fragile body. He was born in Riyadh in 1957, the 17th son of one of the Middle East's greatest magnates, Mohammad bin Oud bin Laden, and his 11th wife, a tiny Syrian woman.

Osama's father, an engineer and architect originally from the southern Yemeni province of Hadramaout, moved to Jiddah when Saudi Arabia was established as a kingdom by Abdelaziz Ibn Saud in 1932. Some sources close to the bin Laden clan claim he initially worked as a labourer or porter to make ends meet, but through dint of hard graft he built up a small construction business and eventually caught the eye of the royal family.

The Saudis, particularly the royal family, were not used to settling down and building a nation-state: they were hunters, travellers, the Bedouins of folklore. Yemenis, by contrast, were hard workers and excellent builders, and Mohammad bin Laden used his expertise and cheap labour to undercut the competition and win a lucrative contract to build an opulent royal palace in Jiddah.

With the palace finished Mohammad bin Laden found himself admitted to the king's inner circle of advisers and confidants. Contracts flowed, and with them came huge wealth. Bin Laden became one of the most powerful men in the kingdom, even helping to put King Faisal on the throne in the early 1960s and paying the wages of the entire Saudi civil service for the following four months because of a hole in the nation's coffers. It was a stunning risk that was richly rewarded: Faisal was so grateful he decreed that all construction contracts should go to bin Laden, and even briefly made Mohammad the Minister for Public Works.

Mohammad bin Laden's company has since become a massive commercial entity, responsible for building much of Saudi Arabia, and rebuilding Kuwait and Beirut, with offices and palaces across the Middle East and an estimated turnover in the mid-1990s of $36 billion.

Yet despite his wealth and power Mohammad bin Laden remained at heart a conservative Muslim. He took 11 wives during his life, and bore 52 sons and daughters, all of whom were raised and educated in the demanding Wahhabite tradition. 'He was fascinated – obsessed – by religion,' said a businessman who worked with the clan for many years. 'He loved obscure religious debate, and spent huge sums financing these regular evening meetings called "halqas" where the greatest preachers and religious leaders in the Saudi kingdom would gather to debate theology. I guess it satisfied some philosophical streak within him.'[7]

Osama's father exercised a profound influence on the lives of his children, despite occasionally forgetting some of their names, and was a figure of enormous power and respect within his family and the kingdom. 'King Faisal was still alive when my father died [in a plane crash in the early 1970s when Osama was in his early teens],' Osama bin Laden has said. 'King Faisal cried at the death of only two persons, one was Mohammad bin Ibrahim and the other was my father Mohammad bin Oud bin Laden. King Faisal said upon the death of my father that today I have lost my right arm.'[8]

While his father had strong religious beliefs, Osama bin Laden was not always a raging Islamic fundamentalist. Although he now likes to portray himself as a pious Muslim, he also seems to have enjoyed the sinful pleasures of secular life. British and American intelligence agents, who have been trying to build up a picture of bin Laden's early life, have discovered evidence of his time in Beirut, during and following his graduation from secondary school in Jiddah in 1973, revealing him to be not quite so zealous a young Muslim.

'You have to understand that his personal behaviour is not of enormous interest to us except when it helps to construct a picture of his investments, support and business dealings,' said one intelligence source.[9] However, 'there are some kind of weird things that don't quite add up. When we dug into his past we discovered bin Laden was travelling to Beirut regularly after he left school in 1973 for, how can I put it, "rest and recreation".'

At the time the Lebanese capital was full of seedy and exotic clubs and bars, dripping with wealth, prostitutes and glamour. When bin Laden arrived it was a playground: decadent, Western and exciting – and there would be two years of high living before the outbreak of civil war in 1975. 'Those who knew him when he was in Beirut all said the same thing. He was spreading cash in clubs and bars. He drank quantities of alcohol, [he was] a binge-drinker, and he had an eye for the ladies.' Bin Laden, it appears, was a serial womanizer during his time in Beirut. Sources also talk of him being involved in at least three drunken fights with other young men after disputes over attractive women, including bar-girls, dancers, and even one woman believed to be a prostitute.[10]

One businessman acquainted with other members of the family remembers some of bin Laden's older brothers 'complaining about what he was up to in Beirut'.[11] 'I remember hearing that they [the bin Laden family] were having this trouble with the "son of the slave", as they called Osama. He was up to no good in Beirut. He was a bit of a nuisance,' he said.[12]

According to Neil Herman, there are obvious similarities between bin Laden's background and Yousef's. 'Those are some of the antics Mr Yousef was engaged in. They came from very different backgrounds, but they do seem to have some similarities, with the bar-hopping.'

'It's the classic thing,' according to a source close to the bin Laden clan, who said Osama's behaviour was mirrored by other members of his family. 'They [wealthy young Saudis] have all this money and they think they are the kings of the world, and they start spending money like water. As soon as they leave Saudi they forget their religion. They would go to Beirut and buy whores and get drunk, and then eventually they have this religious crisis – and some of the young [bin Laden] brothers became very religious. I remember one of the brothers went off and spent weeks praying in the desert.'[13]

Unlike Yousef, bin Laden soon bored of the excesses of youth, wed a young Syrian girl – a distant relative – in a marriage arranged by his family, and enrolled at the King Abdul Aziz University in Jiddah to study management and civil engineering. Most of his brothers chose to study abroad, particularly in London, where they could enjoy the nocturnal pleasures of a Western city, but Osama opted to study in a more Islamic environment. Civil engineering might seem an unlikely subject for a future terrorist leader, but it was a natural choice for one whose father had made billions of dollars from vast construction projects. The degree has since proved useful: in 1998 he devised a plan to divert the River Helmand from Iran into south-western Afghanistan, apparently because he was convinced this would irrigate 0.2 million acres of land and benefit Afghan peasants.[14]

Like Ramzi Yousef, bin Laden's time at university was also crucial in developing his militant beliefs. After the Lebanese civil war began in 1975 many Saudi Muslim scholars began preaching that it was God's punishment for the depravity of Beirut. In March of the same year King Faisal was assassinated by his mentally deranged nephew.

Again, the scholars suggested it was because the nephew had spent too much time in America, and indoctrination by Western culture had unbalanced his mind. Bin Laden seems to have been affected by these claims and sought religious guidance among his friends and other students. When they introduced him to members of the Muslim Brotherhood at the University, he was eager and receptive. The Brotherhood played on bin Laden's guilt about the vices he had enjoyed in Beirut, his troubled identity, and his growing sense of isolation from his family, and transformed him into a hard-line Islamist.

While he was studying bin Laden was also learning about the family empire, attending business meetings dressed in sober Western suits and ties. However, according to a businessman who has worked with the clan, while bin Laden was at university he began to feel he was living in the shadow of his older brothers, particularly his glamorous elder half-brother Salim, a tall, muscular man who flew his own private jet and was well known in the Gulf for his playboy lifestyle.[15]

Another visitor to the Saudi kingdom describes meeting young Osama thus: 'Mohammad bin Oud bin Laden's eldest son, Salim, was my host at the family's lavish offices. Clean-shaven and soft-spoken, Osama was dressed in a well-tailored Western suit and tie. There was no mistaking the unease with which Osama regarded his elder half-brother. After our brief introduction, Salim dismissed Osama with a wave of his hand, and the young man backed away with a look of cold frustration in his eyes.'[16] Salim married an English art student called Anne Carey, the half-sister of the Marquess of Queensberry's son Ambrose, and was widely regarded as his father's anointed successor. Osama knew he could not compete with Salim for affection and position within the family, and seems to have decided to find his own cause in life.

The irony is that although Osama was never in the running for leadership of the family empire, he could well have played an important role. He is a highly intelligent, manipulative man, and although the bin Laden family is huge, power is centralized. When Salim died after he flew a hang-glider into power-lines in Texas in 1989, just before his wife gave birth to a child, Osama was off fighting in Afghanistan and the mantle of head of the family passed to Osama's brother Bakr Mohammed bin Laden. Anne Carey followed Saudi tradition and married another of the brothers.

Back in the late 1970s, however, Osama was frustrated with his lack of status within the family. His father had died and, in true Saudi style, the warring siblings had been placated by gifts of vast sums of money from the family coffers. Osama is thought to have been given upwards of £300 million.

His brothers might have ignored his talents, but others were more sympathetic. Prince Turki Ibn Faisal Ibn Abdelaziz, the head of the Saudi secret service, first met Osama properly in 1978 and the two men were quickly drawn to each other.[17] Bin Laden saw in the older prince a man uncorrupted by money, power or contact with the West, and grew to admire him. The friendship was reciprocated: Prince Turki apparently viewed bin Laden, who was then little more than a troubled young man, as a useful contact who could be cultivated for future use.

Osama however needed a cause, he needed purpose, and it was Soviet premier Leonid Brezhnev who handed it to him on a plate by ordering Soviet troops into Afghanistan on 26 December 1979. Bin Laden, just like the Western powers and millions of Muslims, was furious. He consulted his friend Prince Turki and asked for advice. How could he help to fight one of the two superpowers left on earth? According to American intelligence sources, it was Prince Turki who first suggested to the young bin Laden that he use his wealth to establish a network to locate, train and supply Muslim fighters from across the world to protect the Afghan people by fighting against the invading army. 'When the invasion of Afghanistan started, I was enraged and went there at once – I arrived within days, before the end of 1979,' he has said.[18] 'I decided to wage jihad against Russia . . .'[19]

Bin Laden arrived in Pakistan, just over the border from Afghanistan, as a wealthy but fresh-faced 22-year-old. He may have been no veteran guerrilla, but he was bright enough to realize that his family's vast wealth and contacts within the Saudi government and royal family could be a unique way of obtaining and channelling support for the Afghan Muslim rebels.

Bin Laden soon met Abdallah Azzam, a 40-year-old Palestinian who had arrived in Pakistan from Jordan with a small group of followers, and whose name would eventually pass into Afghan legend. Azzam, who was initially operating out of a single shop in Peshawar, was an aggressive man well known in militant circles for the sermons he gave in Zarqa, a small town near Amman that had been a rallying point for many Palestinian refugees. He believed the Palestine liberation movement, which then consisted almost solely of Yasser Arafat's PLO, was too Marxist, and advocated the total Islamization of Palestine – a belief that put him outside mainstream Palestinian politics.

This did not deter bin Laden, who may have known Azzam from when he taught at King Abdul Aziz University. Bin Laden realized Azzam could be his link to a seething underground of disparate Islamic fighters, men who were committed to the cause of fundamentalism, but who were disempowered by a lack of financial support.

Bin Laden returned to Saudi Arabia and held talks with senior members of the Saudi government who promised him further financial help and support. Prince Salman, King Fahd's brother and number four in the kingdom's hierarchy, would eventually become the principal fundraiser for the mujaheddin. Bin Laden then flew back to Pakistan to put a secret proposal to his new Palestinian friend: Azzam would supply the manpower, and bin Laden would help pay for them to fly into the region, train them, supply them with weapons, and even pay their families any lost incomes. It was to be a winning combination.

To manage the vast sums required to fight the campaign, bin Laden established the Islamic Salvation Foundation, and helped Azzam establish an organization called Mekhtab Al-Khidemat Al-Mujahideen (known as MAK, the Services Office, or the Office of Services of the Mujaheddin). Ultimately, it acted as the leading recruitment agent for the mujaheddin, winning bin Laden huge kudos among fighters, and building the popular support that surrounded him for the next two decades.

'He was involved right from the outset,' said Edward Juchinewicz, a former CIA official who worked with the mujaheddin forces against the Soviets. 'He was raising money, and raising volunteers for one of the factions.'[20]

The MAK eventually established recruitment centres around the world that enlisted, sheltered and transported thousands of individuals from more than 35 countries to Afghanistan to fight the Soviets. It also organized and funded paramilitary training camps in Afghanistan and Pakistan. Recruiting offices were established under the name Al Kifah in Britain, France, Germany, Norway, Sweden and in every country in the Middle East. Dozens of major centres were established across the United States, while 30 American cities hosted smaller Al Kifah offices. The New York end of the operation, the Al Kifah Refugee Centre on the second floor, above the Fu King Food Shop, at 566 Atlantic Avenue, Brooklyn, became a place of pivotal importance to the Afghan struggle. Funds and fighters flowed through it to Peshawar and on to Gulbuddin Hekmatyar, one of the main mujaheddin leaders in Afghanistan.[21]

These were heady times. Saudi Arabian Airlines offered young men flying to Peshawar a 75-per-cent discount on the price of their flights. More than 25,000 foreign jihadis from more than 35 countries fought in the war. Young Muslims from across the world felt the conflict was a religious duty, and they were encouraged by magazines and publications devoted to the war, including Al Kifah's full-colour Arabic monthly magazine *Al Jihad*, which carried page after page of gory photographs of young Muslim fighters with their limbs blown away by Soviet shells or bullets. The accompanying text was a continual exhortation to potential fighters to join the war.

Bin Laden threw money into the campaign, flying between Pakistan and the Middle East to raise more funds, and by 1982 he had begun importing bulldozers and other heavy equipment to build roads, tunnels, hospitals and storage depots through Afghanistan's mountainous terrain to move and shelter fighters and supplies. To the beleaguered Afghan rebels he must have seemed like a holy saviour. According to a retired CIA official, bin Laden 'housed newly arrived recruits near Peshawar and funded the Ma'sadar Al-Ansar military training camp', on the other side of the legendary Khyber Pass in Afghanistan.[22] 'He built landing strips to allow rebel leaders to meet each other and the representatives of Muslim nations and businessmen supporting the struggle. With the help of Iraqi engineer Mohamed Sa'ad he blasted massive tunnels into the Zazi mountains of the Bakhtiar province and built command centres, while his technicians built a telecommunications network for the mujaheddin.' Bin Laden even funded hospitals to patch up wounded fighters.[23]

For the first time in his life bin Laden felt a sense of achievement and purpose. 'One day in Afghanistan was like one thousand days of praying in an ordinary mosque,' bin Laden said later. The fighting in Afghanistan grew and developed into a bloody war, but even as the body-count rose on both sides, bin Laden found his celebrity further enhanced. It was, after all, a holy war against Soviet invasion, and he spent months flying around the Gulf, encouraging kings, princes, businessmen and entire corporations to donate vast sums of money to the battle.[24]

There can be little doubt that his celebrity helped his family's business dealings. In 1983 Bin Laden Brothers for Contracting and Industry secured the most important contract in its history: a $3 billion

(£1.8 billion) deal to restore Mecca and Medina, the two holiest sites in the Islamic world. King Fahd, who had taken power in 1982, is said to have personally given the contract to the bin Laden clan, and Osama seems to have benefited from the huge deal. In 1983 he asked the French-born wife of a friend of his, a Saudi oil executive, to move $30 million (£18 million) by transferring the money from bank accounts in Switzerland to others in France and Monaco.[25] Intelligence sources believe the money was bin Laden's payment for helping to secure the contract, and he moved it from one account to another to create an untraceable 'fallback' fund for the future.

While bin Laden is now lauded among militant Muslims for his fighting prowess, his major role during the Afghan war was as a backroom organizer rather than a front-line warrior. The battles he did fight, however, proved crucial. In early 1986 bin Laden and Abdallah Azzam were among a small force of 50–100 fighters defending the Afghan mountain village of Jadji from a concerted Soviet attack. The Afghan Arabs held out for more than a month, capturing and killing several dozen Soviet soldiers. The Red Army eventually gave up, and inspiration shone forth for the jihadis: the Soviets could be beaten. The CIA has spent several years trying to identify every one of the Afghan Arabs who fought with bin Laden at Jadji, because the men became bin Laden's closest friends – men he trusts implicitly.

His experiences at Jadji and in other battles in Afghanistan turned bin Laden into a man without fear for his own security. 'As Muslims, we believe that when we die, we go to heaven,' says bin Laden. 'Before a battle, God sends us "seqina", tranquillity.'[26] During another attack in the area around Jadji, bin Laden was in a trench with his troops. 'Tanks attacked from the front and [the Soviet] air force also started bombing,' he has since claimed. 'We could hear the enemies' footsteps. Despite the situation, I fell asleep. When I awoke the enemy had disappeared. Perhaps I could not be seen by them. On another occasion a Scud missile exploded very close to me but I remained safe. Such incidents have removed my fear of death.'[27]

Another story tells how bin Laden personally led an offensive against tough Soviet forces in the battle of Shaban in 1987. The attack degenerated into hand-to-hand fighting, but the mujaheddin managed to defeat the Soviets despite suffering heavy losses. Bin Laden is said to have taken the AK-47 assault rifle he now poses with for photographs from the body of a dead Soviet general killed in the fight.

But other sources tell a different tale. Bin Laden, they say, was bossy and arrogant, and many elements of his imported 'fighting force' were often as much of a hindrance as a help. At the battle of Jalalabad in early 1989 bin Laden's men caused so much disruption among the Afghan fighters that the mujaheddin turned their guns on their supposed colleagues, killing around a dozen of Osama's troops.[28]

Bin Laden's power and influence was also stronger in some areas than others. In some parts of Afghanistan, where he was not widely known, he was treated as little more than an annoying interloper. John Simpson, the World Affairs Editor at the BBC, remembers a bizarre meeting with bin Laden in July 1989: 'I was filming a group of muja-heddin in Afghanistan as they fired mortars at the nearby town of Jalalabad. An impressive-looking Arab in beard and white robes [bin Laden], one of the many fundamentalist volunteers fighting alongside the mujaheddin, suddenly appeared. Jumping up on a wall, he screamed that we were infidels and that the mujaheddin should kill us at once. They grinned and shrugged their shoulders, so he ran over to a truck driver and offered him $500 (£312) to run us down. The truck driver grinned, too. Then the tall Arab ran off to the mujaheddin's sleeping quarters and threw himself on to one of the beds, beating his fists on the pillow in frustration. My colleagues and I stood and watched him with a mixture of embarrassment and relief.'[29]

He might have been a caricature of a mad mullah, but bin Laden still had power and a masterly talent for making friends. Many of the alliances he developed during the Afghan war ensured him lasting support. In the early 1980s he made an investment in the obscure Binnori mosque, in the Newtown area of the sprawling Pakistani port-city of Karachi, and bought a house in Karachi for the mosque's head, one Mullah Mohamed Omar, who would later lead the fundamentalist Taliban militia (or 'soldier monks') in a takeover of Afghanistan. The two men quickly became friends.[30]

By the mid-1980s bin Laden had also met and befriended Ayman al-Zawahiri, a fundamentalist from a prominent Egyptian medical family. Al-Zawahiri graduated from Cairo University in 1978 with a Master's Degree in surgical medicine and travelled to Afghanistan in the early 1980s to help in the war. He flew back and forth between Egypt and Afghanistan, gradually rising in the ranks of Egyptian fundamentalists until he eventually became the head of Islamic Jihad. He probably met bin Laden in 1985, and seems to have persuaded him to take a more active role in the fighting. Crucially, as head of Islamic

Jihad, he also 'loaned' bin Laden two men who would later become linchpins of his terrorist gang: Muhammad Atef and Abu Ubaidah al Banshiri.[31]

Bin Laden and the Afghan Arabs also forged an astonishing relationship with the American government, whose emissaries and spies were backing the war against Soviet forces in a secret operation (code-named Cyclone). It was a couple of years into the war before American involvement really took off but between 1986 and 1989 America linked its funding with Saudi Arabia and the two countries ploughed around $500 million (£300 million) per year into backing the mujaheddin, particularly Gulbuddin Hekmatyar, a crazed extremist and one of the mujaheddin's main leaders.

In 1985 senior Republican Senator Orrin Hatch, now chairman of the Senate Judiciary Committee, even travelled to Asia at the behest of President Reagan to arrange assistance for the mujaheddin. The Afghan war created strange bedfellows: the senator actually met with spy chiefs in Beijing and secured their personal support for weapon supplies to the Afghan rebels.[32]

Other American emissaries are understood to have travelled to Pakistan for meetings with mujaheddin leaders, who told them they needed advanced weapons to fight the Soviet forces, including Stinger ground-to-air heat-seeking missiles (a devastating shoulder-launched weapon capable of blowing a Russian fighter out of the sky, or – in the wrong hands – a Boeing passenger jet). One source even suggests the US emissaries met directly with bin Laden, and that it was bin Laden, acting on advice from his friends in Saudi intelligence, who first suggested the mujaheddin should be given Stingers.[33] The Reagan administration decided to send dozens to Afghanistan, complete with instructors. But America could not send in its own forces – it would be a diplomatic disaster if they were captured by the Soviets. Instead soldiers from Britain's élite Special Air Services Regiment (SAS) were flown in to do the job.

The SAS had been providing weapons training for the mujaheddin in Afghanistan from the beginning of the war, until Soviet forces found the passports of two British instructors in a training camp in 1982 and tried to turn the event into a diplomatic incident. British forces withdrew, but the CIA persuaded Margaret Thatcher's Conservative government to continue training the rebels in secret encampments in the Scottish borders and highland regions.[34] SAS soldiers are believed to have resigned from the regiment while they were involved in the covert operation – a standard SAS tactic to allow 'plausible deniability' should details become public.

Dozens of mujaheddin were secretly flown into Britain and trained to attack tank columns, shoot down aircraft and helicopters, and use heavy artillery and mortars. Any culture shock felt by the wild fighters of the Afghan hills was dissipated slightly by the hospitality of their hosts; a chef was apparently on hand to serve halal meat bought from a Muslim butcher.

By the time Reagan authorized the supply of Stingers to Afghanistan, the SAS were an integral part of the CIA operation. One former member of the SAS has even recounted how he took six Stinger missiles and £1 million in gold coins from the CIA (krugerrands for the mujaheddin to buy weapons from the Chinese) into Afghanistan for the rebels.[35] The Stingers proved enormously popular with the Afghan rebels, helping them to down more than 270 Soviet aircraft and further bolstering bin Laden's image. His file at the State Department apparently includes a 1986 photograph seized from Ramzi Yousef's uncle's house by Rehman Malik's FIA agents, showing bin Laden posing with a Stinger perched jauntily on his shoulder.[36]

The relationship between America and bin Laden in Afghanistan is now a source of some embarrassment to both sides. 'Of course it's not something they want to talk about,' said one source, describing both bin Laden and the CIA. 'They [US agents] armed [bin Laden's] men by letting him pay rock-bottom prices for basic weapons. By 1987 we were facilitating [the] supply of some 65,000 tonnes of weapons into Afghanistan.'[37] Bin Laden's faith in his American friends was shattered, however, when the war finished.

'The United States was not interested in our jihad. It was only afraid that Russia would gain access to warm waters,' says bin Laden. 'The United States helped the mujaheddin in order to contain Russia. The mujaheddin started their resistance much earlier. As soon as [former Soviet President] Gorbachev announced the withdrawal of Russian forces from Afghanistan, the United States and Saudi Arabia stopped their assistance for [the] mujaheddin.'

With Soviet forces out of Afghanistan, the US wanted to form a broad coalition government consisting of General Najibullah (whom the Soviets had originally put in power) and several mujaheddin groups. 'I made all the mujaheddin groups agree on the point that an alliance with Najibullah [was] not acceptable,' says bin Laden. 'We were fighting against the communists and [suddenly] the United

States was pressuring us to co-operate with those very same communists. The United States has no principles. To achieve its own interests, it forgets about every principle.'[38]

Up to 3 million Afghans were killed or seriously wounded during the war; another 6 million fled into Iran or Pakistan. By the end of the conflict Afghanistan had been destroyed, but the Muslim rebels still revelled in their victory. Bin Laden, however, had no time for celebrations: he was devastated by the assassination of his friend Azzam in a remote-controlled car-bomb attack in Peshawar on 24 November 1989 (the bomb also killed two of Azzam's four sons). But the incident brought bin Laden closer to Azzam's son-in-law Abdallah Anas (real name Bounoua Boudjemaa), an Algerian militant who was involved with Algeria's radical Group Islamic Army (GIA) and went on to edit its *Jihad News* from Poland.

Crucially, Anas then persuaded bin Laden to invest some of his vast wealth in the Islamic militants' campaign to topple the Algerian regime and replace it with a fundamentalist government. As the years ticked by bin Laden became extremely close to the Algerian militants, allegedly providing financing for terrorist bombings that rocked Paris in 1995,[39] and trusting Algerians to comprise the bulk of his 'praetorian guard'.

The final withdrawal of Soviet troops from Afghanistan prompted bitter factional fighting among the different Afghan tribal groups, and in 1990 bin Laden withdrew many of his men to Peshawar in Pakistan, then flew on alone to Saudi Arabia with a small group of followers to seek the counsel of his family and friends. He was now in his early thirties, wiser and more worldly, and was greeted as a hero. Friends demanded he appear in their homes and mosques to tell stories of his adventures. More than 250,000 cassettes of his speeches were produced, and sold out in shops and market stalls as soon as they appeared.

But after returning from a spartan existence in Afghanistan, bin Laden was unhappy with what he found in the kingdom. Everywhere he looked he saw apathy, evidence of Western cultural imperialism and moral degradation: women disobeying Islamic law in their dress and Westerners flaunting themselves on the streets and drinking alcohol. It was like an American colony, he would later claim.[40] By the time he made his tape recordings bin Laden was clearly furious at

American perfidy. 'When we buy American goods, we are accomplices in the murder of Palestinians,' he can be heard shouting on one
of the tapes, now banned in Saudi Arabia. 'American companies make
millions in the Arab world with which they pay taxes to their government. The United States uses that money to send $3 billion a year to
Israel, which it uses to kill Palestinians.'

Bin Laden had still not discounted a return to the family business,
but he was not the sort of militant who could happily go home to
Saudi and settle into a normal business life. 'Fire was raging within
him,' according to one associate of the bin Laden family.[41] With the
end of the conflict in Afghanistan, bin Laden revamped an organization he established during the war called al Qaeda ('The Base'), with
the help of Muhammad Atef, the militant earlier 'loaned' to bin Laden
by Ayman al-Zawahiri, the head of Islamic Jihad.

Although for many years al Qaeda was little more than an umbrella
organization for various bin Laden projects, by the end of the 1990s
the FBI and CIA had publicly identified it as bin Laden's main vehicle
for international terrorist operations during the 1990s. Although the
reality is not quite so clear-cut, it can, in broad, simplistic terms, be
described as bin Laden's terrorist organization, and several of bin
Laden's terrorist followers have used its name and admitted membership under interrogation in the US and Middle East.[42]

From the moment it was established during the chaos of the Afghan
war, the aim of al Qaeda was to support, both militarily and financially, oppressed Muslims around the world. When the war finished
its membership consisted largely of the Afghan Arabs who had previously fought with bin Laden and it was given a 'majlis al shura', or
consultation council, which discussed and approved major under-
takings, including ultimately 'terrorist operations', according to
American investigators.[43] Bin Laden and Atef both sat on the council,
while another 'military committee' was also established that considered and approved specifically 'military' matters. Atef and Abu
Ubaidah al Banshiri, bin Laden's second principal military commander (also 'lent' to him by al-Zawahiri), both sat on the committee, until
al Banshiri mysteriously drowned in a ferry accident on Lake Victoria
in the spring of 1996.

After re-establishing al Qaeda one of bin Laden's first actions was
an attempt to guarantee the security of his men living in Pakistani
refugee camps by throwing money at the election campaign of Nawaz
Sharif, an energetic Pakistani politician standing for Prime Minister in

the October 1990 general elections. Money was passed from bin Laden via Sami ul Haq, a senior politician and Muslim cleric, to Sharif and the Islamic Democratic Alliance (IJI), which became Sharif's governing coalition when he won the election.[44] Sharif had said he would introduce a hard-line Islamic government, and Osama bin Laden is understood to have supported him for several years. According to senior Pakistani intelligence sources there are three remaining copies in existence of a photograph showing the two men chatting together; however there is no suggestion Sharif has done anything wrong.

Bin Laden's plans to expand al Qaeda beyond Pakistan were interrupted by a watershed event in Middle Eastern politics. In August 1990 Iraqi President Saddam Hussein ordered his troops into Kuwait, an act that heralded the arrival of thousands of American, British and allied troops in Saudi Arabia, ostensibly as protection against further attack, but ultimately to launch a strike into Iraq and secure the liberation of Kuwait.

It was another turning-point for bin Laden, who was furious at the presence of the troops. The Saudi government and royal family, which had previously supported and encouraged bin Laden, now discovered they were on the receiving end of his ire. The young militant barged into Saudi defence ministry offices with maps and flowcharts to demonstrate how the kingdom could defend itself against Iraqi aggression.

'There is no need for American troops!' he cried as he marched into the office of Prince Sultan, the Saudi Defence Minister, carrying a 10-page report that described how he and his small rag-tag army of Afghan Arabs could train Saudis to defend themselves. His family's bulldozers and earth-moving equipment could be used to dig vast trenches along the border with Iraq and Kuwait and lay 'sand traps' against invading tanks and infantry, said bin Laden. Prince Sultan studied the plans politely, and then queried how the kingdom would defend itself against air attack, or even a naval assault. 'Bin Laden just kept saying that American troops were not needed like some sort of desperate mantra,' says one source.[45]

'What do you plan to do about Iraq's chemical and biological weapons?' asked the prince.

'We will defeat them with faith,' said bin Laden defiantly. He was politely shown to the door.[46]

Prince Turki and other senior Saudis tried in vain to placate bin Laden, promising that the American forces would leave as soon as Kuwait was liberated. But US troops did not leave. The Marines stayed in Dharan. American warships patrolled the Gulf. Bin Laden's fury grew, and this time his anger was directed at the Saudi establishment and was channelled into Saudi opposition groups based in London, which he began supporting financially while still nominally working for the family business in Jiddah.

The Saudi government decided it could no longer tolerate his actions. It was one thing for bin Laden to struggle against other governments; it was quite another issue for him to be battling against their regime. In the autumn of 1991 Saudi security police linked bin Laden to an attempt to smuggle weapons into the kingdom from Yemen, presumably as part of a plan to destabilize the country. Despite the protestations of bin Laden's friends, the Saudi government expelled the militant in 1991, citing his political activities, and in 1994 actually revoked his Saudi citizenship.

Bin Laden was no longer wanted in Saudi Arabia, and Pakistan made it clear he was not welcome there. 'Go to Sudan,' advised one of bin Laden's remaining friends in the Saudi government, 'you can organize a holy war from there.'[47] Bin Laden flew from Saudi Arabia to the scorching heat of Khartoum in his private Gulfstream G-8 jet and was greeted with open arms by Hassan al-Turabi, an avuncular University of London and Sorbonne-educated intellectual who was the father of Sudan's June 1989 Islamic revolution and leader of the country's ruling National Islamic Front (NIF) party. Bin Laden bought a comfortable brick-and-stucco three-storey house in the Riyadh section of Khartoum and another house on the banks of the Blue Nile where he could spend weekends with his family. It was far from luxurious, with the former Afghan fighter even deciding against installing air-conditioning. 'I don't want to get used to the good life,' Jamal Khashoggi, a Saudi journalist, quotes him as saying.[48]

By the time bin Laden landed in Sudan he was in his mid-thirties and married to three wives: one Syrian and two Saudis. Osama had followed his father's example by building a large family, and his 15 children – including his three eldest sons, Mohammed (then just seven years old), Omar and Saad, and the entire entourage – moved into their new home and settled into the local community. Bin Laden's wives even taught the Koran to women in the local mosque.

Osama, however, was concerned about his followers, hundreds of whom were still in Pakistan, living in tents and hostels and awaiting a leader. The Pakistani authorities wanted to be rid of them, because their militant views were causing trouble in the border region between

Pakistan and Afghanistan, and bin Laden asked the Sudanese authorities for permission to fly them to the country. Fortunately for bin
Laden, Sudan had abandoned visa requirements for Arabs and was
actively encouraging Islamic militants from around the world to live
within the safety of its vast borders. Even Carlos the Jackal, the original international terrorist, would arrive in Khartoum in the autumn of
1993 seeking refuge. A mysterious city nestling at the confluence of the
White Nile and the Blue Nile, Khartoum would soon be home to militants from across the world.

Bin Laden turned to one of his closest followers, Ali Mohammed, a
balding former soldier, and asked him to organize the Afghan Arabs
into groups ready to travel to Sudan. Even by comparison with some
of the other characters working for al Qaeda, Ali Mohammed was
extraordinary. Much of his life remains cloaked in mystery, but according to FBI sources he was born in Egypt, served in the Egyptian army,
and then in or around 1980 he walked into the US Embassy in Cairo
and offered to be a spy for the CIA. Sources within the agency claim
his offer was refused after agents decided he was 'too unreliable'.
However Mohammed then travelled to America on an 'exchange
program' – probably in 1980 – and in 1981 graduated with the rank of
Captain from the élite Special Forces Officers School at Fort Bragg in
North Carolina, the base for the US Army's Special Operations
Command.

In 1984 he left the Egyptian military and the following year he
settled permanently in America – some sources claim he entered the
United States on a visa program controlled by the CIA. In 1986
Mohammed joined the US Army, receiving the rank of Sergeant and a
posting in US Army Special Operations back at Fort Bragg.
Mohammed's role in the Special Forces (SF) remains unclear, with
some suggesting it was lecturing SF soldiers on Islamic culture, but it
is obvious the US Army trusted him implicitly: he was granted security clearance to level 'Secret'.[49]

In 1989 Mohammed travelled to New York and provided military
training to local Muslims preparing to travel to Asia to fight the
Soviets in Afghanistan. Confusion arises, however, over whether that
training was part of his military duties, or a personal sideline. In
November the same year he received an honourable discharge from
the US Special Forces. What seems most likely is that Mohammed was
first introduced to American Muslims through his connections with
the CIA, and a professional relationship – based on mutual desire to

kick the Soviets out of Afghanistan – soon developed into personal friendship.

The FBI were left to pick up the pieces: on 8 November 1990, they raided the New Jersey home of El Sayyid Nosair, the Muslim militant arrested for shooting the extremist Rabbi Meir Kahane in New York. The Feds found documents from Fort Bragg, some classified 'Secret', 'Sensitive', and 'Top Secret for Training', which included reports on the location of American SF units in the Middle East, US intelligence reports on Soviet military strength in Afghanistan and data from US Central Command on the situation in Afghanistan. The documents included hand-written notes allegedly made by Ali Mohammed.[50]

From 1990 onwards, Mohammed allegedly began travelling to Pakistan and Afghanistan, where he was introduced to Osama bin Laden, who wanted to thank him for his assistance in training soldiers for the jihad. Initially bin Laden was still suspicious of the Egyptian-born former American soldier, but Mohammed quickly won him over. By the time bin Laden moved to Sudan Mohammed is alleged to have been an important figure within al Qaeda: he collected a rag-tag army of approximately 500 Afghan Arab veterans together in the border area between Pakistan and Afghanistan and bin Laden happily flew them to Sudan.

But not everyone in al Qaeda was content to exchange life on the Afghan border for the heat of Sudan. According to Mamdouh Mahmud Salim, an alleged associate of bin Laden's who was arrested and interrogated by German police and security officials in September 1998, many al Qaeda members were unhappy with the move because there was no jihad to fight in Sudan: 'this group didn't have a purpose except to carry out the jihad,' Salim told his interrogators.[51]

Those who did make the move soon made their presence felt in Khartoum. According to Salim there were three types of men in al Qaeda at the time: 'people who had no success in life, had nothing in their heads and wanted to join just to keep from falling on their noses ... people who loved their religion but had no idea what their religion really meant', and people with 'nothing in their heads but to fight and solve all the problems in the world with battles'.[52] In Khartoum the new arrivals spent most of their time in mosques preaching a hard-line version of Islam. Many Sudanese found the Afghan Arabs an intense and arrogant bunch, and nicknamed them 'Halabi', a derogatory, sniggered term for light-skinned Arabs.[53]

Bin Laden was transferring more than just aggressive fighters to

Sudan: he was moving his entire empire, channelling money into shifting his training camps from the region around Peshawar to Sudan, again with the alleged help of Ali Mohammed. Three new training camps for terrorists from Algeria, Egypt, Palestine and Tunisia soon opened in Sudan.

According to a report by Human Rights Watch, based largely on an interview with a defecting Sudanese military officer, bin Laden 'was able to establish a powerful military and political presence in Sudan in the early 1990s, using a variety of business ventures to finance his activities'.[54] Among the hundreds of Afghan Arabs he moved into Sudan were 'Tunisians, Algerians, Sudanese, Saudis, Syrians, Iraqis, Moroccans, Somalis, Ethiopians, Eritreans, Chechnyans, Bosnians and six African-Americans . . .'

Fighters were organized into groups and dispersed to camps throughout Sudan, the main one being a 20-acre site near Soba, 10km south of Khartoum, along the Blue Nile. Weapons were bought from Iran and China, with bin Laden apparently spending $15 million on one arms shipment for his fighters which included Chinese and Iranian weapons, and Czechoslovakian explosives (almost certainly Semtex).[55] Iranians previously based in Lebanon's Beka'a Valley were among those training guerrillas at this camp in the use of explosives, forgery, coding, and other terrorist skills.[56] Bin Laden was preparing a terrorist army for war.

References

1 Author interview.
2 Ibid.
3 Ibid.
4 Interviewed by John Miller, and quoted on *ABC News*, 28 May 1998.
5 Author interviews with American intelligence sources.
6 Author interview.
7 Author interview.
8 Hamid Mir, interview with Osama bin Laden, Pakistan, 18 March 1997.
9 Author interview with an American investigator.
10 Ibid.
11 Author interview with a businessman close to the bin Laden family.
12 Ibid.
13 Ibid.
14 Author interview with a former CIA official.
15 Author interview with a businessman close to the bin Laden family.
16 Arthur Kent, 'A Deadly Organisation's Flawed Leader', *St. Louis Post-Dispatch*, 27 August 1998.

[17] Author interview with a businessman close to the bin Laden family and American investigators.

[18] Robert Fisk, 'Anti-Soviet warrior puts his army on the road to peace', *Independent*, 6 December 1993.

[19] Mir, op. cit.

[20] Stephen J. Hedges, 'Saudi Militant Millionaire Defended Muslims in Afghanistan', *Chicago Tribune*, 21 August 1998.

[21] Author interviews with American investigators and Alison Mitchell, 'After Blast, New Interest in Holy-War Recruits in Brooklyn', *New York Times*, 11 April 1993.

[22] Author interview.

[23] Author interview with a former CIA official

[24] Ibid.

[25] According to Horst Roos, a senior prosecutor in the German city of Trier, near the French border, the woman revealed her role in 1997 during questioning about a jewellery fraud.

[26] Fisk, op. cit.

[27] Mir, op. cit.

[28] Author interview with a former CIA official.

[29] John Simpson, 'The day bin Laden tried to have me killed', *Sunday Telegraph*, 23 August 1998.

[30] Author interview with a former CIA official.

[31] Ibid.

[32] Senator Orrin Hatch is understood to have visited Beijing with several key US intelligence officials, including Morton Abramowitz, Director of Intelligence and Research at the State Department, Michael Pillsbury, assistant to the Defense Undersecretary for Policy Planning, Fred Ikle, the CIA station chief in Beijing, and the deputy chief of the CIA's Operations Directorate. Such was the importance the US attached to supporting the Afghan fighters.

[33] Author interview with a former CIA official.

[34] Ibid.

[35] Gaz Hunter, *The Shooting Gallery*.

[36] Author interview with a senior Pakistani intelligence source and a former CIA official. As the war finished American officials desperately launched Operation MIAS (Missing-in-Action Stingers) to buy back the 1,200 mph missiles. It was a hopeless task. Senior Pakistani intelligence sources now claim that a massive explosion in April 1988 at the Ojhri military warehouses outside Rawalpindi (from where US arms were supplied to the mujaheddin), which killed 100 local people and was said to have destroyed 10,000 tonnes of weapons and dozens of Stingers, was actually a deliberate attempt by members of the Pakistani Inter-Services Intelligence agency to disguise the fact they had removed many more Stingers and sold them to contacts in Iran and Afghanistan. Stingers remain a potent weapon: on 28 May 1999, during an upsurge in tension between India and Pakistan, Muslim guerrillas used one to down an Indian attack helicopter in the disputed province of Kashmir.

37 Ibid.
38 Mir, op. cit.
39 Author interview with a former CIA official.
40 Based on comments bin Laden made to the weekly magazine *Al-Ahram Al-Arabi* in April 1997, an issue that was banned in Saudi Arabia.
41 Author interview.
42 Author interview with an American intelligence source.
43 Ibid., and US indictment: S(2)98 Cr. 1023 (LBS).
44 Author interview with senior Pakistani intelligence source. There is no suggestion ul Haq or Sharif did anything wrong.
45 Author interview with a businessman close to the bin Laden family.
46 Ibid.
47 Ibid.
48 Faiza Saleh Ambah, op. cit.
49 Author interview with American investigator.
50 Ibid.
51 Author interview with British source who has seen an unexpurgated copy of the German interrogation report.
52 Ibid.
53 Author interview with American investigator.
54 Human Rights Watch report, Sudan, August 1998, Vol. 10, No. 4(A), interview with Tessenei (Eritrea), 10 March 1997.
55 Frank Smyth, 'Culture Clash – bin Laden, Khartoum and the war against the West', *Jane's Intelligence Review*, 1 October 1998. Bin Laden also shipped 20 tonnes of C-4 plastic explosive from Poland to Qatar, but intelligence sources remain unclear whether this massive haul surfaced in Sudan.
56 Human Rights Watch, op. cit.

NINE

Al Qaeda

BIN LADEN'S activities in Sudan did not stop at arming and training a disparate gang of Afghan Arabs. A consummate networker, he was training terrorists and simultaneously telling politicians he wanted to help develop the country and improve Sudan's crumbling infrastructure.

Bin Laden forged business alliances with wealthy politicians and began working on a number of large projects. He invested more than $50 million in the Al-Shamal Islamic Bank in Khartoum, a joint venture with senior members of the National Islamic Front (NIF). With other NIF members he was heavily involved in founding Wadi al-Aqiq, a holding company, and Taba Investment, which soon secured a virtual monopoly over some of Sudan's most crucial exports – corn, sunflower and sesame products. US intelligence agents allege that bin Laden then invested in al Themar al Mubaraka, an agricultural firm, Qudarat Transport, a fleet of fishing boats, and a factory to process goat skins.

He also ploughed funds, although Western intelligence agencies are unsure to what extent, into Al-Hijrah for Construction and Development, which eventually built a new airport at Port Sudan and a road 750 miles long between Khartoum and Port Sudan.[1] The Sudanese government paid bin Laden in sesame seeds which he then sold on the commercial market. 'These companies were operated to provide income to support al Qaeda and to provide cover for the procurement of explosives, weapons and chemicals and for the travel of al Qaeda operatives,' according to American investigators.[2]

Perhaps most crucially, bin Laden cannily invested in Gum Arabic

Company Limited, a Khartoum-based firm which has a virtual monopoly over most of Sudan's exports of gum arabic, which in turn comprises around 80 per cent of the world's supply. Gum arabic comes from the sap of the Sudanese acacia tree. A colourless, tasteless gum, it makes newspaper ink stick to printing presses, keeps ingredients in drinks from settling at the bottom of a can, and forms a film around sweets and medical pills, keeping them fresh. It is a crucial ingredient in dozens of products Western consumers use every day, and within two years of arriving in Sudan, bin Laden is believed to have secured an effective monopoly over the entire Sudanese output.

Even now the State Department in Washington and analysts at the CIA remain unsure whether bin Laden is still profiting from his investment. Thirty per cent of the shares in Gum Arabic Company Limited are held by the Sudanese government, who may or may not be siphoning profits into bin Laden accounts. The other 70 per cent is held by individual shareholders and banks, any or all of whom may be acting as fronts for bin Laden. It is still possible that every time someone buys an American soft drink, they are helping to fill Osama bin Laden's coffers.

After establishing his business interests in Sudan, bin Laden began expanding the international side of his secret al Qaeda organization. 'The crucial year was 1994,' says an American source.[3] Wadih el Hage, a softly spoken man with a withered arm, arrived in Sudan that year from Arlington, Texas, to act as bin Laden's personal assistant and secretary. Born in the Lebanon in 1960, and a student at the University of Southwestern Louisiana in Lafayette in the late 1970s, El Hage had converted to Islam from Christianity, fought with bin Laden in Afghanistan and then moved to Tucson, Arizona, where he lived from 1987 to 1990 and helped in the local Al Kifah centre.

He made regular trips overseas, and is believed to have worked with al Qaeda in Pakistan and Afghanistan, before returning to the US to live in Arlington and work in a tyre store. El Hage is suspected by some intelligence agents of acting as bin Laden's chemical weapons 'scout', and has been accused by American investigators of scouring the world looking for supplies to build bombs.[4]

According to American investigators El Hage was crucial in helping to organize al Qaeda's affairs in Khartoum. This enabled bin Laden to turn his sights on London ('the most important city in the Middle East', notes a British intelligence source in reference to the proliferation of Middle Eastern opposition groups in the capital).[5] Bin

Laden had decided London would be the perfect base from which to wage a military and propaganda campaign against the illegitimate governments of the Middle East.

In early 1994 Khalid Al-Fauwaz, a plump, bearded Saudi civil engineer who fought with bin Laden in Afghanistan and travelled with him to Sudan in 1991 (US investigators allege he then swore 'bayat' – an Islamic fighter's oath of allegiance),[6] was despatched to London by bin Laden. His instructions were to establish a regional office of the Advice and Reformation Committee, which had the task of campaigning openly for the introduction of strict Islamic law in Saudi Arabia. Documents obtained by the FBI, dated 11 July 1994, and signed by bin Laden, authorize Al-Fauwaz to open the office and name him as its director.[7]

In a fashion reminiscent of the 'sleepers' sent to the West by the Soviets during the Cold War, Al-Fauwaz and his wife Wejda, both graduates of the King Fahd University in Dharan, Saudi Arabia, moved to a semi-detached house in Neasden, north London. From this model of English suburban living they enrolled on an English language course in Golders Green, a predominantly Jewish enclave of north London. Al-Fauwaz allegedly opened an account at Barclays Bank in fashionable Notting Hill, west London, which from late 1994 onwards, claim the Feds, was used to channel funds to al Qaeda operatives around the world.

Al Qaeda was now going global. Bin Laden's eyes next alighted on the impoverished state of Yemen, which shares a long, disputed and porous border with Saudi Arabia. He saw it as the perfect state from which to encourage a revival of Islamic militancy in the adjoining kingdom, and began founding or buying several Yemeni firms, including publishing and ceramic businesses, and several mysterious 'import–export' firms. He also turned his attention to Albania, an impoverished country home to militant and oppressed Muslims, lax immigration controls, an incompetent police force prone to corruption, and political leaders eager for bribes: the perfect European military base for al Qaeda.

Bin Laden visited Albania in April 1994 as a member of an official Saudi Arabian delegation, and was introduced to one senior government minister as a friend of the Saudi government who would finance the building of apartment blocks and a health-care centre.[8] With hindsight, bin Laden's visit reveals not only the speed of al Qaeda's growth, but also bin Laden's continuing influence among the Saudi establishment. 'Why was he a member of that delegation?' storms one retired American intelligence officer.[9] 'The Saudis are supposed to be our allies. They told us he was persona non grata, and yet here he was working the crowds on an official visit.'

Using either money or ideology bin Laden managed to form a loose friendship with Bashkim Gazidede, then the head of the Albanian Secret Service. Western intelligence sources have since accused Gazidede of facilitating entry to Albania for several Islamic militants, including four men believed to be responsible for the 1993 assassination of Rifat el-Mahgoub, the speaker of the Egyptian parliament, and of helping numerous Islamic charities establish themselves in Albania as cover for militant activity.[10] Even Sali Berisha, who was then President of Albania, had close links with groups that later proved to be fronts for extreme fundamentalists.

Bin Laden's tentacles were spreading across Europe, Africa and the Middle East. Profits from companies he established in Sudan, Kenya, Yemen and Albania were channelled through his finance and accounts department – based in Sudan and several European capitals including Rome – which was staffed by 17 employees led by a Sudanese friend of bin Laden called Abu-al-Hasan.[11]

Establishing himself in business was only a diversion from bin Laden's real passion while he was living in Khartoum: launching and leading a holy war against the Western infidels he could now see camped out in his homeland, near the holiest shrines in the Muslim world. The Gulf War had been over for years but the gum-chewing American forces were not leaving Saudi Arabia, and nothing made bin Laden more angry. He was, and remains, desperate to force American troops out of his homeland. They had no right to be there, he would shout, berating Sudanese militants and government officials who did not share his views.

In December 1992, still emboldened by their success against the Soviets in Afghanistan, some of the Afghan Arab members of al Qaeda conducted what most intelligence sources believe to have been the group's first attempt at a direct attack on the US. Muhammad Atef, one of bin Laden's military commanders, quietly travelled to Somalia to investigate how al Qaeda operatives could attack US and United Nations forces stationed in the country, where they were participating in Operation Restore Hope – a humanitarian mission to save the country from lawless brigands.

After allegedly consulting with bin Laden and al Qaeda's 'majlis al shura', or consultation council, al Qaeda operatives then placed a bomb in a hotel in Yemen where US troops had been staying on their way to Somalia; it exploded on 29 December, after the soldiers had left, blowing two Austrian tourists to pieces. Almost simultaneously, a small group of terrorists trained by al Qaeda was caught at Aden airport preparing to launch rockets at US planes. Atef promptly flew back to Somalia with other members of bin Laden's gang, and provided further 'military training and assistance to Somali tribes', according to American investigators.[12]

Within weeks American soldiers in Mogadishu, the capital of Somalia, were caught in a vicious firefight that saw helicopters shot out of the sky. On 3 and 4 October 1993, 18 US servicemen were killed and scores more injured by men 'trained by al Qaeda (and by trainers trained by al Qaeda)'.[13] Television channels showed footage of the body of an American soldier being dragged through the streets of the city. US foreign policy in the region fell to pieces.

'It is true that my companions fought with Farah Adid's forces against the US troops in Somalia,' bin Laden said later. 'But we were fighting against US terrorism. Under the cover of [the] United Nations, the United States tried to establish its bases in Somalia so that it could get control over Sudan and Yemen. My associates killed the Americans in collaboration with Farah Adid. We are not ashamed of our Jihad. In one explosion 100 Americans were killed, then 18 more were killed in fighting. One day our men shot down an American helicopter. The pilot got out. We caught him, tied his legs and dragged him through the streets. After that 28,000 US soldiers fled Somalia. The Americans are cowards.'[14] Bin Laden falsifies the fatality figures, but the withdrawal of American troops certainly emboldened his gang. In their eyes they had pushed the Soviets out of Afghanistan, and now they had forced the Americans out of Somalia.

By the time of the Yemeni hotel bomb attack, America had still not identified bin Laden as a serious threat. Other countries, however, were waking up to the monster America had helped to create in Afghanistan. A secret Egyptian and Saudi Arabian investigation into bin Laden's activities from around this time discovered he had given money to a group of Egyptian militants to buy printing presses and weapons. Initially, the report was not passed to any other nation, but instead the Egyptians put tremendous pressure on the Saudis to silence their errant son, and the Saudi authorities eventually took the

Blind Muslim preacher Sheikh Omar Abdel-Rahman, who several of Ramzi Yousef's World Trade Center gang followed, and around whom another terrorist conspiracy unfolded.

(FEDERAL BUREAU OF INVESTIGATION)

Khalid Sheikh Mohammad, who the FBI believe was involved in Ramzi Yousef's 'Bojinka Plot'. He is now a fugitive with a reward of up to $5 million on his head.

(FUGITIVE PUBLICITY OFFICE, FEDERAL BUREAU OF INVESTIGATION)

Abdul Rahman Yasin is associated with Ramzi Yousef's World Trade Center terrorist gang. Yasin was interviewed by the FBI shortly after the bombing, but was subsequently released. He promptly fled to Baghdad, Iraq, where he still lives. A reward of up to $2 million is offered for his capture.

(FUGITIVE PUBLICITY OFFICE, FEDERAL BUREAU OF INVESTIGATION)

One of few photographs known to exist of Mohammad Atef, Osama bin Laden's right-hand man and military commander in his al Qaeda terrorist organization.

(FEDERAL BUREAU OF INVESTIGATION)

One of the matchbooks
dropped over Pakistan
showing Ramzi Yousef's
photograph and giving details
of his crimes.

(FUGITIVE PUBLICITY OFFICE, FEDERAL BUREAU
OF INVESTIGATION)

A flyer issued during the hunt for the men behind the 7 August 1998 bombings
of American embassies in Kenya and Tanzania.

(FUGITIVE PUBLICITY OFFICE, FEDERAL BUREAU OF INVESTIGATION)

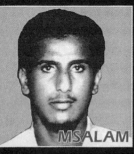

Posters issued during the hunt for the men behind the bombings of American embassies in Kenya and Tanzania.

(FUGITIVE PUBLICITY OFFICE, FEDERAL BUREAU OF INVESTIGATION)

MURDER

Nairobi & Dar es Salaam bombings, 1998
220 killed and 5,000 wounded

MURDERER

Usama Bin Laden

UP TO $5 MILLION REWARD

Usama Bin Laden and Muhammad Atef have been indicted for the August 7, 1998 bombings of the U.S. embassies in Kenya and Tanzania. These brutal attacks killed more than 220 innocent Americans, Kenyans and Tanzanians and seriously injured more than 5,000 men, women and children.

Bin Laden, Atef, and their organization, al Qaeda, also allegedly conspired in the killings of American military personnel in Saudi Arabia and Somalia.

To preserve the peace and save innocent lives from further attacks, the U.S. Government is offering a reward for information leading to the arrest or conviction of Bin Laden and Atef. Persons providing information may be eligible for a reward of up to $5 million, protection of their identities, and may be eligible for relocation of themselves and their families. Persons wishing to report information on Usama Bin Laden, Muhammad Atef, or other terrorists, should contact the authorities or the nearest U.S. embassy or consulate.

Within the United States, contact the Federal Bureau of Investigation or call the U.S. Department of State, Diplomatic Security Service at 1-800-HEROES-1. Information may also be provided by contacting:

HEROES

Post Office Box 96781
Washington, D.C. 20090-6781 U.S.A.
email:heroes@heroes.net
www.heroes.net

UP TO $5 MILLION REWARD
ABSOLUTE CONFIDENTIALITY

Osama bin Laden, who became the most wanted terrorist in the world after the capture of Ramzi Yousef.

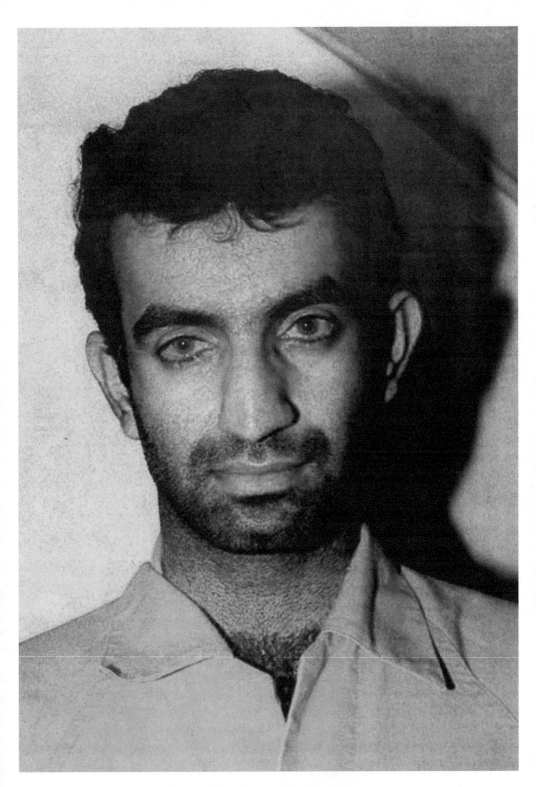

Ramzi Yousef in a photograph taken shortly after his capture and return to the United States.

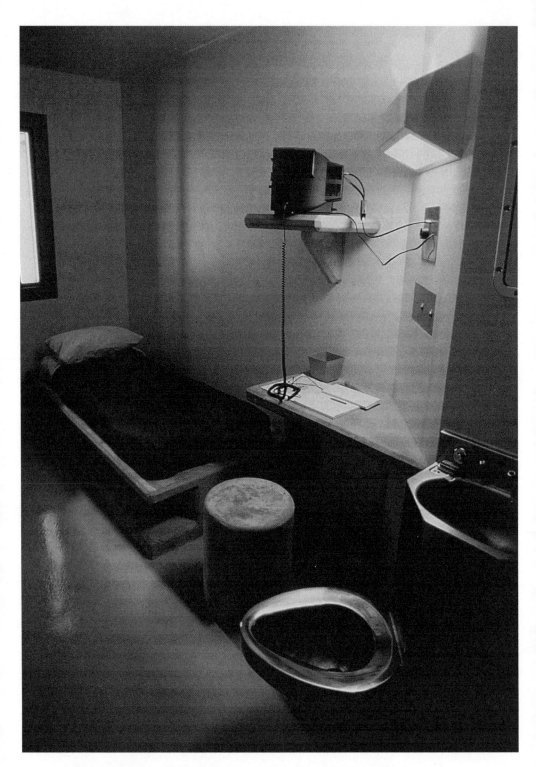

One of the cells at the 'Supermax' prison in Florence, Colorado, the most secure jail in the world. A room like this now holds Ramzi Yousef; another waits for Osama bin Laden.

highly unusual step of revoking bin Laden's Saudi citizenship.

The CIA was slightly behind, but they were catching up fast. By 1993 CIA analysts in Africa and the Middle East had realized there had been a tremendous upsurge in Sudanese support for Islamic militants, and the State Department put Sudan on its list of countries that sponsor terrorism, preventing many companies from trading with the country. It was a heavy blow for the regime in Khartoum.

However it was not until after Neil Herman's FBI team began investigating the February 1993 bombing of the World Trade Center that the CIA really identified bin Laden as a major problem. The initial investigation into Yousef's gang of conspirators – which revealed that many militants in New York had fought in Afghanistan with US backing – woke the CIA to a massive 'blowback' problem from Afghanistan, as former intelligence assets turned against their sponsors. James Woolsey, then the head of the CIA, quickly flew to Cairo with more than 20 CIA Middle East specialists for secret briefings on the Afghan Arabs from the Egyptian Mukhabarat al-Amat, the political police. 'Bin Laden was top of the Egyptian list,' said a US intelligence source.[15]

Then, as mentioned in a previous chapter, Neil Herman's Joint Terrorist Task Force found bin Laden's telephone numbers amid the huge number of phone-calls made by Yousef and his men from their New York safehouses. For the CIA it was proof bin Laden had turned on them. From the summer of 1993 CIA agents began monitoring bin Laden and building a file on his activities.

Their prey remained busy. From the comfort of his home in Khartoum bin Laden began considering plans for assassination attacks on Middle Eastern leaders he opposed. In June 1993 he was involved in an attempt to murder Crown Prince Abdullah of Jordan, now the leader of the country since the death of King Hussein in 1999. He also helped to fund another attempt on the life of Egyptian President Hosni Mubarak on 26 June 1995 while the President was visiting Ethiopia.

Emboldened by his success in Somalia and the growth of his empire, bin Laden also began funding militants working within Saudi Arabia. On 13 November 1995, a truck bomb exploded outside Saudi Arabia's National Guard Communications Centre in central Riyadh, killing two Indians and five American servicemen. Four Saudi men were captured by the authorities and beheaded before they could be interrogated by American investigators. Some Western intelligence sources suggest that bin Laden's few remaining friends in the Saudi government and intelligence services arranged a swift execution for the men to prevent the full extent of bin Laden's involvement – and his links to senior Saudis – becoming widely known. The few words the men did say to investigators suggests they were, at the very least, bin Laden supporters. Three had fought with the mujaheddin in Afghanistan; the other had fought with Bosnian Muslim forces in the civil war in the former Yugoslavia; and all expressed their admiration of and support for bin Laden.

Many senior Saudis were furious at the attack and knew of bin Laden's involvement. Concerned that bin Laden's campaign against America might expand into terrorist attacks on the Saudi royal family, they had already decided to give him a 'warning'. Around the time of the explosion in Riyadh, a 1981 Toyota HiLux pick-up stopped a few metres from bin Laden's home in Sudan,[16] and four Yemeni mercenaries in the car opened fire on both the house and bin Laden's security guards with AK-47 assault rifles. A firefight ensued that ended with the deaths of three of the attackers and two of the guards; the other attacker was executed by the Sudanese government. Security around bin Laden's home was increased: barriers were erected on the roads around the house, trenches were dug at each end of the street to halt traffic, and more armed guards were stationed around bin Laden's house to protect the foreigner. At night for months afterwards, even pedestrians walking along the road were questioned and searched.

By 1995 the FBI and CIA were convinced bin Laden was heavily involved in terrorism. He had been linked 'to numerous terrorist organizations'[17] and he was directing 'funding and other logistic support through his companies to a number of extremist causes'.

'Every time we turned over a rock, there would be some sort of connection to bin Laden,' said one CIA official. 'The conventional wisdom at the time was that he was some sort of financier and little else, a kind of Gucci terrorist. The more we dug, the more it became clear that there was more there.'[18]

In January 1996, a decision was taken by senior staff of the CIA's 200-strong Counterterrorist Center, located in sprawling windowless offices on the ground floor of the agency's headquarters in Langley, Virginia, to form a special bin Laden taskforce. Ever since, the Osama bin Laden desk, manned by élite staff of more than eleven federal agencies, has mounted the largest, most expensive and most extensive investigation ever into a single individual charged with international terrorism.

With personnel drawn from the CIA's Directorate of Intelligence (analysis), Directorate of Operations (case officers and agents) and Directorate of Science and Technology (scientists and technicians), the new team's initial task was to identify the scale of bin Laden's operation ('the nature of the beast', says one American intelligence official). Analysts pored over their own files and talked to representatives from Britain's MI6, the Israeli Mossad, Germany's BND and BfV, the Italian DIGOS, and the French DST and DGSE, all of whom are understood to have investigated the Afghan Arabs.

Much intelligence work is tedious, involving scrutiny of reams of figures and paper. In the CIA's Counterterrorist Center the tension is lessened slightly by 'street signs' hanging from the ceiling, including 'Tamil Tiger Terrace' and 'Abu Nidal Boulevard', which point to the respective CIA team studying a particular group.[19] 'The initial work on bin Laden was really boring,' said an American intelligence source.[20] 'The guys [in the Counterterrorism Center] read and digested everything bin Laden had ever said or written.' Meanwhile the CIA's sophisticated 'link-analysis' computers began printing out complicated diagrams of bin Laden's organizational links with other militants. The bin Laden desk then began analysing the source of his funding, where it was coming from, where it was stashed, and – perhaps most importantly of all – if he was receiving state sponsorship or money from Gulf states such as Saudi Arabia. Their conclusion, according to sources close to the investigation, was that large sums were still flowing into bin Laden's accounts from businessmen and senior politicians in Saudi Arabia, Kuwait and Qatar.[21]

As the investigation proceeded, the CIA began holding talks with American Special Forces and Janet Reno, the US Attorney General, about launching a military operation to capture bin Laden abroad. Agents kept a close watch for him in the Gulf, where it was thought the US could exert pressure on local authorities to assist in an arrest, but bin Laden failed to leave his sanctuary in Khartoum.

Although US operations against bin Laden had been dramatically scaled up, the US is not thought to have been involved in the attempt on bin Laden's life that took place in the spring of 1996. Details of the unsuccessful attack are sketchy, but it is thought the assailant was one of his bodyguards and that the Saudis, who were growing increasingly fearful of bin Laden's influence within the kingdom, were probably behind it. An olive branch had previously been extended to their wayward son: bin Laden had been visited in Khartoum by senior Saudi officials and told his passport and property in Saudi Arabia would be returned, and that he could move back to the kingdom, so long as he publicly expressed allegiance to king and government. Bin Laden scornfully refused.[22]

After this second attempt on bin Laden's life Saudi emissaries flew to Khartoum and warned Hassan al-Turabi, the leader of the country's ruling National Islamic Front, that unless Sudan withdrew its support for bin Laden Saudi Arabia would take action. The exact nature of their threats is not known, but they were combined with increased pressure from America, which warned Turabi that sanctions would be tightened again unless bin Laden was 'squeezed and silenced', according to one US source.[23] Sudan may have given Carlos the Jackal to the French in August 1994, but Turabi was not going to allow bin Laden to go the same way.

Bin Laden and Turabi had become friends, indeed they still are: 'Bin Laden is inspired by Turabi's expansive vision; he sees eye to eye with him,' said Kenneth Katzman, a former analyst for the CIA who is now the in-house terrorism expert for the Congressional Research Service.[24] 'Turabi has Islamic credentials bin Laden could never have. They are allies. They are close associates. They are business partners. Bin Laden is Turabi's alter ego, his field commander, his operations chief.' But American, Egyptian and Saudi pressure on the government in Khartoum had become intense and Turabi had no choice: in April 1996 Sudan politely asked bin Laden to leave.

Bin Laden considered his options: 'Iraq is out of the question. I would rather die than live in a European state. I have to live in a Muslim country and so the choice is between Yemen and Afghanistan,' *Al Quds al-Arabi* quoted him as saying in an interview.[25] He chose Afghanistan, where he knew he could rely on the support of his old comrades. Many of them had now reorganized into the fundamentalist Islamic militia known to the West as the Taliban, which was imposing harsh Sharia law in the country: forcing men into mosques at gunpoint five times a day, banning music and alcohol, and preventing women from working. In May 1996 Osama bin Laden flew into the eastern city of Jalalabad with his wives and around 150 supporters on a chartered C-130 transport plane.

American strategists had made a huge mistake. By increasing the pressure on Sudan they had allowed the most dangerous terrorist financier in the world to move to an impenetrable stronghold from which he could direct terrorist attacks with near impunity. It was months before analysts realized the scale of the error.

Even as bin Laden moved from Sudan to Afghanistan, al Qaeda terrorists were preparing more attacks. During the night of 25 June 1996, a massive 5,000lb truck bomb exploded in Dharan, near a US military housing complex called Khobar Towers. It destroyed the entire front of the building, killing 19 American servicemen and injuring scores more. Bin Laden was immediately suspected of involvement and he initially described the attack as heroic. Some analysts believe his involvement was limited to providing advice, gaining moral support for the attack among other Islamic militants in Saudi Arabia, and possibly providing technical support.

However, one American investigator points to a classified report from the CIA's Counterterrorism Center, based on telephone-calls intercepted by the National Security Agency. It states that Ayman al-Zawahiri, leader of Egyptian Islamic Jihad, and Ashra Hadi, a leader of the Palestinian Islamic Jihad, both of whom are close friends of bin Laden, called him within two days of the attack to 'congratulate' him on the operation.[26] Saudi investigators promptly flew to Pakistan to share intelligence on the Afghan Arabs with Rehman Malik of the Federal Investigation Agency.

Within weeks of the attack the FBI and Mary Jo White, the US Attorney for the Southern District of New York, had initiated a grand jury investigation into bin Laden and the involvement of al Qaeda in international terrorism.[27] Bin Laden soon gave them some useful evidence: 'Only Americans were killed in the explosions,' he said. 'No Saudi citizen suffered any injury. When I got the news about these blasts, I was very happy. This was a noble act. This was a great honour but, unfortunately, I did not conduct these explosions personally. But I would like to say to the Saudi people that they should adopt every tactic to throw the Americans out of Saudi territory.'[28]

Bin Laden settled back into life in the hills of Afghanistan. He knew the Americans might try to capture him at any time, so he recruited a small army of supporters as protection. One bin Laden follower has recounted how he was offered $100-a-month support to move his family into Afghanistan from Egypt.[29] 'Bin Laden spread the word that militants who were having trouble could live with him safely in Afghanistan,' said a British intelligence source.[30]

After bolstering the ranks of his own private army, bin Laden wanted to ensure he had the support of one of the most powerful forces in the region: the spies, agents and politicians of Pakistan, particularly the heads of the all-powerful Inter-Services Intelligence agency (ISI), the major backer of the Taliban. According to Pakistani and British intelligence sources, bin Laden travelled into Pakistan to renew old acquaintances within the ISI, and also allegedly met or talked with Nawaz Sharif, the former Prime Minister of Pakistan – who was then campaigning for re-election over the incumbent Benazir Bhutto. 'There were very close links between bin Laden and the Pakistani intelligence services,' Bhutto now claims.[31]

Moreover, militants associated with the Binnori mosque in Karachi, where most of the Taliban's senior leaders studied, allegedly joined al Qaeda as a direct result of encouragement from senior figures in the Karachi office of another of Pakistan's internal intelligence agencies, the Intelligence Bureau (IB), which was supposed to be 'monitoring' militant and terrorist activity.[32] The relationship was only discovered by American and other Pakistani agents investigating the murder of American diplomats in the same city on 8 March 1995 – an attack ordered in retaliation for the arrest of Ramzi Yousef. The IB provided safehouses in Karachi for al Qaeda members, and even armed and trained young militants.[33]

By 1999 Benazir Bhutto was out of office and being tried on corruption charges in Pakistan, and felt more able to speak of the events of 1996. She now recalls one time earlier in her administration when she heard that $10 million had been donated by Saudi Arabia to opposition politicians to approve a vote of no confidence in her government. 'I was told that a plane had come in with crates of fruit, and the money had come in with the fruit,' she said. 'So I sent my minister of law to see the Saudi king, and he said we have not given any money, she is like our daughter, her father was like my brother, our kingdom would never give any such money. And while he [Bhutto's emissary] was there, others told him that a rich Arab, who had fought in the Afghan war, and had money, had given the money. And when he asked for a name he was told it was Osama bin Laden.'[34] At the time the name meant nothing to Bhutto: '... my response when I was told was "Who is Osama bin Laden?"!'

While the sceptical view is that Bhutto is now trying to portray herself as a moderate victim of fundamentalists to win favour in the West ('I was caught in a sea of sharks,' she says), her claims are supported by other Pakistani and Western intelligence sources. Bhutto also alleges that bin Laden's influence went further than merely providing money to ensure her downfall, claiming, 'Even people in my party today who were with Nawaz Sharif yesterday . . . [name of a confidant of Bhutto][35] says, "I met Osama bin Laden with Nawaz Sharif in discussing plots to get rid of you [Bhutto]." He tells me, "It was no secret, I met Mr Osama bin Laden when he was in Pakistan to get rid of you."' Again, there is no suggestion that Nawaz Sharif has done anything wrong, but the allegation does support claims that bin Laden was trying to destabilize the Bhutto government to ensure the election of politicians who would be more amenable to his presence in Afghanistan.

As well as trying to secure political support next-door in Pakistan, bin Laden was careful to cultivate his friendship with the most powerful man in Afghanistan, Mullah Mohamed Omar, the Amir-Ul-Momineen (Commander of the Faithful), and supreme leader of the Taliban. Bin Laden had sustained Omar financially and had bought him a house in Karachi nearly a decade previously. He had also encouraged Omar's friendship with gifts, which in 1997 included an offer to take over funding of an irrigation canal in Helmand province.[36] His money also bought a splendid new house in Kandahar's Shahar-i-nau (New Town) area for Omar and his three wives, a daughter and five sons.[37] In the city of Kandahar, where women are rarely seen on the streets because of the Taliban's ferocious restrictions, bin Laden also began upgrading the electricity and water supplies, and began funding the construction of a vast new mosque complex in the south-west of the city in 1998.

His generosity has paid dividends. Some sources suggest the two men became so close that bin Laden married one of his daughters to the mullah; others claim bin Laden also married one of Omar's daughters in an extraordinary display of bonding. However, Mullah Omar, who is now in his early forties, is a tough and pragmatic man unlikely to be swayed by gifts and possibly even marriage bonds. During the Afghan war the mullah was a relatively obscure guerrilla commander, but when Soviet forces left, and Afghanistan descended into a nightmarish orgy of violence and corruption, he left his troops and retreated to the remote village of Singesar in the Maiwand district 56km to the west of Kandahar.

There he lived, studying the Koran in a mud-walled religious school until the early months of 1994, when some of his neighbours told him that two young girls had been kidnapped, shaved, and raped by the mujaheddin rebels manning a local checkpoint. The mullah was furious and rallied a small group of former veterans. Together they attacked the checkpoint with a few rusty AK-47s and freed the girls. The ringleader was hanged from the barrel of an old Soviet tank while the mullah's comrades cheered.

The incident was a turning-point in Afghan history, for the mullah's new followers multiplied rapidly. At the time there was general revulsion in Afghanistan at the moral degradation of some elements of the former mujaheddin: while the mullah was rescuing the two girls, two mujaheddin commanders were squaring up to each other with tanks in a bazaar in Kandahar in a dispute over a young teenage boy both wanted to use for homosexual sex. In the battle that followed up to forty bystanders were massacred.[38]

Mullah Omar led his new troops in battles to defeat other ragged and corrupt former Afghan soldiers, and within 30 months of hanging the checkpoint commander he was the supreme Taliban leader and had conquered 20 of Afghanistan's 32 provinces. His personal bravery is unquestionable. He has been injured seriously four times in the last 20 years. One legend relates how he was wounded in the eye by shrapnel when a Soviet shell hit his mosque during the Afghan war. The mullah felt blood trickling down the side of his face, knew the eye was useless and would soon be infected, and tore it out of its socket with his own fingers. Visitors to Singesar can still see a bloody fingerprint inside the mosque where the mullah is said to have wiped his blood.[39]

Support for the Taliban came from unlikely quarters, including Pakistan, Saudi Arabia, and perhaps even the United States. One senior Pakistani intelligence source claims the CIA backed the Taliban, thinking it would both provide a useful bulwark against the extremists in Iran and stop the drugs trade. American firms also wanted to lay a massive pipeline to pump natural gas from Turkmenistan through Afghanistan to Pakistan, a deal that would have been impossible without a dominant regime in power. The source claims that while Pakistan and Saudi Arabia backed the Taliban with money, in late 1994 the CIA provided, via Pakistani contacts, satellite information to the Taliban giving the secret locations of scores of Soviet trucks, holding tonnes of arms and ammunition, which were hidden in vast caves near the border with Pakistan at the end of the war. The astonishing speed with which the Taliban conquered Afghanistan is explained by the tens of thousands of weapons found in these trucks, which are believed to have numbered up to 400.

If it was the CIA who told the Taliban where to find the guns, they backed the wrong team. By 1999 Iran had a moderate new leader who travelled to the Vatican to meet the Pope and allowed visits from an American wrestling team. It was the Taliban who became the extremists, banning women from schools and jobs, outlawing music and kite-flying, and making the regime in Tehran look like a Scandinavian democracy.

By spring 1999, the Taliban controlled more than 90 per cent of Afghanistan and had become the worst oppressors of women in the world. Under their dehumanizing rule, based on literal Islamic Sharia law, women were forced to cover their faces and wear the burqua, an all-enveloping body sheath. Women were also forbidden from leaving their homes unless accompanied by a male relative, girls were not allowed to go to school and men were forced into mosques to pray and told to grow beards. However, drugs production in Afghanistan continued – indeed, many analysts believe the Taliban actively tried to increase production. 'The Americans do seem to balls things up in Afghanistan,' a British intelligence official observed laconically.[40]

Saudi Arabia has made similar mistakes in Afghanistan – viewing the Taliban as a useful means of defeating Afghan groups supported by Shiite Iran. It is also thought that senior members of the Saudi government also helped to protect bin Laden, interceding on his behalf with the Taliban to guarantee his protection against growing American interest in his role in international terrorism. With the weight of his government's chequebook behind him, some Western intelligence sources suggest Prince Turki may have personally met with senior Taliban leaders to extract guarantees of support for bin Laden.[41]

'Osama refused to meet Prince Turki for several years after 1995 because he felt so alienated from the Saudi regime,' said an American source. But during his meetings with Taliban leaders Prince Turki is believed to have pressured them to look after bin Laden but 'discourage' him from continuing his campaigns against the Saudi government and royal family.[42] The pleas fell on deaf ears. Bin Laden was soon 'throwing money' at Saudi opposition groups, which were emboldened by increasing discontent with the regime both internally and internationally.[43]

By the summer of 1996, bin Laden was a powerful figure funding many Islamic militants, but his level of day-to-day control over al Qaeda must be questioned. When bin Laden returned to Afghanistan, he appears to have devolved command over some areas of al Qaeda to Khalid Al-Fauwaz in London. A question-mark remains over just how much control was passed to Fauwaz, but some indication can be gained from FBI claims that he was a pivotal figure in the al Qaeda cell in Kenya that organized the attacks on American embassies in east Africa in 1998.

American agents investigating the east Africa bombings found files on a computer seized from the house of an al Qaeda operative in Nairobi that allegedly indicate Fauwaz's seniority and command. Clearly not learning from the mistakes made by Ramzi Yousef, who lost his laptop when his Manila flat was raided, the operative had stored a report on the computer expressing his concern that the Kenyan cell of al Qaeda had been identified by the CIA and was under heavy surveillance. 'I forced them [other members of the group] to burn that [telephone number] immediately and informed Khalid that I had prohibited them from calling me here as I am 100-per-cent sure the telephone is tapped.'[44] The writer of the report went on to explain his reasons for committing his fears to paper: 'He [Khalid] asked me also to write periodically about the security situation of the cell and the whole group here in general in east Africa.'

Khalid may have been the point man, but bin Laden was the eminence grise, retaining overall control from the shadows. That changed on 23 August 1996, when bin Laden decided Allah was calling him back to the fore, and he issued a declaration: 'to His Muslim Brothers in the Whole World and Especially in the Arabian Peninsula: Declaration of Jihad Against the Americans Occupying the Land of the Two Holy Mosques; Expel the Heretics from the Arabian Peninsula'.[45] It was a strong and specific call to arms that told Saudis they had a moral right to strike at the 5,000 Americans stationed in the country.

'I had decided to myself, after the Saudi government clamped down [in September 1994] on the country's [Muslim scholars], dismissing them from their posts in universities and mosques and banning distribution of their tapes, virtually preventing all of them from speaking, that I would start saying what was right and denouncing what was wrong,' said bin Laden in November 1996.[46]

Bin Laden moved his base into a cave – which had been tunnelled into the side of a mountain to protect it against air attacks – located above the city of Jalalabad in eastern Afghanistan. The cave, approached down a narrow ravine road guarded by several hundred men armed with machine guns, heavy weapons and tanks, extends back into the mountain, but is believed to consist of just three large rooms.[47] Unlike the 'show camps' in the region, which bin Laden used to meet and greet journalists, the cave could be loosely identified as his headquarters. Bin Laden salvaged only a few trappings of modern life: two laptop computers, at least one satellite phone, low beds with thin mattresses and a library of bound Islamic books.[48]

For months he lived simply amid Afghanistan's mountains and vast plains, waking early for prayers and a simple breakfast. It was a life far removed from the glamour and opulence of his upbringing in Saudi Arabia. It was not exactly luxurious. 'It was freezing,' said Abdelhari Atwan, editor of *Al Quds al-Arabi*, who stayed in the cave in November 1996 when he was interviewing bin Laden.[49] 'I reached under my camp-bed hoping to find an extra blanket. Instead, it was crammed with Kalashnikov rifles and mortar bombs.'

Other former comrades and interviewers have noted that bin Laden rarely spent two nights in the same place for security reasons. He would shuttle around Afghanistan in a convoy of up to twenty vehicles, with a small mobile force of men armed with small arms, rocket launchers, and Stinger surface-to-air missiles to protect against air attack. When they stopped overnight bin Laden always seemed to choose caves with the most scorpions and rats lurking in the shadows.

Bin Laden's declaration of war led to 'a concentration of attention', according to one intelligence expert,[50] and America decided to pursue him on the ground. At the end of June 1997, just after bin Laden had moved from the eastern province of Nangarhar to the southern Taliban stronghold of Kandahar, a party of three diplomats and CIA officers stationed in New Delhi flew to Peshawar to make contact with indigenous Afghan tribes and the Taliban. Their mission was simple: spread the word that America would pay dearly for information on bin Laden's location, and would be even more generous if one of the tribes decided to kidnap the terrorist and turn him over to the American authorities. The three men spent at least 10 days in the region, meeting with ageing tribal warlords and even a senior minister from the Taliban, but they flew back to India empty-handed.

In the months that followed bin Laden's support grew, and in February 1998 he met with several other Islamic leaders in Afghanistan to discuss how they could build a broad coalition against the West and the regimes they despised. According to Western intelligence, those present at the meeting included Ayman al-Zawahiri, head of Islamic Jihad; Abdul Salam Mohamed from Bangladesh; Abou Yassir Ahmed Taha from Egypt's Al-Gama'a Al-Islamiya, who was representing all of the Islamist groups in north Africa; and Fadhi Errahmane Khalil, the leader of the Pakistani movement Ansar.[51]

The talks went well, and bin Laden was soon ready to reveal a new coalition to the world, the International Islamic Front for Jihad Against the Jews and Crusaders. 'For over seven years the United States has been occupying the lands of Islam in the holiest of places, the Arabian peninsula, plundering its riches, dictating to its rulers, humiliating its people, terrorizing its neighbours, and turning its bases in the peninsula into a spearhead through which to fight the neighbouring Muslim peoples,' read the text of the group's first edict – essentially a fatwa from bin Laden – issued on 23 February 1998. Good Muslims must fight and kill American civilians and soldiers whenever they can, it said, 'in accordance with the words of Almighty God'.

Some analysts within the CIA likened the threat to a declaration of war.[52] The next day the CIA released a memo to Senator Jon Kyl, who was chairing a Senate hearing on foreign terrorism in the United States, noting that this was the first time bin Laden had authorized attacks on American civilians anywhere in the world. Pressure was brought to bear on the Saudi regime to silence bin Laden once and for all, and within a few days Prince Turki flew by private jet to Kandahar in Afghanistan for an audience with Mullah Mohamed Omar.

The prince demanded a meeting be arranged between himself and bin Laden. After several hours of debate and shouted conversations with bin Laden's lieutenants via satellite telephones, a meeting was arranged at bin Laden's base near Khost. 'The prince told bin Laden his family's business would suffer if he did not show more "restraint",' said an American source.[53] 'But bin Laden was evasive and rude to his old friend.' The prince returned to Saudi Arabia with scant evidence that bin Laden would behave himself.

By then, however, there were mutterings of discontent among some senior but disparate sections of the Taliban, who realized they would never achieve their aim of United Nations recognition as the rulers of Afghanistan while they were harbouring the man threatening to start a war with the West.

Sensing this discontent, bin Laden visited Mullah Mohamed Omar and suggested he could leave Afghanistan if his presence was causing the Taliban too many problems. The mullah, however, was unequivocal, reportedly telling bin Laden: 'You are one of our own and one of our own you will remain.'[54]

By now US law enforcement officials had decided they had enough evidence to mount a prosecution against bin Laden in the United States, and at a meeting in Washington in the early spring of 1998 authorization was given for an operation to extricate the terrorist leader from Afghanistan and return him to America. 'Special Forces were tasked with responsibility for planning his capture, and their conclusions were aired at a meeting between the President, senior military staff, and officials from the Justice Department and the CIA,' said a US intelligence source.[55]

President Clinton noted that the last time the US Army had invaded a country to arrest a suspect was in Panama, when they went after the dictator Manuel Noriega. In Panama they had used loud music piped through loudspeakers to wear down their prey. Afghanistan would be a rather different situation. In April 1986 three élite battalions of Soviet commandos fought their way into Zhawar Kili, the same area where bin Laden's training camps were located in 1998, in a ferocious battle that lasted three weeks and cost hundreds of Soviet lives. Clinton decided the risk of American casualties was too great to launch an immediate attack, and instead opted for a twin-track approach to the problem: continue planning a military 'snatch' operation while simultaneously launching a diplomatic offensive to have bin Laden thrown out of Afghanistan.

In mid-April 1998 Bill Richardson, the US Ambassador to the United Nations, a man used to dealing with difficult characters, travelled to Pakistan and then on into Afghanistan for talks with senior officials from the Taliban on how bin Laden could be handed over to the US. As Richardson met the Taliban several teams of US Special Forces soldiers arrived in Pakistan and were 'smuggled' into the heavily defended US consulate in Peshawar in preparation for a cross-border raid. Richardson promised the Taliban their international isolation would end if they turned bin Laden over, but the mullahs would not co-operate. Bin Laden, they said, would remain their 'protected guest'.

References

1 Based on author interviews with intelligence sources and US indictment: S(2)98 Cr. 1023 (LBS).

2 Ibid.

3 Author interview with retired CIA official.

4 Based on an author interview with a US intelligence source. Also September 1998 statement of Prosecutor Patrick Fitzgerald during a bail hearing: El Hage was 'being investigated for his involvement in attempting to obtain chemical weapons and for his involvement in providing logistical support to the people who were attacking people in Somalia'. Mahmud Abouhalima, one of the World Trade Center bombers, also told FBI agents he had twice visited El Hage in Texas to obtain weapons.

5 Author interview.

6 Author interview with American investigator.

7 Author interview with retired CIA official.

8 *Gazeta Shqiptare* newspaper, Tirana, Albania, 3 November 1998.

9 Author interview with retired CIA official.

10 There is no suggestion Gazidede has done anything illegal. However, after the collapse of illegal pyramid investment schemes in Albania Gazidede fled the country and is now believed to be hiding in Damascus, Syria.

11 Author interview with retired CIA official.

12 Indictment, op. cit.

13 Ibid.

14 Hamid Mir, interview with Osama bin Laden, Pakistan, 18 March 1997.

15 Author interview with retired CIA official.

16 Karl Vick, 'Letter from Sudan', *Washington Post*, 27 August 1998.

17 Ambassador Philip C. Wilcox, Jr., Coordinator for Counterterrorism, *1995 Patterns of Global Terrorism*, US Department of State, release date: April 1996.

18 Vernon Loeb, 'The Federal Page: Where the CIA Wages Its New World War', *Washington Post*, 9 September 1998.

19 Author interview with retired CIA official.

20 Ibid.

21 Ibid.

22 Ibid.

23 Ibid.

24 Tim Weiner, 'How bin Laden moved from ally to foe', *International Herald Tribune*, 21 August 1998.

25 Barry May, 'Saudi dissident sets up foothold in Yemen', Reuters, 21 March 1997.

26 Author interview with retired CIA official.

27 US indictment: S(2)98 Cr. 1023 (LBS).

28 Mir, op. cit.

29 Egyptian intelligence interview with Ahmad Ibrahim al-Najjar, related to author by British intelligence source.

30 Author interview.

31 Author interview with Benazir Bhutto.
32 Author interview with Pakistani investigator.
33 Ibid.
34 Author interview with Benazir Bhutto.
35 Name removed by author for legal reasons.
36 Author interview with retired CIA official.
37 The mullah, however, has since moved back into a large house next to the most important shrine in Kandahar.
38 Author interview with a retired CIA official.
39 Ibid.
40 Author interview.
41 Author interview with retired CIA official.
42 Ibid.
43 Ibid.
44 Detail from a 300-page FBI report on Khalid. Author interview with US investigator.
45 Proclamation of Osama bin Laden issued on 23 August 1996, from his base in the Hindu Kush mountains. Described in US indictment: S(2)98 Cr. 1023 (LBS).
46 Interview with bin Laden by Abdelhari Atwan, editor of *Al Quds al-Arabi*.
47 Author interviews with a CIA official and a Pakistani journalist who has worked among the Taliban.
48 Atwan, op. cit.
49 Kenneth R. Timmerman, 'This Man Wants You Dead', *Reader's Digest*, June 1998.
50 Author interview with CIA official.
51 Ibid.
52 Ibid.
53 Author interview with US intelligence source.
54 Author interview with a Pakistani journalist.
55 Author interview.

TEN

Unravelling Terror

AFTER ISSUING his 'declaration of war' against America in February 1998, there was little chance that Osama bin Laden would keep quiet for long. He might have been living in relative isolation in Afghanistan, under threat of abduction by American forces and under intense satellite scrutiny, but bin Laden needed to hit the Americans hard if he was to back up his threats with actions.

Bin Laden decided to put his al Qaeda terrorist cell in east Africa into action. The cell had been established in 1994, when Mohamed Sadeek Odeh, a slender young militant Palestinian from Jordan, moved into a modest house in the city of Mombasa on the Kenyan coast. Odeh had received terrorist training in Afghanistan before he joined al Qaeda in 1992, allegedly pledging allegiance to bin Laden at a camp in the Hindu Kush mountains. His first assignment had been Somalia, where US intelligence sources claim he trained fighters who killed 18 American soldiers. In Kenya he bought a seven-tonne boat and set up a fishing business 'with al Qaeda money'. Catches from the boat were used to support other al Qaeda members who then began arriving in the country.[1]

In the years that followed other bin Laden militants quietly settled in Kenya. Fazul Abdullah Mohammed, for example, had fallen under bin Laden's spell while he studied in Khartoum. The young militant, originally from the town of Moroni on the stunning island of Comoros in the Indian Ocean, arrived in Kenya with his wife Hamila and two young children, and began living with and working for Wadih El Hage, the senior al Qaeda man in the country. El Hage had arrived in Kenya from Khartoum and taken command of the east Africa cell, renting a comfortable house on the Fedha Estate near Nairobi airport for £300 a month ($500), opening businesses that would act as fronts for al Qaeda, and pretending to work for a charity called Help Africa People. His five children went to local schools and his wife April even joined the local Parent–Teacher Association.[2]

It was an astonishing international operation paralleled by the actions of other al Qaeda 'sleeper' units in countries such as Britain and America. These men spent years establishing themselves in an alien country, living perfectly respectable lives, waiting for nothing more than a call to arms from Osama bin Laden. Yet they were not completely in the shadows. The FBI, CIA, MI6, and the intelligence services of almost every country in the Middle East were either monitoring or investigating al Qaeda by 1996, and by 1997 American investigators knew al Qaeda was established in Kenya and east Africa. Wadih El Hage was even questioned by the FBI in New York on several occasions in September 1997, and in Texas again in October of the same year: on all occasions he allegedly lied about his contacts with al Qaeda. The CIA also had informants working within the east Africa cell, but they apparently failed to warn of bin Laden's plans.[3]

By the end of July 1998, the east Africa al Qaeda cell had been turned into an operational terrorist unit ready to attack US embassies. Mohamed Rashed Daoud Al-'Owhali, an aspiring terrorist who had asked bin Laden for 'a mission', arrived in Nairobi from Lahore, Pakistan, on 31 July, having filmed a videotape with a man called 'Azzam' to 'celebrate their anticipated "martyrdom." '[4] The gang converged at 43 Rundu Estates, Nairobi, a two-storey unfurnished house and garage surrounded by a high wall and hedge, which Fazul Abdullah Mohammed had rented. They were not planning a long stay. The east African cell assembled in the house and began making their final preparations. The brother-in-law of their landlady was among those the gang would kill.

By the evening of 6 August 1998, both the bomb and the gang were ready. Odeh, the senior terrorist, had been told to leave the city, and using an assumed name he flew out of Nairobi on Pakistani International Airways flight 746, heading towards Pakistan. Early the next morning Fazul Abdullah Mohammed climbed behind the wheel of a white pick-up truck parked at the gang's villa. Carrying four stun grenades and a handgun, Al-'Owhali jumped into a larger Toyota truck driven by Azzam – a massive bomb sat in the back. Together the two vehicles wound their way through Nairobi's busy streets, and headed towards the American embassy in the city.

At 10.30 a.m. the battered bomb truck pulled up at the back of the embassy, and Al-'Owhali jumped out, lobbed a stun grenade in the direction of a Kenyan security guard, and turned and ran. Instead of immediately reaching for the detonator, Azzam fired his handgun at the windows of the embassy, giving Al-'Owhali precious seconds to round a corner. He escaped the worst of the massive blast that followed seconds later when Azzam detonated the bomb, blowing himself to pieces, demolishing a multi-storey secretarial college, and severely damaging the US embassy and the Co-operative Bank Building. At least 213 people died and more than 4,500 were injured.

Within 10 minutes of the Nairobi blast a second van bomb exploded outside the US embassy in Dar-es-Salaam in Tanzania, killing 11 people and injuring another 85. The blast was so powerful that the body of the suicide-bomber driving the van was cut in two, and the top half of his torso hit the embassy building still clutching the steer-ing-wheel in both hands.

For the Kenyan police and scores of FBI agents who arrived within hours to investigate the bombing, Osama bin Laden was the immedi-ate suspect. 'He was top of a short list' of men capable of pulling off the double attacks, according to an American source familiar with the investigation.[5] There was concern, however, at the depth of planning for the double attack. 'Two at once is not twice as hard,' said Milton Bearden, a retired senior CIA official who has served as the agency's ranking officer in Afghanistan, Pakistan and Sudan.[6] 'Two at once is a hundred times as hard.'

The bombings showed that despite years of investigation and moni-toring by the world's intelligence services, al Qaeda was still a power-ful terrorist force worthy of a James Bond movie. American intelligence later realized al Qaeda had also been planning other attacks on American interests in Kampala, Uganda, to coincide with the bombings in east Africa, but they were delayed at the last moment, giving police the time to swoop and arrest 18 terrorists over the following two weeks. 'The attacks were planned to be more serious and devastating than those in Nairobi and Dar-es-Salaam,' Muruli Mukasa, the Ugandan State Minister for Security, said later.[7]

Despite the sophistication of al Qaeda's attack, the escape plans of the terrorists left a lot to be desired. When Odeh fled to Pakistan, he took a direct flight and carried documents that did not even bear his photograph. He was arrested, interrogated by Pakistani intelligence agents, and later deported to the United States to face charges. 'I did it all for the cause of Islam. [Osama bin Laden] is my leader, and I obey his orders,' he allegedly said.[8]

In Kenya Fazul Abdullah Mohammed escaped the immediate drag-net via the Comoros.[9] Al-'Owhali, the would-be suicide bomber, survived the Nairobi blast and was taken to the MP Shah Hospital. Suspicious doctors noted that his injuries appeared to indicate he had been running away from the bomb when it exploded. When the FBI came calling a few days later the doctors mentioned the Arab patient, a taxi driver remembered taking him to an address in Nairobi from the hospital, and the police picked him up. Within days of the bombings the FBI had two strong suspects in custody, and were actively seeking their supporters and backers. Al-'Owhali broke down and gave crucial details. Other suspects were picked up across east Africa and the cell began to unravel.

By the time President Clinton launched Tomahawk cruise missiles against bin Laden's base at Zhawar Kili, south-west of the Afghan town of Khost, his administration had accumulated a wealth of infor-mation on al Qaeda. The President's instructions were simple: take it down.

At CIA headquarters in Langley after the missile strikes, agents, analysts and senior officials crowded into the room used by the Counterterrorism Center for crisis management (nicknamed the 'fusion centre'). Stuffed with phones, more than a dozen computers linked directly to giant mainframes in the basement, and large moni-tor screens displaying satellite photos and the latest media reports, the fusion centre has been witness to both hideous failure and spectacular success.[10] A burn mark on the carpet marks the spot where George Tenet, the down-to-earth, burger-loving Director of the CIA, dropped his cigar in excitement at the news that Mir Aimal Kansi, who killed two CIA employees outside the Langley HQ, had been captured in Pakistan in June 1997.[11]

Imagine the palpable sense of disappointment in the fusion centre when translators heard bin Laden talking in a radio message beamed out over Afghanistan and Pakistan after the missile strikes: 'By the grace of Allah, I am alive!' he said.

Bin Laden had been warned that America was tracking him via his phone just hours before the attack, allegedly by supporters working for Pakistani intelligence, and he switched it off. 'He turned the lights out,' said one intelligence source.[12] Bin Laden also cancelled a meeting at Zhawar Kili after discovering that 180 American diplomats were withdrawing from Islamabad on a chartered plane. He correctly assumed it was to prevent retaliation after an imminent strike, and was actually hundreds of miles away in northern Afghanistan when the missiles landed.

The wisdom of the attacks on Sudan must also be questioned. The US government initially said simply that the Al Shifa pharmaceutical factory was connected with bin Laden and was producing chemicals used to manufacture chemical weapons. However, CIA agents involved in identifying the factory as a risk were not aware it was producing medicines for human and veterinary use until they checked the factory's Internet web-site after their missiles had ripped it to pieces.[13] In the rubble reporters found packaging for the company's 'Profenil' brand of ibuprofen, a common anti-inflammatory drug and pain reliever, and boxes of veterinary antibiotics plastered with pictures of goats, camels and sheep.

If the missile strikes were designed as a surgical operation to crush al Qaeda, they failed. Most of the bases hit in Afghanistan had no connection with bin Laden. Among the survivors from those bases who were linked to bin Laden, support for him was redoubled. Mohammad Hussain, an 18-year-old militant training in the camps when the bombs fell, was left with deep wounds in his back and chest. Six of his friends were killed. 'I could smell perfume from the blood of those martyrs,' he said.[14] 'We will take revenge from America and its president. They should not think we are weak. We will emerge as heroes of Islam like Osama bin Laden.'

Bin Laden would never be an easy man to kill; he is no fool. Consider the experience of Peter Jouvenal, a British cameraman who went to interview him. 'We were called at our hotel and left in the middle of the night,' said Jouvenal.[15] 'We were blindfolded and the car stopped on a mountain road. There we were body-searched and a metal detector was passed over us, three times. We were told to confess if we had any tracking devices. When we met [bin Laden] I was not allowed to use my own camera. They had their own one, which worked. They're not stupid. They know all about modern technology and they know what they're doing.'

Optimistic Westerners who dismiss bin Laden as a paper tiger should consider the wars he has already fought and study his words. 'Having borne arms against the Russians for 10 years,' he has said, 'we think our battle with the Americans will be easy by comparison . . .'.[16]

The fanaticism of bin Laden's closest followers and soldiers is also unlikely to wither away. 'We spent a lot of time waiting to see [bin Laden] which gave us a chance to really sit around and talk with bin Laden's soldiers,' said John Miller of America's *ABC News*, one of just a handful of Western journalists to have interviewed the al Qaeda leader. 'They talked a great deal about the battles in Afghanistan, in Somalia, in other places where they've fought and their level of commitment to him. They regard him as almost a god.'

Bin Laden's success following the US missile strikes was twofold. Firstly, he secured a large personal following throughout the Muslim world. Many who had never met him, whose only contact was through one of his interviews, a radio broadcast or Internet home-page, pronounced themselves ready to die for his cause. His second major success was to unify disparate groups of Islamic militants, even groups such as Islamic Jihad and the Islamic Group in Egypt, under his broad banner. Bin Laden's policy on this was clear: he views the Muslim world as a 'single nation' with one religion, and points to the continued presence of American troops in Saudi Arabia, US support for Israel and the stalled peace process, and continued American action, both military and diplomatic, against Iraq, as reasons for fighting the US.

His influence within the militant Muslim world cannot be underestimated. Even among many moderate Muslims bin Laden is viewed with grudging respect as a man prepared to stand up to the arrogance of the world's only remaining superpower. Scores of Pakistanis have named their newborn sons Osama, while many others have actually changed the names of their sons to carry bin Laden's.[17] Books about bin Laden and his beliefs have sold out in Pakistan, as have tens of thousands of stickers and pictures of the man. There is also the Osama Cloth House, the Osama Mosque and even the Osama Poultry Farm. It is some small indication of how the 'cult' and legend of bin Laden is spreading around the world.

'Many Muslims see the American strikes against Afghanistan and Sudan as a huge arrogance of power,' said Yousef al-Khoei, the influential head of the al-Khoei foundation, which represents the moderate face of Islam. 'Muslims who carry out these attacks are the fringe. But those who applaud are the disenfranchised Muslims everywhere who see the double standard of the United States taking unilateral action against an Islamic nation. Now, anyone who stands up to the US becomes a hero.'[18]

Some American experts agree. 'Informed students of the subject have known for years that although the various militant Islamist movements around the world share a common ideology and many of the same grievances, they are not a monolithic international organization,' according to Raymond Close, a CIA veteran.[19] The American attacks 'may have inflamed their common zeal and hastened their unification and centralization – while probably adding hosts of new volunteers to their ranks. We are rolling up a big snowball.' Close was right. By late 1998 more than twenty different militant factions were nestling under the broad umbrella of al Qaeda. Some of the most dangerous terrorists in the world were flocking to support bin Laden.

So America and its allies went to war against Osama bin Laden and al Qaeda. With the help of at least one, possibly two, medium-level moles within the organization, American investigators arrested and questioned 20 of bin Laden's closest associates and began inquiries in 28 countries. Simultaneously the CIA began organizing its first covert assassination attempt against bin Laden, despite memories of a plot code-named 'Mongoose' (the CIA's disastrous attempts to assassinate Fidel Castro).

The operation against bin Laden in November 1998 involved American technology and know-how in concert with Saudi finance and manpower, thus avoiding any difficult questions in the US Congress about state-sponsored assassinations. The attack, which bin Laden apparently blames on Saudi Prince Salman bin Abdul-Aziz, the governor of Riyadh, involved an assassin called Siddiq Ahmed who was paid $267,000 to poison bin Laden. It was only partially successful, causing the target acute kidney failure. For the next few months bin Laden hobbled around Afghanistan leaning heavily on a stick.[20] When the Pakistani journalist Rahimullah Yusufzai later filmed bin Laden looking frail, al Qaeda's security chief personally erased those sections of the videotape.

CIA agents also went after bin Laden's finances. When the bin Laden desk was originally opened in the CIA's Counterterrorism Center in 1996, agents analysed bin Laden's bank accounts in order to track and identify his funding. Then in 1997 bin Laden's chief financial aide,

Sayed Tayib al-Madani[21] 'was turned' away from bin Laden and began talking with Saudi intelligence and the CIA. Some sources suggest Madani was a Saudi intelligence agent all along who had been secretly 'loaned' to bin Laden by senior elements within Saudi intelligence. An alternative theory, no less beguiling, is that the Saudis identified Madani as a key man in the bin Laden organization, and persuaded him to swap sides. According to intelligence sources, Madani has since disclosed details of many of bin Laden's crucial financial secrets, and using his information the FBI has discovered accounts and funds stashed in banks in Europe, the Caribbean, Detroit, Jersey City and Brooklyn which had links to bin Laden.

After the American embassy bombings 'the gloves came off', and agents 'went after him in cyberspace', said a US investigator.[22] President Clinton signed an executive order freezing any American assets owned by bin Laden and experts visited the offices of the Treasury Department's Financial Crimes Enforcement Network (FinCEN) to study his holdings.

'We began working with the intelligence community and the Office of Foreign Asset Control from the early 1990s,' said Stanley E. Morris, the former director of FinCEN and the US Marshals Service.[23] 'FinCEN has become one of the stops that you make if you are an investigative agency. They want to make sure there's nothing there that might be helpful. FinCEN is an organization that tries to fill in a couple of pieces. It has large databases, some analytical capability. What would happen is that we would get a request to provide some information, perhaps from the FBI, or the intelligence community or the Secret Service. People would give us names, and just say to us "go and search everything you can", and then we'd go and check our data-bases. Eventually we might be able to go back and say to them, for example, the wife of this person entered the US three or four times, there has been the following bank account activity, etc.'

But investigating bin Laden abroad was a difficult task. 'Probably no area of the world has less records for money-laundering reporting and financial investigative capacity than the Middle East,' said Morris.[24] 'They basically have the old standard of secrecy, and there's far less transparency in that part of the world than elsewhere.' Even the problem of translating Arabic names to English, and vice versa, plays a part. 'It has come down to simple things like the different spellings of a particular Saudi name,' said one source acquainted with the investigation.[25] 'The translated name might be Muhammad, but because they register it as Mohammad with an "o" or with a more subtle spin, it becomes real hard to locate.'

American agents moved on to disruption tactics, which ranged from jamming and blocking cellular and satellite phones in parts of Afghanistan, to hacking into bank accounts and deleting and shifting funds. One source familiar with the operation says that US agents fed special computer programs into the systems of several European and Middle Eastern banks. When money was moved from an account under investigation one part of a 'sniffer' program would follow the funds, while another part would alert American agents that a transfer had occurred.

Meanwhile, the Pentagon-based National Imagery Office (NIO), which co-ordinates all US satellite activity, and the National Security Agency (previously more concerned with monitoring Saddam Hussein via satellites several miles above Baghdad), had already been snapping away at bin Laden's bases and monitoring his phone-calls for more than two years – ever since they obtained a poor copy of one of the tapes of his speeches that were distributed in Saudi Arabia on his return from Afghanistan in the early 1990s.

Bin Laden's 'voice-print' (a computerized record of his voice) was then entered into the acres of computers located beneath the NSA's headquarters in Fort Meade, Maryland, and satellites scanned cellular and satellite phone-calls emanating from Afghanistan for a match. On numerous occasions the NSA and CIA were able to monitor bin Laden's personal phone-calls, despite his use of an Inmarsat satellite phone and two electronic 'scramblers' designed to protect the security of conversations.

Unfortunately for the Americans, however, these weapons were designed to fight the relatively sophisticated Soviet KGB during the Cold War, and although they monitored many of his calls bin Laden was careful not to use the phone too regularly. Eventually he simply reverted to issuing his commands in person or by messenger. It slowed down his operation, but it also made him almost untraceable and untrackable because the West desperately lacked human intelligence (Humint) on the ground in Afghanistan.

The American investigation continued, however, with a twin-track approach: the CIA pursued intelligence on bin Laden and al Qaeda, while the FBI pursued a criminal investigation from the Bureau's office in New York – chosen largely because of Neil Herman's success with the JTTF.

By early 1999 American investigators had apparently identified at least three holding companies used by bin Laden in Amsterdam and Luxemburg. Europeans, described as 'local expertise' totally unconnected with al Qaeda, were acting as 'front men'.[26] Investigators also found that his financial support from Saudi Arabia, while considerably diminished, had not disappeared. Pakistani and American intelligence sources suggest one of his major backers was a senior figure in the Saudi car industry, while money was still flowing into bin Laden's coffers from members of the Saudi royal family, despite his stated opposition to the regime. 'We've got information about who's backing bin Laden, and in a lot of cases it goes back to the [Saudi] royal family,' according to Dick Gannon, the former Deputy Director for Operations at the State Department's Office of Counterterrorism.[27] 'There are certain factions of the Saudi royal family who just don't like [America].'

Bin Laden's entire empire was mapped and detailed in secret briefing papers passed back and forth between the FBI, CIA and State Department. According to the American investigators, by early 1999 bin Laden still had his trading companies in Kenya, a ceramic manufacturing firm in Yemen (a claim denied by the Yemeni government),[28] money in a Sudanese bank, a construction company, investment firms, and the White Nile Tannery in Khartoum, where the skins of goats and cattle are turned into leather. He was also alleged to be a partner in a lapis lazuli mine in Afghanistan.

Nevertheless bin Laden was no longer the hugely wealthy individual he had been at the start of the Afghan war. When he was forced out of Sudan in 1996 he lost up to $150 million on his investments and in deals where the Khartoum government failed to pay their debts. 'We know he lost a lot when he pulled out of Khartoum,' said one intelligence source.[29] But establishing details of bin Laden's finances still proves remarkably difficult.

Some sources happily speculate that bin Laden has vast personal reserves totalling more than £500 million ($800 million) and investments across the globe. But the consensus of those close to the US intelligence and criminal investigations into bin Laden is that by the time of the east Africa embassy bombings he was no longer such a powerfully rich man. He did, perhaps, have £30 million ($48 million) scattered across banks, investment companies, obscure trading firms and property, but even that is a generous figure; one senior investigator, while refusing to put a figure on his wealth, snorted with derision at the suggestion he had more than a few million pounds to his name.[30]

However, by late 1998 and early 1999 the size of bin Laden's bank balance had almost become an irrelevance. He no longer needed to be rich because many of al Qaeda's cells were virtually self-sufficient. His soldiers were working for a reward from Allah, not for financial gain. Bin Laden himself was required to pay little more than initial start-up costs and the price of an occasional air-fare.

Bin Laden had also become a powerful figure within the ranks of international Islamists, someone who thousands of militants turned to for leadership. So if he needed more money he had ready access to the huge financial reserves of the world's numerous Islamist groups, esti-mated variously at between $5–$16 billion (£3–£10 billion). Month by month, these reserves, which are spread through hundreds of bank accounts in the Middle East, Pakistan, Switzerland, the Benelux states, and the Caribbean, increase in size. Independent militants in Kuwait are understood to be donating at least £16 million (£10 million) every month while militant businessmen from other Gulf states – including Saudi Arabia – are collectively giving an average of at least $1.6 million (£1 million) every single day to Islamist coffers. [31]

As the Taliban become more professional in their management of the Afghan drug trade, which Western analysts estimate is worth $6.5–$10 billion (£4–£6 billion) annually, extra funds will flood into Islamist accounts. According to some intelligence reports, bin Laden and al Qaeda benefit from this drug money because bin Laden is understood to have helped the Taliban arrange money-laundering facilities through the Russian and Chechen Mafia. One American intelligence source claims that bin Laden's involvement in the estab-lishment of new financial networks for drug distribution and sales has been pivotal, and that by the spring of 1999 bin Laden was taking a cut of between 2 and 10 per cent from all Afghan drug sales ($133–$1,000 million, or £80–£600 million a year).[32] Such sums would be enough to fund al Qaeda's militant activity for many years to come.

By spring 1999 Osama bin Laden was still running and leading a powerful international terrorist organization. In Algeria, where Afghan Arabs had led an orgy of slaughter since the government cancelled general elections in 1992, the funding bin Laden has already channelled to several groups will keep them active for at least two years – even if bin Laden is captured and taken to America.[33]

He does not appear to have given money blindly. Bin Laden initially funded the murderous Armed Islamic Group (GIA), run by Antar Zouabri,[34] but by 1998 he is understood to have become concerned at the appalling image of the group, even in the Islamic world. So he persuaded a fundamentalist leader called Hassan Hattab, a 33-year-old former GIA commander and native of Rouiba, 30 kilometres east of the Algerian capital, to set up the Salafist Group for Preaching and Combat (GSPC). According to a renegade member of the GSPC bin Laden tried to persuade Hattab to concentrate attacks on 'legitimate targets': members of the Algerian security forces. However, the group has since been responsible for the murder of several dozen civilians at roadblocks in the Kabylie region of Algeria.[35] Intelligence experts suggest the group already has some 3,000 armed supporters, and will soon lead Algeria's Islamist guerrillas in an even bloodier struggle against the Algerian government.

The scale of bin Laden's involvement in Algeria and other parts of the world actually grew after the American cruise missile attacks on his bases in Afghanistan. In Italy, for example, the number of junior al Qaeda operatives actually rose.[36] The country had been an important element in bin Laden's global organization for several years, with one of his most trusted underlings, an Egyptian militant, working out of a flat in northern Italy and another apartment just across the border in Switzerland. With a fax machine and two telephone lines, he acted as the 'Italian exchange', receiving brief messages and commands from bin Laden or one of his senior lieutenants and then disseminating the instructions to other bin Laden militants or workers in Europe and the US.

Bologna, a beautiful city in northern Italy with portico-lined streets and perhaps the oldest university in the world, also provided sanctuary to several hundred of bin Laden's fighters. During the fighting in the former Yugoslavia men would stop and rest in Italy on the way to or from the war, which bin Laden viewed as another holy battle fought by Muslims threatened with oppression and slaughter. Italy became a key stopover point because of its proximity to the Balkans and Albania, and militants would arrive illegally by boat and make their way to safehouses in Bologna, where they would be fed, bathed and provided with new documents. From there they would fly out of Italy on one of numerous airlines offering cheap flights. One airline offering regular cheap tickets out of the city apparently became known to Italian intelligence officers as 'Jihad Air' because it was used by so many Islamic fighters.

Even by early 1999 bin Laden's operations in Italy were still relatively intact, despite an investigation code-named Operation Sphinx involving several undercover Italian police officers of North African origin, which led to the arrest of 11 Islamic militants from the Islamic Cultural Institute on Milan's via Jenner. This focused attention on several other militants connected with bin Laden. According to the Italian General Investigations and Special Operations Division (DIGOS), and the Central Bureau of General Investigations and Special Operations (UCIGOS), there were still up to 4,000 Arab militants in Italy by early 1999.[37] Most of the militants were 'guest-workers' living in Rome and Milan and belonging to more than twenty 'charity' groups or religious centres, bearing names such as 'The Mujaheddin Battalion' and the 'A.D. Group'. In early 1999 several dozen senior Arab veterans of the Afghan and Bosnian wars who pledge allegiance to bin Laden were still living in Bologna.[38]

Albania, just across the Adriatic Sea from Italy, has also been crucial in the modern development and growth of al Qaeda. Afghan Arabs were attracted to the region because of fighting in the neighbouring former Yugoslavia and battles between Muslims and Serb aggressors. Bin Laden saw the conflict as a 'European Afghanistan', and sent Arab Afghans into Albania and then Bosnia to fight alongside their Muslim brothers against the Serb aggressors.

The CIA had just begun to realize that the Afghan Arabs were a threat – largely because of investigations into the World Trade Center bombing – and that many were gathering around bin Laden. Terrified the region would turn into another Afghanistan the CIA, supported by British and Italian intelligence agents, as well as elements of the Albanian police, began evicting bin Laden and al Qaeda from Albania and the Balkans.[39] American agents are understood to have worked with British and even Serbian intelligence units to identify many of the Afghans.[40]

Many Afghan Arabs in the region came under pressure after the 1995 Bosnia peace accord was signed in Dayton, Ohio, and they moved to Kosovo, although one, Sabri Ibrahim al-'Attar, claims he was arrested by CIA agents working with Serbian intelligence officers and handed to the Egyptians.[41]

Under a highly dubious interpretation of international law, the CIA arrested and quietly shipped dozens more Afghan Arabs back to Egypt (some were even kidnapped by masked agents), where they were held without trial as Muslim fundamentalists or tried for terrorism against the state. The success of CIA and MI6 operations in the Balkans is understood to have been the reason why the Afghan Arabs did not immediately enter the conflict that flared up in late 1998 between Muslim Albanians in the Serbian province of Kosovo and the Serbian government of Slobodan Milosevic and which in March 1999 resulted in NATO attacks on Serbia. 'They [Afghan Arabs] were champing at the bit, but they couldn't risk exposing themselves again by getting involved,' said a British intelligence source.[42]

Despite the best efforts of the CIA to dislodge them, in spring 1999 al Qaeda was still well established in Albania. There were, however, a few mishaps for bin Laden. In October 1998, Salah Muhammad al-Sa'id, one of bin Laden's principal lieutenants in the country, shot himself in the head when police were called to his Tirana home after locals reported seeing a man with a gun wandering around inside the building. But this loss is unlikely to affect bin Laden's activities. Bin Laden is understood to have retained a large investment in the Islamic Bank in Tirana, and a mysterious figure by the name of Sheikh Claude Ben Abdel Kaden, a French national of Algerian extraction, has travelled the country recruiting young Muslim militants for al Qaeda.[43]

But Albania and Italy were not the only countries hosting al Qaeda members by Spring 1999. Afghan Arabs and bin Laden supporters also live in France, Germany, Switzerland, Spain, Holland, Denmark, and Britain. The network of Islamic militants originally established by bin Laden in Britain in 1994 after the arrival of Khalid Al-Fauwaz developed into a particularly impressive operation. Disparate militant groups linked to bin Laden emerged from 1995 onwards. Some limited their activities to vociferous protests at the decadence of the West and corruption in Middle Eastern governments. Others, however, were more sinister.

It is only since a group of young British Muslims were arrested in the Yemen in December 1998, that the full scale of British Islamic militancy became apparent. Ranging in age from 17 to 33, the eight young men, Sarmad Ahmed, Shahid Butt, Moshin Ghalain, Ghulam Hussain, Ayaz Hussein, Mohammed Mustafa Kamel, Shazad Nabi, and Malik Nasser, were accused of belonging to a group called Supporters of Sharia (SoS), run by Abu Hamza, a mysterious London-based militant cleric. The Yemeni authorities claimed the men were caught with mines, rocket launchers, dynamite, guns, satellite phones and laptop computers, and said they had travelled to Yemen for military training and to launch a bombing campaign against the British consulate in Aden, two hotels and the local Anglican church.[44] Some of the men also allegedly travelled to Albania in 1997 for military weapons training. Video cassettes were seized by the Yemeni authorities that purportedly showed the men playing with hand grenades. In early August 1999 they were all convicted and several were sentenced to long jail-terms.

Although Yemeni intelligence officers are not averse to making inventive claims about their suspects, and the Britons protested they were tortured and raped in custody, the arrests did draw attention to a shadowy network recruiting young British Muslims for military training, both in the UK and abroad. Up to 2,000 British Muslims are now believed to have received military training each year between 1995 and 1998, involving learning survival arts and unarmed combat in Britain (where obtaining firearms is extremely difficult), and receiving weapons training in countries such as Yemen, Pakistan and Sudan. Some of the Britons are believed to have fought with the Bosnian Muslims against the Serbs in the former Yugoslavia. But the majority were far removed from the normal image of militant Muslims: they were not Afghan Arabs, hardened veterans of the war in Afghanistan; rather the new recruits were British citizens, young men drawn inexorably to the flame of militancy.

The revelations were news as much to the vast majority of British Muslims as they were to the general public, investigative journalists, and most sections of the police and intelligence services. However the security services had known of the links between Abu Hamza, head of Supporters of Shariah, and Osama bin Laden. The two men probably met in Afghanistan during the 1980s. Hamza arrived in Britain to study engineering in the 1970s and claims to be a veteran of the war (he has metal claws for his hands, which he says were lost during the fighting). He preached at the mosque in Finsbury Park, north London, and openly professed sympathy and even support for bin Laden. There was clear evidence of connections between bin Laden and supporters in Britain, and the British police sensibly took no chances. In October 1998 a team of élite detectives from SO13, Scotland Yard's anti-terrorist branch, arrested and questioned seven men with alleged links to bin Laden, including Khalid Al-Fauwaz.

Despite the scale of his organization, the future for Osama bin Laden himself looks bleak. He cannot stay in Afghanistan for ever, and Western agents and mercenaries operating covertly from bases in

Peshawar will eventually capture or kill him. The only question is how much damage he will do before then, and whether the fire he has lit under Western–Islamic relations can be quenched. Many militant Islamists claim we are witnessing only the beginning of a new struggle.

'They have developed Osama bin Laden as a champion, as a symbol of Islam for all young people, in the whole Muslim world,' said Hassan al-Turabi, one of the leaders of Sudan.[45] 'Even if they reach him and they kill him, they will generate thousands of bin Ladens, thousands of them.'

Turabi has a point: killing bin Laden could prompt a catastrophic response from his followers. Although the links between al Qaeda and other militant organizations are often vague and based on nothing more than a common religion and a mutual hatred of America, there is no doubting the strength of bin Laden's support. 'It is a challenge to the entire Muslim world . . . bin Laden is a hero of the Muslim world. If anything happens to him, America will be responsible,' said Omar Warsi, a leader of Sipah-e-Sahaba ('Army of the Companions of the Prophets'), the militant Pakistani Sunni Muslim group of which Ramzi Yousef was an active member.[46] After the American cruise missile attacks on bin Laden, Sipah-e-Sahaba is understood to have promised him the help and protection of 10,000 armed fighters.[47]

There are many more bin Laden fighters living freely in the West, prepared to attack if their leader is threatened. 'The reason we don't talk about [sleeper agents] is because it would scare the hell out of people. There may be a large number of people that we are not aware of,' said Marvin Cetron, a terrorism expert and the author of the Pentagon's highly classified 'Terror 2000' report.[48]

So killing bin Laden may be just as dangerous as allowing him to remain alive. Either way the West must try to prevent more terrorist attacks, and while police and law enforcement agents have certainly prevented several since the east Africa bombings, they must be lucky every time.

Bin Laden's group has several factors working in its favour which lead many analysts to believe it is now just a matter of time before another massive terrorist attack. The first is its structure: however quickly Western investigators unravel one element of al Qaeda and the global Islamist movement, another will uncoil, simply because a broadly based terrorist organization without a rigid central command structure is often impossible to contain.

The second is the size of its support base: bin Laden already had thousands of trained fighters before the American missile attacks; now he has been deluged with volunteers, and camps on the borders between Afghanistan and Pakistan are once again swelling with young militants eager for jihad.

Perhaps the most immediate danger is bin Laden's own burning ambition – particularly his desire to launch apocalyptic terrorist attacks on the West – and the close links he has formed recently with Saddam Hussein, the renegade Iraqi leader.

In pursuit of his apocalyptic aims, Osama bin Laden has been determinedly pursuing ownership of weapons of mass destruction ever since he moved to Sudan in 1991. 'In my personal view [bin Laden] is very much interested in obtaining weapons of mass destruction and he has the money to pay for them,' said Peter Probst, a senior terrorism expert at the Pentagon.[49] With the help of a small coterie of his senior lieutenants and a small group of engineers and Western-educated physicists in the Sudanese government, bin Laden initially plotted to build an atomic bomb.[50]

Central to his scheme, according to Western intelligence sources, was a plot to buy highly enriched uranium, a crucial ingredient, from the former Soviet Union.[51] 'We don't consider it a crime if we tried to have nuclear, chemical, biological weapons,' bin Laden has said, appearing to confirm the Western claims.[52] 'Our holy land is occupied by Israeli and American forces. We have the right to defend ourselves and to liberate our holy land.' He added: 'acquiring weapons for the defence of Muslims is a religious duty. If I have indeed acquired these [atomic] weapons, then I thank God for enabling me to do so. And if I seek to acquire these weapons, I am carrying out a duty. It would be a sin for Muslims not to try to possess the weapons that would prevent the infidels from inflicting harm on Muslims.'[53]

Bin Laden's first serious attempt to obtain weapons of mass destruction began in late 1993, when he allegedly agreed to a plan put to him by several other members of al Qaeda that the group should consider buying a complete nuclear missile or highly enriched uranium from the former Soviet Union.[54] The project was given a green light.

In pursuit of this 'Islamic bomb',[55] one of bin Laden's senior lieutenants is understood to have travelled to at least three Central Asian states to meet with officials suggested as good contacts, probably by bin Laden's friends in Pakistani intelligence (Pakistan had its own relatively sophisticated nuclear programme). On and off for the next year the lieutenant shuttled between bin Laden's base in Sudan, Middle Eastern capitals and cities and towns in the Central Asian states.

Fortunately no intercontinental ballistic missiles were available for immediate sale, and the man from al Qaeda was instead treated as something of a naïve curiosity who could be fleeced of his money. 'One gang offered al Qaeda more than 100kg of enriched uranium, which sent Israeli intelligence into spasms of panic,' said a British source.[56] 'But it was just a con. The uranium was actually low-grade fuel from a nuclear reactor that could never have been used in a nuclear bomb.'

Other al Qaeda emissaries were also sent to Kazakhstan on the same mission, prompting Israel to despatch a senior minister to the country to try to head off any deal. The Israeli intervention appears to have worked in that case, but bin Laden still secured a network of friends and paid accomplices in the former Soviet Central Asian states and the Ukraine.

Al Qaeda was unlikely to get hold of a working nuclear missile (sophisticated technology would anyway be needed to launch it). What was more conceivable, and perhaps only slightly less frightening, was that bin Laden could detonate the warhead of a missile as part of a conventional attack (on Washington or London perhaps), boosting the effect of a bomb and scattering radiation over a large populated area. Such an attack would have devastating physical and psychological consequences.

After al Qaeda's second failure to obtain a nuclear device in Kazakhstan, the organization appears to have changed tactics and shifted countries. Reports emerging from Israel and Russia suggest that bin Laden gave his contacts in the Chechen mafia several million dollars in cash, and heroin with a street value of more than $500 million (£300 million); in exchange the Chechens launched an all-out campaign to obtain 'nuclear suitcase' bombs for al Qaeda.

The existence of these weapons was denied for years by Soviet and then Russian governments, but Western experts now believe they were developed during the Cold War for possible use by Soviet Special Forces or 'sleeper agents' within America and the West.[57] Estimates of their explosive potential vary, but one expert suggests that if detonated under the World Trade Center, one of these suitcase bombs would have destroyed everything within a radius of 250 metres.

Because the Chechens need bin Laden to facilitate their drug deals with the Taliban leadership, they are extremely unlikely to have accepted his money and his heroin if they were unable to supply the suitcase bombs. According to one senior American intelligence source close to America's bin Laden investigation, officials from al Qaeda, or possibly senior members of the Taliban, obtained several of the nuclear suitcase bombs in the autumn of 1998, and transferred them into storage in the Taliban's main secure complex near Kandahar in Afghanistan.[58]

There appears to be some confusion, however, within the intelligence community over whether the bombs are still programmed with a Soviet-era coding system that requires a signal from Moscow before detonation is possible. The Russian government refuses to comment on the allegations, but by early 1999 there were strong rumours in the Central Asian states that Chechen rebels (in this case, the mafia) were hoping to recruit former Soviet Special Forces. It is possible al Qaeda or the Taliban need these recruits to explain and work the coded control system of the suitcase bombs.

However, even if they fail to get the suitcase bombs working, bin Laden, or rather, his supporters, are believed to have already successfully obtained chemical and biological weapons. According to a British intelligence source privy to the records of Egyptian interrogations of captured Afghan Arabs, members of al Qaeda operating from Albania have obtained phials of anthrax and the lethal viral agent botulism from a laboratory in the Czech Republic for $7,500 a sample.[59] Representatives of the Moro National Liberation Front in the Philippines, which has close links to al Qaeda, are also understood to have obtained anthrax 'in some form' from an Indonesian pharmaceutical company.[60] The quantities obtained are unknown.

The problem for the Islamists, including bin Laden and al Qaeda, has been perfecting a system of delivering these weapons on to their target. By early 1999, however, Osama bin Laden was in the process of forging a secret alliance with Saddam Hussein, an alliance that may yet see the terrorist acting as an arm of vengeance for the despot and Iraqi scientists assisting in the development of terrorist weapons of mass destruction. It is a prospect that appals Western analysts and intelligence agents. 'Bin laden has money and he has followers. The worst thing would be if he links up with Saddam Hussein,' said Marvin Cetron.[61]

Contact was first made between the two sides in the early 1990s, when Hassan al-Turabi put bin Laden in contact with operatives from the Mukhabarat (the Iraqi Secret Service).[62] The meeting was unproductive, but in 1993, when bin Laden was living in Sudan and there were the first signs of pressure on him to leave, Iraqi agents visited him at his house in Khartoum and offered him sanctuary in Baghdad. Bin Laden rejected their offer, almost certainly because of his contempt for Saddam Hussein's secular Ba'athist regime.

However contacts between bin Laden and Iraq were maintained by representatives of the Iranian terror group MKO, which has its headquarters near Baghdad, and wanted to use bin Laden and the Taliban to incite violence on the border between Iran and Afghanistan – just as they had used Ramzi Yousef. Their contacts appear to have worked, because bin Laden then began expressing open support for Iraq in his public comments. 'The British and the American people loudly declared their support for their leaders' decision to attack Iraq,' bin Laden announced in December 1998 in the Arab newspaper *Asharq al Awsat*. According to his logic, this made it imperative that all Muslims 'confront, fight and kill' Britons and Americans.

Just as his comments were being digested in the Arab world, Saddam Hussein's son Qusayy, who by December 1998 was responsible for much of Iraqi intelligence operations, despatched Farouk Hijazi, a senior Iraqi intelligence officer newly appointed as ambassador to Turkey, to meet with bin Laden. Hijazi allegedly flew to Pakistan and travelled into Afghanistan with a colleague and a local guide to meet first with Mullah Omar and then personally with bin Laden.[63] According to an American intelligence source, at the meeting on 21 December 1998, Hijazi, who was formerly director of external operations for Iraqi intelligence, 'first offered bin Laden asylum in Iraq, and then put forward a list of targets' bin Laden might consider attacking, including Radio Free Europe, based in Prague, which beams anti-Saddam propaganda directly into Iraq.[64] Hijazi is also said to have given bin Laden a 'collection' of blank Yemeni diplomatic passports – worth more than gold to an exiled militant – as a gift and sign of Baghdad's good faith.

'That [meeting] was followed by further meetings between approximately three senior Iraqi intelligence agents and a small number of bin Laden's lieutenants in Khartoum, Sudan, in mid-January 1999,' according to the source.[65] Iraq had moved several tonnes of precursor chemicals for chemical weapons into Sudan for storage just before the outbreak of the Gulf war and Western intelligence agents feared Iraq could covertly assist bin Laden's chemists in the construction of crude chemical weapons using 'ingredients' stored in Sudan.

Bin Laden certainly seems to have begun mobilizing his men in support of Iraq by the end of 1998. According to the Kuwaiti police several hundred Afghan Arabs connected to al Qaeda began receiving military training in southern Iraq at the end of 1998, with the intention that they would conduct a terrorist campaign along the Kuwaiti border. The plot was foiled after Kuwaiti intelligence arrested a terrorist 'cell' of 25 Egyptian militants in the first weeks of January 1999.

Bin Laden also appears to have mobilized his followers in Yemen in support of Iraq: Scotland Yard detectives and FBI agents who investigated the kidnap of 16 British, American and Australian tourists in the country in late December 1998 are convinced the motive was to use the men and women as a 'human shield'. The kidnappers were armed with sophisticated weapons including rocket-propelled grenades, a satellite phone and laptop computer, and were allegedly trained in bin Laden's camps and undertook the operation on the direct orders of senior members of al Qaeda. Warnings were to be issued that the tourists would be killed if there were further air attacks on Iraq; however, a shoot-out with the Yemeni military ended with the deaths of several of the tourists and the capture of the group's leader.

With America breathing down bin Laden's neck and the Taliban quietly hoping he will leave Afghanistan, the Saudi dissident may soon have to ask Saddam Hussein to return the favour and give him asylum. Bin Laden seems to be running out of places to hide. In late February 1999 he went missing within Afghanistan, hiding with a small group of his closest supporters (including Ayman al-Zawahiri) in the desolate north of the country, and seems to have spent the next few months debating where to go next. Bin Laden would personally like to stay in Afghanistan and hide in a major new command headquarters his men are building in vast caves in the Pamir mountains near the border with Tajikistan.

Another possibility is that bin Laden will try to return to his ancestral lands in southern Yemen (he had been quietly cultivating contacts with the powerful Sanhane tribe for precisely this purpose). But the Yemeni authorities would never be able to protect bin Laden, even if they wanted to, from concerted American and Saudi attention.

Another bolt-hole could be the former-Soviet republic of Chechnya, devastated by years of war, where bin Laden forged alliances with militia groups and the ferocious mafia, helping them to obtain 'rights' over the Afghan heroin trade in return for money and sophisticated weaponry. Or perhaps Dagestan, where hundreds of Afghan Arabs had gathered in the Kadar–Bunyakisk–Karamaki 'triangle' by spring 1999.[66] By August 1999 the fighters had begun battling against Russian troops in pursuit of their aim of turning Dagestan into an independent Islamic state. Egyptian fundamentalists even suggested he have plastic surgery and move to one of four towns in Upper Egypt – al-Minya, Asyut, Suhaj or Qina – where he could hide with other militants.[67] But bin Laden will never find security in Yemen, Chechnya or Egypt, or, for that matter, Libya or Sudan. He may have no choice but to put aside his contempt for Saddam Hussein's regime and move to Baghdad.

By early 1999 there were signs that old differences between Iraq and Islamic militants were being laid quietly to one side in preparation for bin Laden's move. A link between Hussein and bin Laden could be part of Saddam Hussein's 'grand plan' to ignite global Islamic anger against the West. On 5 January 1999, Hussein marked Iraq's Army Day with a violent speech in which he called on Arabs and Muslims to rise up and revolt against their governments and the West. With his new apocalyptic vision, which he apparently agreed with his sons Qusayy and Udayy in November 1998, Hussein also won over former enemies among Islamic militants in London. By February 1999, several of these groups were diluting their previously anti-Hussein rhetoric and preparing their supporters for a full conversion to the righteousness of Hussein's war on the West.

Hussein, meanwhile, was busy wooing other terrorists, seducing them into his new alliance. One of his first moves was to forge an alliance with Abu Nidal, who was responsible for dozens of international bombings and assassinations and was the most feared terrorist in the world before the mantle passed to Ramzi Yousef and Osama bin Laden. In the summer of 1998 Nidal moved from Sudan to Baghdad, and was quickly joined by more than fifty of his followers from Palestinian refugee camps in Lebanon and Syria. If Saddam Hussein pursues his vision of a war between Muslims and Christians, he will try to encourage Abu Nidal and Osama bin Laden to fight on his side. It is hard to imagine a more deadly triumvirate.

References

[1] US indictment: S(2)98 Cr. 1023 (LBS), and author interview with American investigators.

[2] Ibid, and Karl Vick, 'A Plot Both Wide And Deep', *Washington Post*, 23 November 1998.

[3] Author interview with a CIA official.

[4] US indictment, op. cit.

[5] Author interview with an American investigator.

[6] Tim Weiner, 'Tracking Terrorists: Too Many Blind Alleys', *International Herald Tribune*, 13 August 1998.

[7] Simon Kaheru and Ofwono-Opondo, 'Terrorists Name City Targets', *New Vision*, Uganda, 25 September 1998.

[8] Author interview with an American investigator. A question-mark hangs over the veracity of Odeh's interrogation by Pakistani investigators.

[9] Ibid.

[10] Ibid.

[11] Ibid.

[12] Author interview with retired CIA official.

[13] Ibid.

[14] Anon, 'Survivors report huge fireball in missile strike', AFP, 22 August 1998.

[15] John Sweeney, 'From the bazaars to the hillsides, they see a long war looming', *Observer*, 30 August 1998.

[16] Abdelhari Atwan, interview with Osama bin Laden.

[17] Rahimullah Yusufzai, 'Mission: "Get Osama"', *The News*, 8 November 1998.

[18] Marie Colvin, 'The Radical New Face of World Terror', *Sunday Times*, 30 August 1998.

[19] Raymond Close, Hard Target, *Washington Post*, 30 August 1998.

[20] Author interview with American investigator.

[21] *Aka* Sidi al-Madani al-Ghazi Mustafa al-Tayyib, *aka* Sidi Tayyib, *aka* Abu Fadel, *aka* Mohammad bin Moisalih.

[22] Author interview with American investigator.

[23] Author interview with Stanley E. Morris.

[24] Ibid., and Jack Nelson, 'US Moves to Seize Assets of Main Terrorist Suspect', *Los Angeles Times*, 22 August 1998.

[25] Author interview.

[26] Ibid.

[27] Bruce B. Auster and David E. Kaplan, 'Saudi royalty gives money to bin Laden', *US News & World Report*, 19 October 1998.

[28] For more on the Yemeni denial see the Bahraini *Al-Ayam* newspaper, 25 August 1998, which quotes senior official sources in Sana-a.

[29] Author interview with CIA official.

[30] Author interview.

[31] Author interview with an American intelligence source.

[32] Ibid.

[33] Based on a briefing paper prepared by French intelligence on the February 1999 trial of Mohamed Berrached, in the Kabylie region of Algeria, and passed to a British intelligence source interviewed by the author.

[34] Who has since been killed.

[35] French briefing paper, op. cit.

36 Author interview with British intelligence source.

37 Ibid.

38 Ibid.

39 Ibid.

40 Ibid.

41 Author interview with British intelligence source basing his information on the interrogation of al-'Attar by Egyptian police.

42 Author interview with source basing his information on the confessions of Ahmad 'Uthman Isma'il, a militant arrested in Albania and handed back to Egyptian security police.

43 Author interview with American intelligence source. Confirmed by several reports in the Albanian newspaper *Shekulli* during November 1998.

44 Marie Colvin and Dipesh Gadher, 'Britain's Islamic Army', *Sunday Times*, 17 January 1998.

45 Jane Corbin, 'Osama bin Laden', *Panorama*, BBC Television, October 1998.

46 Kathy Gannon, 'Bin Laden "hero" to some who warn US against his capture', Associated Press, 5 November 1992.

47 Author interview with American intelligence source.

48 Author interview with Marvin Cetron.

49 Author interview with Peter Probst.

50 Information for this section is sourced from author interviews with several Western intelligence sources.

51 Author interview with German source.

52 Jamal Ismail, 'I am not afraid of death', *Newsweek*, 11 January 1999.

53 Rahimullah Yusufzai, 'Conversation with Terror', *Time*, 11 January 1998.

54 Author interview with American intelligence source.

55 According to an American investigator this term has been used during interviews of arrested members of al Qaeda.

56 Author interview.

57 Alexander Lebed, Russia's former national security chief, prompted shudders around the world in 1997 when he confirmed that mini-nuclear weapons or 'suitcase bombs' existed, and said that up to a hundred had gone missing.

58 Author interview.

59 Author interview. The source refused to name the laboratory.

60 Author interview with American investigator.

61 Author interview with Marvin Cetron.

62 Author interview with American intelligence source.

63 Author interviews with American and Pakistani sources, and Riyad 'Alam-al-Din, 'Bin Laden and Iraq', *Al Watan Al Arabi*, 1 January 1999. Guido Olimpio, 'A Secret Pact with bin Laden, the terror Sheikh', *Corriere della Sera*, 28 December 1998.

64 Author interview.

65 Author interview with American intelligence source.

66 Ibid.

67 Khalid Sharaf-al-Din, 'Bin Laden backed-down on entering Egypt', *Al-Sharq al-Awsat*, 8 March 1999.

ELEVEN

Militant Islam

AMID THE rush to hold all Muslims responsible for the crimes of self-proclaimed fundamentalists such as Osama bin Laden, it is perhaps worth considering the real scale of the threat Islamic militancy poses to Western democracies and world peace.

There are more than one billion followers of the Prophet Mohammad on the planet, and the vast majority want global harmony and reconciliation between different religious groups. A tiny proportion of this number have taken up arms and launched themselves against the West but in waging the holy war these terrorists believe they are reversing a Christian tradition that began with the Crusades.

While these militants may view themselves as holy warriors, to the West they are little different from the communists who haunted the free world during the Cold War. The similarities are striking. Islam is the world's only major political religion: it makes no distinction between religion and state, and covers every aspect of life. Communists and Islamic terrorists are both, it seems, highly organized, highly trained, and determined – at any cost – to destroy the Western way of life. With the fall of the Berlin Wall and the collapse of the Soviet empire, Western media and politicians have been hunting for a new enemy. Now it is Muslims who are deemed to be the danger.

While such stereotyping is deeply insulting to Muslims, it would be foolhardy to deduce that the minority of Muslims who can be broadly identified as 'Islamic fundamentalist' do not pose a serious threat. According to Neil Herman, who spent more than two decades investigating terrorism for the FBI in New York, Islamic fundamentalism is indeed the greatest terrorist threat to the West. Peter Probst, a special-ist on international terrorism with the Pentagon's secretive Special Operations and Low-Intensity Conflict Office, and eight other senior intelligence and terrorism experts from Britain, Germany and the US also agree.[1]

Furious at US support for Israel and what they see as double-stan-dards in American treatment of the Palestinians, outraged by the presence of Western troops in Saudi Arabia and the military and economic attacks on Iraq, and brought together by the globalization of militant Islam in recent years, Muslim extremists are growing in numbers. The threat is increasing.

Among those who characterize themselves as Islamic fighters there are three broad strands of militancy.[2] The first consists of groups tradi-tionally supported by Iran, which nestle under the umbrella of Hezbollah, an international organization with branches, offices and supporters in at least seventeen countries around the world. Hezbollah has had the avowed intention of fighting against Israeli forces since it seized parts of southern Lebanon. The bulk of its support and membership is drawn from Shiite Muslims, although within its ranks there are Sunnis and even several hundred Christians who have converted to Islam.

The second grouping consists of the Afghan Arabs, the fighters who travelled from across the Islamic world to Afghanistan in the 1980s to fight the Soviet invaders. Osama bin Laden heads al Qaeda, the main Afghan Arab group, but there are at least five others based in Afghanistan and led by Safwat Abdel-Ghani, Talaat Yassin Hammam, Muhammad Mekkawi, Talaat Fouad Qassem, and Muhammad Muhieddin, who has created his own little empire inside Afghanistan with the help of several hundred followers and local tribesmen. These leaders swear no allegiance to bin Laden, indeed they are still declar-ing 'fatwas' on each other and fighting their own internecine wars.

The third strand of Islamic militancy is the broadest, comprising more than a hundred groups and gangs, many of which have national-specific agendas. These groups have their bases in such countries as Albania, Algeria, Bosnia, Brunei, Chechnya, Dagestan, the Central Asian republics, India, Indonesia, Malaysia, Pakistan and the Philippines.

Despite the widely differing nature of their campaigns, it would be wrong to imagine these groups have no co-ordination. Representatives of Hezbollah meet early each year in Tehran, the

Iranian capital, for a short conference. The different Afghan Arab groups have all sent representatives to meetings in Khartoum, Sudan, organized by Hassan al-Turabi's National Islamic Front and also attended by radicals from Algeria, Egypt, Libya and Tunisia. Even many members of the third strand, the most disparate of all, have met and plotted together at huge conferences held in Dallas, Texas, in 1988 and 1990. The Dallas meetings were the largest of their kind ever held, hosting more of the world's radical Muslims than had ever previously assembled under one roof. The different strands also send representatives to meetings of the other strands.[3]

The aim of men such as Osama bin Laden is now to harness these disparate groups, with their widely differing aims, into a broad coalition with one central objective: to attack the West. In trying to build this coalition bin Laden has been assisted by the communications revolution and globalization, which is not only a powerful force in popular culture and the world economy, but is an important trend in the international Islamist movement. For example, the 18th convention of the Islamic Group of Pakistan (Al-Jama'ah al-Islamiyyah), held in Islamabad between 23 and 25 October 1998 was attended by delegates from more than thirty other militant Islamic organizations. 'All of them spoke about their countries, their movements and the need to unify the message of the Muslims,' according to Ibrahim Ghosheh, the spokesman for Hamas (the Palestinian terrorist group) in Jordan, who was attending the conference for the first time, and wrote a report on it for the December issue of the London-based *Filastin al-Muslimah*, Hamas's main publication.[4]

As these militant groups unify, so they pose more of a threat to fragile governments. 'We can see several countries where [Islamists] now threaten to effect a take-over,' said a US intelligence source.[5] The most serious example is obviously Afghanistan, where the Taliban have nearly strangled the entire country. But Afghanistan is one of the most insular nations on earth. Even if the Taliban took complete control of the country and continued with their repressive policies, the West would feel little of the pain, although heroin from the region kills and hospitalizes thousands of addicts around the globe.[6] The main victims of the Taliban will be the Afghanis, nearly 19 million souls who have suffered as much in recent decades as any people on earth.[7]

Afghanistan's neighbour, Pakistan, however, is not an insular nation, but a powerful nuclear-armed state courted and cajoled by the

West. It is an important Western trading partner with armed forces totalling more than 587,000, and another 513,000 in reserve.[8] It is also a nation heading inexorably towards the establishment of a militant Islamic system of government.[9] In March 1999 President Rafiq Tarar, a religious conservative and former judge, was openly urging a speedy change to Islamic government, including the segregation of men and women. According to the former Prime Minister Benazir Bhutto, if Pakistan adopts a hard-line Islamic system of government, the consequences for the majority of Pakistanis will be dire.[10] 'The Western powers think they are the only ones confronting Osama bin Laden and his kind, but it is not just a battle between the Islamists and the West, it's a battle between the majority of Muslims and the Islamists,' she said. 'They want to totally control our way of life, what we wear, what we do, what we think.'

The establishment of an Afghan-style government in Pakistan could destabilize the entire region and swiftly lead to conflict with neighbouring India. The two countries have fought three wars in the last 50 years, and many analysts and intelligence experts warn that the next conflict between the two states, perhaps over the disputed province of Kashmir, could swiftly escalate into the world's first nuclear war. By late May and June 1999 these fears appeared to have some justification, as the conflict in Kashmir degenerated into rocket and air-strikes on both sides.

Pakistan's transition to militancy may be unstoppable because it is being encouraged by the alumni of thousands of small madrassas, or religious schools, originally established in the country during the Afghan war by the late Pakistani military dictator General Mohammed Zia-al Haq. Zia rightly supposed the schools could be a useful source of young fodder for the Afghan front, but when the war ended and the Soviets left, the religious schools remained. Pakistan, a country with endemic political corruption, high unemployment, political apathy and a fragile democracy, already had a void in the education sector left by the lack of a decent state system: religious schools filled the gap. With obscure sources of funding (often businesses affiliated to the schools and militant Islamic parties and businessmen), their numbers mushroomed. By 1999 more than 4,000 religious schools were registered with the Pakistani government, teaching more than 540,000 students.[11]

Many poor families send their children to the schools because they know they will be fed and looked after. But the children spend their days learning the Koran and praying, and receive little in the way of a formal education. They leave the schools with only a rudimentary knowledge of the world, but a fanatical belief in the supremacy of Islam and their responsibility to fight and ensure its spread. Many retain military connections with their schools.

It is a situation that worries Benazir Bhutto. Shortly after the American cruise missile strike on Osama bin Laden's bases, Bhutto was travelling on a plane, sitting next to a senior Pakistani militant. 'So I said to him are there people from the madrassas [religious schools] who are going [to support bin Laden], and he said yes,' said Bhutto.[12] 'And I said to him how many people do you have in your madrassas, and he said all together the Pakistani madrassas have 325,000 men under arms. So I said how many went into Afghanistan [during the Afghan war], and he said 75,000.' Bhutto claims she has been told that militants in Pakistan eventually want this huge body of 'soldiers' from the madrassas to replace the official army as some sort of revolutionary guard.

Many political and moderate religious leaders in Pakistan have expressed concern at the huge number of religious schools and their potential to destabilize Pakistan. Nasrullah Babaar, Pakistan's former Interior Minister and police chief, has said they are 'hotbeds of terrorism'.[13] When she was in office Benazir Bhutto tried to restrict their sources of funding, while the current incumbent, Nawaz Sharif, has tried to impose controls over religious school curriculums. Both Prime Ministers were unsuccessful: there are simply too many schools, with too many powerful supporters, and many are effectively hidden in remote parts of the country.

Students leaving these schools are a danger to their own communities, let alone to the country or the wider world. Many of the schools are indoctrinating children with a hatred of America and the West, but they are simultaneously encouraging hatred of other branches of Islam. The streets of Karachi are already riven with factional fighting between rival Sunni and Shiite Muslims, and the only night-time sounds in some districts are the wails of private ambulances collecting the dead from yet another shooting. The city is starting to resemble Beirut during its darkest hours.

Pakistan stands on the brink of an abyss. Its fragile democracy and the lives of its millions of peaceful hard-working citizens are threatened by vociferous militants preaching revolution. Taliban supporters and Islamic militants are gradually infiltrating every stratum of society, including, most worryingly, the army.

According to Benazir Bhutto the Islamists often work through innocuous-looking non-governmental organisations (NGOs).[14] 'They keep making these NGOs because they claim the CIA, during the Afghan war, made NGOs, and the CIA operated through them,' she says.[15] The thinking seems to be that if such subterfuge worked for the CIA it will work for Islamic fundamentalists.

'I didn't realize where the Islamists came from in the beginning,' said Bhutto.[16] 'I thought they were the military, or they were the intelligence services, but then I realized that these Islamist groups are working to try and influence the placing of people within the military, within the intelligence services, within the election commission, and they are creeping towards power in every sphere [of the country].'

This gradual advance of radical Islam ensures another comparison with the Cold War. For decades Western intelligence agencies ran covert operations to prevent communism taking root, like a malignant tumour, in countries such as Italy and France. The same 'domino theory' used during the Cold War to explain the threat of one country, then its neighbours, falling to insidious communism, is now being applied to the spread of militant Islam. If fundamentalists take over in Egypt, so the theory goes, the whole of North Africa and the Middle East will follow. Thus if militants finally complete their take-over of Afghanistan, the Muslim Central Asian states may follow the same path.

'The future for Pakistan is very grim,' said Benazir Bhutto.[17] 'I don't think that a take-over by the Islamists in Pakistan is yet imminent, but I think in the last 10 years they have made tremendous inroads, and given another decade, or perhaps just five years, anything could happen.' According to Bhutto, the Islamists are 'playing a long game'.[18] 'They are not looking for an election, they are looking for a revolution. Their idea is "so what if we have to live like [the] Taliban, at least we'll be left with our honour". But what is honour? Is honour starvation for the people?'

Among moderate Islamic politicians and Western intelligence experts there is now a general consensus that Islamists have identified several countries to target for conversion to a hard-line system of Islamic government. 'I believe Pakistan is the top target [of the Islamists],' confirms a senior American intelligence source.[19] Benazir Bhutto agrees, saying she believes the aim of Islamists is for Pakistan to fall first, and Saudi Arabia to fall second. Most Western analysts seem to believe Egypt is the third target, but Bhutto believes it is actually Turkey.[20]

'And there *is* a "domino effect",' said Bhutto. 'If Pakistan falls then Saudi Arabia will surely be the next one to fall.' Other countries will follow, according to Bhutto: 'After I took over [as Prime Minister for her second term of office in 1993] I had senior Pakistani army and intelligence officers tell me that they wanted a confederation between Pakistan and Afghanistan.' The officers apparently wanted to enter Afghanistan and take the capital, Kabul, by force. 'I vetoed it. They had this dream of going upwards into the Central Asian republics, and I told them that Pakistan cannot have such ambitions, and so they were against me.'

According to Bhutto even Nawaz Sharif, the current Prime Minister, is not safe. 'The Islamists backed Sharif because he promised to make General Hamid Gul the Chief of Army Staff, and pass the Islamic Bill. Now that he has had problems delivering on his promises, the Islamists are turning against him.' Bhutto claims that her sources have told her recently that the Islamists in Pakistan have decided they need to create a moral and social vacuum by killing 100,000 people in the country 'to destroy the institutions in Pakistan so that a revolution takes place'. In this scenario Pakistan will turn into another Algeria – a country riven by terrorist massacres. 'They have got a whole agenda,' she said.[21]

Bhutto has been given a chilling warning of Pakistan's future. 'One man said to me, "Remember there will only be those who believe and those who will die. There will only be the dead and the believers." '[22]

If fundamentalism does spread from Afghanistan to Pakistan and the Central Asian states, it will be a process that takes several more years. Central Asia has felt the influence of Islam for more than a thousand years, but it has usually cohabited with local cultural practices and customs: the first sense of identity possessed by people in the region is usually loyalty to their tribe or region. Within the new republics of the former Soviet Union, fundamentalism, indeed Islam as a whole, has made little headway.

A greater threat to global security, perhaps, is posed by the possible resurgence of fundamentalism in powerful, strategically important countries such as Egypt, or oil-rich states such as Saudi Arabia.

Hosni Mubarak, the current Egyptian President, has no natural successor, and when he retires or dies there appears to be no one capable of taking his place and leading the country as a secular society. 'Egypt will fall soon enough,' said a veteran American intelligence official.[23] 'Everything [President] Mubarak does [to stop the Islamists] is just delaying the inevitable.' The American source believes the world could soon witness a new Cold War, but this time one pitting secular democracies against autocratic Islamic nations. 'We [the US] were victorious against communism, but this will be the struggle for liberty that dominates world politics well into the next century, and I think we've lost the fight already,' said the man wearily. 'It's just a matter of time.'

Some experts believe that such warnings are melodramatic, given the ferocity with which the Egyptian government has attempted to crush the Islamist movement. Since 1991 more than 100,000 Islamists have been detained without trial in Egypt and squashed into the country's crowded jails. By the beginning of June 1999 officials were quietly voicing the belief that Mubarak had won the battle with the Islamists. The conviction and sentencing to death, in absentia, of nine prominent fundamentalists, coupled with the trial in April 1999 of 107 more, seemed to convince Mubarak he was in control. He even released 1,300 low-level suspected fundamentalists from jail.

Mubarak's complacency is dangerous, because the Islamists will never give up their struggle to convert Egypt into an Islamic state. The permanent nature of their global fight was set out as far back as 1968: 'Jihad will never end. It will last until the Day of Judgement,' according to the eminent Sheikh Muhammad Abu-Zahra.

There can be no doubt that an Islamist take-over in Egypt would have far-reaching consequences. Many intelligence experts predict it could have a greater impact on global politics than the 1979 Iranian Islamic revolution. Iran is dominated by Shiite Muslims, the minority sect in the Islamic world, while Egypt, by contrast, has the largest population of any Arab state, and is the world's leading centre of Sunni Muslim learning – its Al-Azhar University is the oldest and most prestigious Islamic university on earth. So a take-over in Egypt by fundamentalists, even if it was by democratic vote, would shatter other Islamic governments around the world.

Saudi Arabia is another leading target for the Islamists. Osama bin Laden, who considers the Saudi rulers to be corrupt Western stooges, has focused on the country for years, and there are now signs the Saudi leadership's power and influence is starting to wane. The Saudi monarchy has specifically tried to draw legitimacy from fundamentalist Islam ever since 3,500 Islamists seized the Grand Mosque in Mecca in 1979. Mullahs on the government payroll denounce the West, the mutuwaeen (the religious police) harass members of the public who fail to stop working or shopping at prayer time, and the government has erected road signs with religious exhortations such as 'God is great'.

However King Fahd is ailing, and many doubt that his likely successor (and the current de facto ruler), Crown Prince Abdullah, can prevent the winds of change blowing through the kingdom. GDP per head in Saudi Arabia is rumoured to have fallen from $15,000 per year a decade ago to as low as $4,000 in 1998; unemployment and discontent is growing among the population, and the regime shows signs of weakness. Vast petroleum revenues that used to earn the nation more than $140 billion a year during the 1980s have now dwindled to just $20 billion a year, according to Western intelligence reports.[24] Saudis who used to travel to smaller Gulf states to party and shop are now being forced into taking employment there, while some are even taking jobs as menial workers – almost unheard of for Saudi citizens. The Saudi government has been forced to announce that at least 80 per cent of every company workforce must be Saudi citizens in a desperate bid to increase employment among its supporters inside the kingdom. The militants smell blood.

Osama bin Laden has not been slow to identify falling oil revenues as a rallying cause. 'Muslims are starving to death and the United States is stealing their oil,' he says.[25] 'Since 1973, the price of petrol has increased only eight dollars per barrel while the prices of other items have gone up three times. The oil prices should also have gone up three times but this did not happen.' According to bin Laden the price of American wheat has increased threefold but the price of Arab oil has increased by no more than a few dollars over a period of 24 years – 'because the United States is dictating to the Arabs at gunpoint'. Bin Laden claims that over the last 13 years the United States has caused Arab nations a loss of more than $1,100 billion. 'We must get this money back from the United States,' he said.

The threat from Islamic militants stems not only from their future establishment in countries such as Saudi Arabia, but also from existing regimes. Sudan still sponsors and trains a small number of terrorists, according to Western investigators, although this has dramatically decreased since the days when Osama bin Laden was resident in Khartoum.[26]

Iranian-sponsored terrorism also remains a significant problem, despite the presence of reformist and moderate politicians in Tehran. Hard-liners still dominate the intelligence services and remain committed to funding terrorism, particularly on Israel's northern border. Iran has been linked to several terrorist attacks in the 1990s, including the killing of three leaders of the Iranian Democratic Party of Kurdistan and their translator in an attack on a Berlin restaurant in 1992, the bombing of the Israeli embassy in Buenos Aires in March of the same year, an assassination attempt on Jaques Kimche, a prominent Jewish leader, in Istanbul in June 1993, and the bombing of a Jewish community centre in Buenos Aires in July 1994, which killed 96 people and wounded more than 200.

Investigations into the Berlin restaurant killings, which were conducted in a brazen fashion reminiscent of a gangland 'hit', revealed the full extent of the Iranian terror operation in Europe. According to investigations by the German Bundesamt für Verfassungsschutz (BfV), the internal intelligence service, the Iranians established a special operations centre in 1986 to co-ordinate terrorism in Europe from the sixth floor of their Bonn embassy, run by a permanent staff of 20 élite 'Revolutionary Guards'.[27]

However, the signs emerging from Tehran since the landslide victory of Mohammad Khatami, a Shiite Muslim theologian and scholar of Western philosophy, in the 1997 presidential elections, have been overwhelmingly positive. 'The world is tired of seeing the perpetuation of violence and terrorism,' said President Khatami during a landmark visit to Italy in March 1999, the first state visit by an Iranian leader to a Western nation since the Islamic revolution in 1979.[28] 'The world, now more than at any other time, needs peace and concord.' American politicians may be wary of embracing a country they have spent two decades turning into a pariah nation, but US analysts remain more confident: 'there are signs Iran is scaling-back its covert operations,' says a senior American analyst and terrorism expert grudgingly.

However the backing Iran gives to many terrorist groups, such as the Lebanon-based Hezbollah (amounting financially to perhaps $7–10 million every month), continues. Hezbollah has been linked to the bombing of a US Marine barracks in 1983, bombings of two American embassy buildings and kidnappings of more than fifty foreigners. By the late 1990s it had moderated its position slightly, and thus become a stronger political force, but it remains a serious threat to peace in southern Lebanon.

While established groups launch and fund attacks around the world, other groups are now successfully infiltrating a country some analysts see as one of the world's future religious battlegrounds: the United States. Until the 1993 World Trade Center bombing the FBI saw little threat to domestic American security from Muslim extremists. But even after the New York attack the intelligence services have been unable to prevent militant groups establishing themselves in the US. According to Oliver 'Buck' Revell, former Associate Deputy Director of the FBI, 'the United States is the most preferred and easiest place in the world for radical Islamic groups to set up their headquarters to wage war in their homelands, destabilize and attack American allies . . .'[29]

Groups now known to have established themselves in the US include: Hamas, Islamic Jihad, Hezbollah, Hizba-Tahrir (the Islamic Liberation Party), the Algerian Islamic Salvation Front and Armed Islamic Group, En-Nahda of Tunisia, the Muslim Brotherhood, Egyptian Ga'mat Islamiya, Abu Sayyaf Group, followers of Osama bin Laden, the Afghan Taliban and Jamat Muslimeen (from Pakistan and Bangladesh).[30]

Hamas has a particularly strong presence in the US, and is believed to have developed the largest network of all militant Islamic organizations in the country. 'Its origins go back to 1981 when it started in Plainfield, Indiana,' according to Steven Emerson, one of the foremost experts on terrorism in the US.[31] Today, Hamas has offices, branch chapters or a major presence in more than twenty American towns and cities.[32]

Islamic militants pose a serious challenge to the intelligence services. 'What makes these groups so troublesome is that they hide under a religion, do not have a traditional linear hierarchy, speak a foreign language and generally go about as far as they can in pushing the limits of the law without our being able to track them when and if they go over the line,' said Oliver Revell.[33] Revell understands the threat better than most, but he has a more worrying thesis: the agenda of Muslim terrorist groups in the United States, he says, 'is to not only build their infrastructure and raise funds but also to be in position to ultimately move against the United States.'

References

[1] Author interviews.

[2] Author interview with American intelligence source.

[3] Ibid.

[4] Translated by Reuven Paz of the Israeli International Policy Institute for Counter-Terrorism (ICT), and published as ICT research paper: 'Islamic Groups, the International Connection', 3 January 1999.

[5] Author interview.

[6] Afghanistan is the world's biggest producer of the drug after Myanmar, formerly known as Burma.

[7] Population based on 1994 UN estimate.

[8] Source: *Jane's*; also quoted by Rahul Bedi and Ahmed Rashid, 'Change of tactics in India's battle to oust guerrillas from Kashmir', *Daily Telegraph*, 27 May 1999.

[9] Author interview with a CIA official.

[10] Author interview with Benazir Bhutto.

[11] Author interview with Pakistani intelligence source.

[12] Author interview with Benazir Bhutto.

[13] Kathy Gannon, 'Boys learn their beliefs may require violent defense', *Salt Lake Tribune*, 11 October 1998.

[14] Author interview with Benazir Bhutto.

[15] Ibid.

[16] Ibid.

[17] Ibid.

[18] Ibid.

[19] Author interview.

[20] Author interview with Benazir Bhutto.

[21] Ibid.

[22] Ibid.

[23] Author interview.

[24] Author interview with an American intelligence source.

[25] Hamid Mir, interview with Osama bin Laden, Pakistan, 18 March 1997.

[26] Author interview with retired CIA official.

[27] Con Coughlin, 'Focus on the Middle East: Terror HQ', *Sunday Telegraph*, 21 April 1996. Germany initially ignored the operation because of its important trading links with Iran (until the mid-1990s Germany was Iran's second-largest trading partner, earning the country more than $2.5 billion a year), however the restaurant massacre prompted a crackdown: a warrant was even issued for the arrest of Ali Fallahian, the minister in charge of Iran's foreign intelligence services.

[28] Steve Pagani, 'World Is Tired Of Terrorism - Iran's Khatami', Reuters, 10 March 1999.

[29] Quoted by Steven Emerson, prepared statement delivered before the Senate Judiciary Subcommittee on Terrorism, Technology and Government Information, 24 February 1998.

[30] Ibid.

[31] Ibid.

[32] Operating largely but not exclusively under the names the Islamic Association for Palestine and the Holy Land Foundation for Relief and Development.

[33] Steven Emerson, op. cit.

TWELVE

Supermax

A NEW breed of terrorist may be launching themselves against the West, but the career of Ramzi Yousef, the first and most dangerous, ended with his capture in Islamabad in early 1995. Yousef made his first appearance in an American court on 9 February 1995. One of the most dangerous men in the world was off the streets.

The Manhattan Federal Court was ringed with marksmen as Yousef, smiling, clean-shaven, and wearing a smart double-breasted suit, entered the courtroom. He refused a translator, waived his right to have the 11 charges against him read out aloud, and replied 'Not guilty' when District Judge John Keenan asked him for a plea. Yousef spoke fewer than ten words, and then shuffled back to his cell in the top security 9-South wing of New York's Metropolitan Correctional Center (MCC), to await his trial.

Yousef did not take well to incarceration. The wardens at the MCC, part of the same complex where he was due to be tried, had been warned of his extraordinary technical prowess. Marshals from the Bureau of Prisons concluded Yousef was one of the most dangerous prisoners in the entire federal system, and as he sat and paced around in his cell, Yousef was kept under 24-hour observation. Wardens isolated him from other Arabic speakers and removed his personal possessions – wristwatch, shaving cream, toothpaste, coffee creamer, cup and spoon – on the grounds they could be used to fashion miniature bombs. Yet Yousef was still dangerous. The very fact that he was in jail provoked revenge acts of terror.

Within days of his arrest more than twenty of his supporters were arrested in Pakistan to try and discourage retaliation. In Quetta, a special team from the Federal Investigation Agency arrested his friend and supporter Abu Safian when he sold Yousef's house in Quetta, presumably to raise money to support Yousef and his family. Abdul Shakur, Yousef's old friend from Kuwait, was arrested by railway police in Peshawar as he boarded a train for Karachi with baggage containing explosives and half a dozen grenades. According to Pakistani intelligence sources Shakur was handed over to agents working for Rehman Malik's Federal Investigation Agency (FIA). After interviewing Shakur, FIA officials under Malik's command then raided the al-Habib hotel in Islamabad, and discovered more evidence linking Ramzi Yousef's gang to Osama bin Laden and plots against the Saudi government. At the hotel, the agents found pamphlets calling for the overthrow of the House of Saud which had been printed on the Edgware Road in London, then sent to Pakistan, from where a bank of fax machines would send them to scores of militants within Saudi Arabia.

Investigations also continued in the Philippines, and six more suspected Arab terrorists were arrested in Caloocan City in connection with Yousef's plot to assassinate the Pope. All were in their twenties and Filipino security officials alleged that M-16 Armalite rifles, dynamite and detonators were found stored at their safehouse.[1] But direct revenge for Yousef's arrest still followed.

Two US consular workers, Gary C. Durrell, a 45-year-old CIA communications technician, and Jackie Van Landingham, 33, a consulate secretary, were shot dead at traffic lights in Karachi on the morning of 8 March. Marc McCloy, a 31-year-old postal clerk, was wounded in the ankle.

On 19 November the same year the Egyptian embassy in Islamabad was virtually destroyed by a devious two-stage suicide-bomb attack. Fifteen people died in the massive blast, and more than sixty were injured. At the time the Pakistani government intimated it was the work of Islamists and Afghan Arabs working against the regime in Cairo. Now, however, Benazir Bhutto, the former Prime Minister of Pakistan, states: 'We saw the Egyptian embassy bombing not as a destabilizing act, but as direct revenge for the Ramzi [Yousef] extradition.'[2]

Other groups also mobilized to campaign for Yousef's release, including militants in Kashmir who tried to make it a condition of the release of Western hostages: Yousef deserved 'praise and applause' and was a 'great son of Islam' according to Abdul Ahad Waza of the Hizbul Mujaheddin group.[3]

Revenge for the assistance of the Philippines National Police in

Yousef's capture and the arrest of the six other terrorist suspects may have been the motive for an appalling Abu Sayyaf attack on the Christian town of Ipil, north-east of Zamboanga in the southern Philippines, at the beginning of April 1995. More than 200 gunmen killed 53 people, injured hundreds more and burnt half the town. There were even macabre reports of cannibalism, with one hostage claiming he had seen a young boy beheaded, roasted and eaten.[4]

A year after Yousef's arrest prosecutors finally decided it was time to try him in court. There would be two cases: the first for his involvement in the 'Manila Air' case - the Bojinka plot, which resulted in the agonizing death of Haruki Ikegami and could have caused thousands more deaths if Yousef's Manila flat had not caught fire; the second for the World Trade Center bombing.

From the very beginning of his first trial, Yousef never stopped grandstanding. Even during initial jury selection, when he was introduced to a pool of 75 potential jurists, Yousef turned to them, flashed a broad smile, and said: 'Good morning.'

The trial started on 29 May 1996, and the next day Yousef announced he wanted to handle his own defence. He was apparently hoping to 'humanize' himself in the eyes of the jury, to convince them that a polite and decent young chap like him could never have committed such appalling crimes. It was a typical display of Yousef's bravado: the last high-profile defendant to do the same was Carmine Persico, a boss of the Colombo crime family; he was convicted and sentenced to 100 years in prison in the mid-1980s.[5]

'You're making a fool of yourself. I can't be any stronger in telling you the difficulty of what you're doing,' the normally avuncular Judge Kevin Duffy told Yousef. 'You are not going to start delivering a political diatribe', he added. The judge feared Yousef's genius for control and manipulation. 'What he is trying to do is manipulate everybody in the place, including you and me, and he's trying to manipulate the system,' Judge Duffy warned.

'I have no intent of permitting this courtroom to be turned into a circus just to permit you to preen your ego,' Yousef was told. 'Is that understood, sir?'

'Yes, your honour,' Yousef replied with apparent sincerity.

Judge Duffy need not have worried that Yousef would use the courtroom to make political speeches. 'He wasn't loud and aggressive, he was actually quite quiet and appeared to be respectful towards the court,' said Neil Herman. The jury was riveted as Yousef, wearing a conservative dark business suit, delivered a 10-minute statement in a low, quiet voice.

'I want you to keep in mind that even though defendant Yousef is not a US citizen, and doesn't speak the way you speak, that he is a person just like you. Concentrate on the evidence. If you do so, the only just verdict is not guilty,' Yousef told the jury. He was forced to refer to himself in the third person, as 'Mr Yousef', or 'the Defendant' but Yousef still managed to do a passable job of his own defence, saun-tering into the courtroom in Foley Square, southern Manhattan, wear-ing tailored suits resplendent with French cuffs. If he wasn't wearing handcuffs, those watching might have mistaken him for a precocious lawyer.

Despite his lack of legal training, he even managed to elicit confir-mation from Maria Delacruz, the air stewardess on the PAL plane Yousef bombed, that the US government had promised to relocate her and her parents in the US and help her to find a job if she agreed to testify.

For the FBI, the trial was a mammoth undertaking. The Materials and Devices Unit, part of the FBI Laboratory based in J. Edgar Hoover headquarters in Washington D.C., conducted approximately 5,000 examinations in connection with the case and put forward more than 1,000 exhibits for the trial, including Yousef's Toshiba laptop computer, digital watches, airline tickets, and charred plastic and metal fragments from the PAL plane.[6] Some of the evidence was mind-numbing in its detail, such as comparisons of the precise percentages of tin found in solder from the watch used in the PAL bomb attack, and solder found on timing devices in Yousef's hotel rooms in Manila and Islamabad.

The case was an extraordinary legal event. It involved allegations of terrorist attacks and planned atrocities committed outside the United States, the death and injury of non-American citizens, plots against the Pope in the Philippines; and yet the trial was taking place thousands of miles away in southern Manhattan because the case involved plots against American airliners.

Yet if any of the jury felt the case involved strange foreigners and strange places far removed from their own lives, that sense was shat-tered on 17 July 1996, when TWA 800 plunged into the ocean off Long Island en route from New York's JFK airport to Paris, killing all 230 passengers and crew. Dozens of FBI agents who began investigating the disaster initially thought the Boeing 747 had been blown out of the sky in protest at Yousef's trial by one of Yousef's undetectable nitroglycerine bombs, placed in the cabin to ignite a fuel tank below.

The case against Yousef continued, and as it wound to a close Yousef personally summed up the defence case from a lectern, glancing at notes in a three-ring binder during a three-hour speech. 'What better way to gain favour with the United States government than to give them someone to blame?' he suggested, claiming the entire Filipino case against him had been fabricated.

'He's a bit heavy-handed, jumping up when he shouldn't and then missing other pieces of testimony that he should object to, but he's not bad,' said one lawyer involved in the case.[7] 'He did a very good job,' said Mary Jo White, the US Attorney with overall responsibility for the prosecution.[8] 'He's a very intelligent person.' But even Yousef's undeniable charm couldn't protect him from the overwhelming evidence.

Fourteen weeks from the start of the trial, on 5 September 1996, Ramzi Yousef and his conspirators Abdul Hakim Murad and Wali Khan Amin Shah were all convicted of plotting to bomb United States-based airliners in Asia. Yousef was also convicted of the PAL bombing and the death of Haruki Ikegami.

'You didn't care who was on those planes,' Judge Duffy told Yousef. 'Those aeroplanes could have been filled with Muslims, indeed, they could have been filled with imams or mullahs or even the Ayatollah. You just wanted to kill for the thrill of killing human beings. When one realizes that the greatest concentration of Muslims in the world is found in Indonesia and that Islam is well represented in the Pacific rim countries, the potential for the passengers on those flights to be Muslims is staggering. What you have shown is your total disdain beyond doubt for the people who Allah has made.'

Neil Herman was standing in a vast hangar called Plant 6 in Calverton, Long Island, part of a former Grumman aircraft assembly plant, when he received a call from FBI agent Frank Pelligrino to say Yousef had been found guilty. By a twist of irony Herman was the Supervisory Special Agent in charge of the FBI's TWA 800 investigation, and inside the hangar agents were reassembling the plane with pieces dredged from the sea. 'I had mixed emotions when I heard the verdict, because I would have liked to have been there,' said Herman. 'Frank rang me. He had been in the courtroom and he gave me a call and said the verdict had come in. He said simply: "It's over. We won.

239

He's been convicted on all counts." It was a great relief and great credit to Mike Garcia and Dieter Snell, the two prosecutors.' Yousef was led back to the MCC cells to contemplate spending the rest of his life behind bars.

The days and then months ticked by until Yousef was ready to face trial for his role in the World Trade Center bombing. Surprisingly, given that he was being held in solitary confinement in the MCC, Yousef's spirit did not break. 'My soul is longing for liberty, yearning for release, and my world is a shackle,' he wrote in Arabic in a poem he sent to the hard-line Arabic monthly newspaper *Politics and the World*, based in New Jersey. Written in the classical Arabic 'tawil' style, the poem focused on Yousef's love of God and his desire to end his earthly existence for the paradise of the afterlife. 'He is certainly not illiterate and seems to be quite well read in classical poetry,' said Philip Kennedy, Professor of Middle Eastern Studies at New York University.[9] 'It's very impersonal and austere – his poetry is something of a rallying cry to people like him.'

Nor did solitary confinement temper Yousef's eye for the ladies. In a pre-trial hearing before the World Trade Center case in late August 1997 his eyes alighted on the pretty courtroom sketch artist, Christine Cornell. Would she like to go on a date with Yousef if he beat the rap, one of his lawyers asked? Cornell sensibly declined the offer with a gracious 'thank you'. But despite his flippant attitude and flirtatious nature Yousef was not blind to the implications of the cases against him.

Dr Laurie Mylroie, an American expert on terrorism and Iraq, formerly with Harvard University and the US Naval War College, remembers: 'I was sitting in the courtroom when the government was contemplating going for the death penalty and the Prosecutor stood up to tell the Judge what they'd decided, because there were questions about the promises that were made to Pakistan to secure Yousef's arrest; and I was watching Yousef and he was really nervous as the Prosecutor stood up, and then said they were going for a life sentence not a death sentence.' Yousef, said Dr Mylroie, 'exhaled and visibly relaxed'.[10]

The World Trade Center trial opened, this time with Yousef choosing to let his lawyers do the talking. Prosecutors passed around 13 graphic photographs of the six victims of the bombing. Four of the photos were facial close-ups of the victims, six depicted the position of one of the victims as he lay in the rubble, another was a close-up of the appalling damage done to a victim's shoulder, and another two photographs showed victims' bodies, including a clearly pregnant Monica Smith, as they lay prostrate on stretchers. Jurors winced and bit their lips. Ramzi Yousef just stared into the distance, his mind apparently elsewhere.

The jury would have been sobbing if they could have heard Monica's husband, Edward Smith, who spoke from the heart during the first World Trade Center trial of Yousef's conspirators. Smith began his short speech by taking the jury back to the autumn of 1992, when he was at night school and called home between classes. It was a phone-call that would change his life. Monica had purchased a pregnancy test but would not take it until Smith was home.[11]

'We took the test and it came back positive,' Smith told the court. 'Our lives and marriage would now have everything we wanted. A new baby was on the way, and I can remember that night as if it was yesterday, because I never felt so close to another human being. We slept in each other's arms, as if we were one person.' Hospital tests showed the delighted couple they were due to have a boy, who they named Eddie. 'From then I would come home at night and sing to our baby. Monica, Eddie and I myself lay in bed too excited about life to sleep. We visited the doctor together and listened to the baby's heart beating contentedly inside his home. Near the end of February, with just a few months to go before Eddie was due, we went shopping for baby furniture.'

Then came 26 February 1993. 'The day started out exciting and happy as I was coming home from a business trip to be with Monica and Eddie. I can remember it better than yesterday. A fellow employee walked into a meeting and said there was a fire at the World Trade Center. A few minutes later the employee came back in and told me there was at that time not a fire, but an explosion. I immediately called Monica's office. There was no answer and there never would be. I raced in my car for New York calling everyone and anyone to see if they had heard from Monica. They had not.'

At 11 p.m. that night the mother of Monica's best friend rang the New York City morgue. 'I was told that I should come right away,' said Smith. 'I asked the man on the phone, what about my son? "Sir," he said. "Do you know how bad it was?".'

'Nobody could have ever prepared me for the feelings I was experiencing. I lost my wife, my best friend, my idol, and my son. I would never get the chance to tell Monica how much I loved her. I would never get to tell her what an inspiration she had been. I would never get to tell her what a best friend meant to me. I would never get the opportunity to hold baby Eddie in my arms. We never got to hear Eddie say his first words, to say mommy. We would never get the opportunity to see Eddie walk or go to school. We would never get to be with Eddie through the love time and the heartbreak and friendship that parents share with a child.'

The pain and suffering, said Smith, will exist for ever. He listed the names of those who died in the World Trade Center: Robert Kirkpatrick, William Macko, Stephen Knapp, John DiGiovanni, Wilfredo Mercado, Monica Rodriguez Smith. 'And Edward Smith, her son, and my son who was killed 26 February 1993 before he was born anywhere but in our hearts.' Hardened FBI agents sitting in the courtroom had moist eyes by the time Smith sat down.[12]

Even though it was nearly five years since the bombing, memories of these victims still haunted the second World Trade Center trial. After months of evidence the verdicts were finally read out on 12 February 1997. Yousef was found guilty.

'Yes, I am a terrorist and I'm proud of it,' said Yousef before he was sentenced.[13] 'And I support terrorism so long as it was against the United States government and against Israel, because you are more than terrorists, you are the ones who invented terrorism and using it every day. You are butchers, liars and hypocrites.'

Judge Kevin Duffy, in response, was equally forthright. 'Ramzi Yousef, you are not fit to uphold Islam,' he said contemptuously.[14] 'Your God is death. Your God is not Allah. You worship death and destruction. What you do you do not do for Allah; you do it only to satisfy your own twisted sense of ego. You would have others believe that you are a soldier, but the attacks on civilization for which you stand convicted here were sneak attacks which sought to kill and maim totally innocent people.'

We know that Yousef is a bright man, said the judge, and his activities in the Manila bombing case show that he is 'intelligent and talented'. But his gifts were 'totally perverted'. 'Your inventiveness and the engineering skill that you displayed there may have been first class, but it was all aimed at accomplishing death and destruction. Death was truly your God, your master, your one and only religion.'

Yousef was, said the judge, merely pretending to be an Islamic fundamentalist. In reality, he 'cared little or nothing for Islam' or the faith of Muslims. Rather, you adored not Allah, but the evil that you yourself have become. And I must say that as an apostle of evil, you have been most effective.

'When you arrived in this country you immediately recruited a group to your evil plans. When you went to the Philippines you brought still others into your adoration of evil. Starting from nothing you have shown you can quickly put together those whom you believe are necessary to carry out your nefarious plans. Obviously you converted them from Allah to evil.'

Duffy, who could not sentence Yousef to death because the death penalty for federal terrorist cases was not introduced until 1994, instead sentenced him to 240 years in prison, and imposed two special restrictions. First he recommended that Yousef be held at a particular prison in Colorado, and 'second, I recommend that your visitors' list be restricted to your attorneys. The prison should not permit friends, gawkers or media reporters to visit with you. While normally a prisoner in administrative detention might have some visitors from his family, in your case I would expect the prison to require proof positive that one is in fact a member of your family. We don't even know what your real name is. You have used a dozen aliases. Having abandoned your family name, I must assume that you have abandoned your family also.

'The restrictions I am imposing are undoubtedly harsh. They amount to solitary confinement for life.' However the evil that Yousef espouses needs to be 'quarantined', said the judge. 'Your treatment will be no different than that accorded to a person with a virus which, if loosed, could cause plague and pestilence throughout the world.'

Eyad Ismoil, who actually drove the van bomb into the World Trade Center, and had been arrested in Jordan at the beginning of August 1995 and returned to the US to face trial, was convicted at the same time. He was, according to his mother, 'an animal lover who especially likes to feed cats'[15] but the evidence proved otherwise. Ismoil read a bizarre rhyming statement in English when he was sentenced, saying: 'standing a trial when the judge is an accuser is unfair . . . but in this world a fair trial is rare . . . I don't think you will ever rest . . . tyrants always end up in trouble . . . your false claims will end like a bubble.'[16]

Judge Duffy fined Yousef $4.5 million, checked whether the prosecution and defence had any objection to the sentence, and then announced crisply: 'All right. Marshal, he is yours.'

Yousef left the court blank faced.

Ramzi Yousef, as he himself proudly proclaims, is something of a genius. An evil man, he has a talent for manipulating both the truth and anyone who crosses his path. Even after he was arrested and knew he would never again taste freedom, Yousef still played games. He would tease his captors, knowing they were hanging on his every word. The money for the World Trade Center bombing had been provided by Mohammad Salameh, he told them. Salameh, the man who went back to collect the deposit on the Ryder truck that carried the World Trade Center bomb, had provided $20,000 through a fraudulent cheque scheme.

Salameh would have trouble signing a cheque, let alone raising $20,000 from fraud.

Yousef also liked to claim that he had arrived in New York with the intent of causing mayhem, but with no connections in the city. A cab driver, he said, had introduced him to Salameh within two hours of leaving JFK airport. It was a preposterous lie, but it proved Yousef's desire to protect some of his backers, who still remain in the shadows. But then Yousef has not shied away from implicating and accusing those he deems expendable. In conversations with FBI agents he confirmed that Salameh, Abouhalima, Ayyad and Ajaj were all involved in the bomb attack, as well as Abdul Rahman Yasin, who was – and still is – a fugitive from justice.

Even in jail Yousef treated the other conspirators like his puppets. In the late summer or early autumn of 1996 Yousef started talking with one of his African-American prison officers, asking him where he was from and whether he was a Muslim.[17] Later the same day, when the officer was serving the inmates their lunch, he handed some food to Ismoil, who refused to eat. Yousef asked the officer for Ismoil's food, but said that 'Ismoil should eat, [because] he was guilty of the World Trade Center bombing, and he [is] going to rot in jail.'[18]

When the corrections officer turned to Ismoil and asked if he was guilty of the bombing, Ismoil nodded his head in the affirmative, smiled wanly, and said, 'Yes.' Yousef continued chatting with the guard, telling him that after the bombing, Ismoil waited in a coffee shop for a report about the damage on the news and then immediately fled the country. In front of the officer Ismoil acknowledged this was correct, said he was brought back to the United States, and then expressed annoyance that the Jordanian Government failed to protect him.

Yousef then turned his attentions on Abdul Hakim Murad, telling the guard that Murad was a pilot. The conversation rambled on, until Murad had had enough, and screamed 'Liar!' at Yousef. Ignoring his former friend's protestations, Yousef said Murad was also guilty of terrorism, and mentioned that Murad had been brought back to the United States from the Philippines. Yousef's game had worked. He had pushed Murad over the edge. Incandescent with rage, Murad began yelling and screaming at Yousef in Arabic.[19]

Apart from driving his conspirators stir-crazy, Yousef's games have also prevented FBI investigators from answering some of the fundamental questions that still surround the young man. Terrorism is an expensive business, especially when it is international in scale and involves false identities, safehouses, and sophisticated technology. Yousef had no real obvious means of support, apart from – according to Pakistani investigators – the investment made on his behalf in a Pakistani company importing holy water from Mecca.[20] So where did he get money from for his bombing campaigns? Who pulled the puppet-master's strings? The FBI remains unsure.

'Yousef, even to this day, is a very shadowy figure that we really don't know that much about, even after all that's been done and all that's been investigated on him,' admits Neil Herman. FBI and CIA investigations traced some of the money given to the WTC conspirators back to Germany and the Muslim Brotherhood. Other funds seemed to come from Iran, Saudi Arabia, Kuwait, but without a new confession from Yousef, or one of his men, the West will probably never know exactly who gave Yousef the money for the World Trade Center bombing. It did not cost much, certainly no more than $15,000, and Yousef has himself admitted that $8,500 of that came from his 'friends and family', without being more specific. He has also said that the date of the bombing was decided because the plotters did not have enough money to pay any rent for March, and had to flee the country.

However, he would have needed large sums of money to fund his later escapades in the Philippines, his regular international flights, and many thousands of dollars just to buy the air tickets for the simultaneous jet explosions demanded of the Bojinka plot.

Osama bin Laden was certainly the major source of much of Yousef's funding after the bombing of the twin towers, but he was not Yousef's only sponsor, according to both American and Pakistani investigators.[21] The FBI and CIA believe Yousef was funded by up to half a dozen other wealthy businessmen from Saudi Arabia, Qatar and the United Arab Emirates during the latter half of his career,[22] as well as senior government ministers from two Gulf states. Some of their names are known to Western intelligence services – they appear to be anonymous militants who gave money to Yousef to punish the infidels in the West. However there is little prospect action can ever be taken against them because of a lack of hard evidence.[23] It is also virtually impossible to stop them making such donations in the future.

A more serious FBI and CIA investigation was conducted into the suggestions that Iraq was involved in Yousef's career, or that Yousef was actually an Iraqi agent from the beginning of his terrorist career. It is a suggestion energetically championed by Dr Laurie Mylroie,[24] and one which was supported, to some degree, by James Fox, the former director of the New York FBI office. 'Although we are unable to say with certainty the Iraqis were behind the [WTC] bombing, that is the theory accepted by most of the veteran investigators,' said Fox.[25]

While the evidence of Iraqi involvement in the rest of Yousef's crimes is virtually non-existent, the evidence of Iraqi involvement in the twin towers bombing is strong.

The timing of the attack is the first clue. Yousef told investigating agents that the date had been forced upon the conspirators because they could not afford to pay their rent for the next month. However Yousef left New York on a first-class ticket, and the FBI discovered $2,615 in cash in the conspirators' apartments. More significant, perhaps, was that 26 February, the date of the bombing, was the second anniversary of the liberation of Kuwait. Saddam Hussein may have been taking his revenge on the United States.

Abdul Rahman Yasin, one of the WTC conspirators – and a man with a $5 million bounty on his head – now lives openly in Baghdad and apparently works for the Iraqi government. He was born in Bloomington, Indiana, in April 1960, and his Iraqi family moved back to Iraq shortly afterwards. Yasin returned to the US only in late 1992. Although Neil Herman likens him to a 'gopher', a minor figure in the plot, it is still possible he was sent to the US by Iraqi intelligence.

Another important link with Iraq may have been Mohammad Salameh, one of Yousef's helpers. He has an uncle now living in Baghdad, Qadri Abu Bakr, who was a leading figure in a PLO terror-ist unit that received funding from the Iraqi regime. Well before Yousef arrived in the US to work on the WTC bombing, Salameh made the first of 46 telephone-calls to Baghdad, most of them to his uncle.[26]

Initially the plot to bomb the World Trade Center was just a plan to launch terrorist attacks involving pipe-bombs, apparently to get El Sayyid Nosair – who killed Rabbi Meir Kahane – out of jail. 'Salameh's telephone bills suggest that the pipe-bombing plot was one of the most exciting events in his life: in six weeks he ran up a bill of over $4,000 and lost his phone service,' notes Mylroie.[27] But after Salameh began making his phone-calls to Iraq, the plan stepped up a gear, and Yousef arrived to turn it into the most devastating ever foreign terrorist attack on American soil.

Pakistani investigators believe this is no coincidence. They point out that Yousef is from Baluchistan, a Sunni area that spreads into Iran, which has been a fertile recruiting ground for the Iraqis, and they are convinced Yousef had close links with the MKO, an anti-Iranian terrorist group supported and run from Iraq. At the request of the MKO Yousef is believed to have murdered dozens of Iranians in a bomb attack on the city of Mashhad – he was a freelance terrorist who would initiate attacks or attach himself to whatever campaign he so chose. 'Yousef was a pretty unique person,' said Neil Herman.[28]

While Yousef was not actually a full-time Iraqi agent, several senior Pakistani and American investigators believe that while he was teaching and receiving tuition in Osama bin Laden's terrorist training camps in spring 1992, Yousef met with a senior Sunni representative of the MKO, who in turn was also working for the government in Baghdad.

Acting under orders from Baghdad, the MKO official, whose name is known to the Pakistani investigators, allegedly asked Yousef to go to the US to prepare a spectacular – a major terrorist attack. 'Yousef Ramzi [sic] was already known to the MKO because of his family in Baluchistan,' said a senior Pakistani investigator, 'and he was the perfect choice for this task. He was young, clever, brilliant with explosives. And, most important, there was nothing to link him directly to Iraq.'

It would not be the first time Iraqi agents have tried to take revenge on America for the Gulf War. In January 1991 a bomb exploded prematurely near the US-sponsored Thomas Jefferson Library in a suburb of Manila. One Iraqi was injured and the body of another, Ahmed J. Ahmed, was blown to pieces and parts were catapulted on to the roof of a nearby house, 20 metres high. Two sons of Hikmat Abdul Sattar, the Iraqi ambassador to Somalia, were arrested by the Philippines police and deported.[29]

Saddam Hussein also wanted to assassinate former American

President George Bush between 14 and 16 April 1993 when Bush was visiting Kuwait to celebrate the allied victory in the Gulf War. Kuwaiti police seized hundreds of pounds of explosives and arrested 16 people, including 11 Iraqi nationals, led by a colonel in the Mukhabarat, the Iraqi secret police, who were preparing to kill Bush.

Some commentators suggest the American government has not pursued the question of Iraqi involvement in the bombing. Agents who investigated the case categorically deny this. Despite their massive resources and sophisticated technology, they cannot perform miracles, they say. The trail was pursued as far as it could be, but Yousef's background lies in Baluchistan, an area virtually impenetrable even by local law enforcement officials, let alone the representatives of a government most Baluchi view as the enemy.[30]

'We were never able, despite all our means and efforts, to determine whether Yousef had funding from Iraq. There are all kinds of errors in that [theory],' said Neil Herman.[31] 'We believe he had these ties to Turbat in Baluchistan, but that's as far as we were able to get. He still had family there. There were several phone-calls made when he was incarcerated to those areas, but we had trouble determining exactly who he called. To understand everything about Yousef you'd probably have to debrief him from six months to a year.'

The exact nature of the relationship between Iraq and Yousef will probably never be known for certain. By refusing to testify in his own defence at his trials Yousef avoided difficult questions about his sponsors. His Toshiba lap-top computer may hold more secrets, but experts have been unable to crack all of the powerful encryption programs on the computer and decode all of the files.[32]

So an element of mystery still surrounds Ramzi Yousef. Even to Neil Herman, he remains something of an enigma. 'He was very Westernized and liked the Western lifestyle,' said Herman. 'He liked the bar scene, he liked women, he liked moving around, he had a girl-friend as well as a wife. He is not someone you would ever describe, in any shape or form, as being religious. Some of the people he associated with were, but he was not. That always bothered us, that he didn't have that background [of Muslim fundamentalism], because it was a sort of dichotomy or paradox that he hated this Westernized world and yet embraced it in his own life. That really bothered us, but he is a very complex person. It still bothers me to this day that if he was the "mastermind" then what was there behind the person. It seemed to me to be something of a personality conflict.'

Questions still surround Yousef's motivation. Neil Herman believes he had strong personal convictions that drove him to terrorism, but others disagree. While chatting with Dr Laurie Mylroie, one female court official involved in the Yousef trial and the previous terrorist case involving Sheikh Omar Abdel-Rahman, said the Sheikh Omar trial was more interesting. 'I said "Why?",' said Dr Mylroie, 'and she said, "Because it was about ideas. Yousef was just a killer, a cold-blooded killer." And that's exactly what he is. Ramzi Yousef is just a killer. He's not Islamic, he's just a killer.'[33]

It is a moot point. While Yousef is certainly a murderer, few men are born evil. 'He's a product, I guess, of his environment,' said a senior American investigator. 'His life was shaped by bigotry, hatred, anger at what he thought was oppression of Muslims and Islam by Washington, and by the actions of Israeli soldiers. Put all that in a pot with technical skill and you're left with a potent mix. We'll see it again.'

What remains beyond doubt, however, is Yousef's intelligence and obscene brilliance as a terrorist. 'You would certainly have to put Yousef right there at the top,' said Neil Herman. 'He was a diabolical, elusive figure, and I'm sure in his mind that he felt he didn't kill enough people. He was very good, well trained, very clever. His acts took a great deal of preparation and he did his homework.

'Here was a person that after his involvement in the twin towers bombing was planning this massive conspiracy to bring down 11 aircraft, moving around from country to country in the Far East. Think about it. The whole airline industry would shut down. It would have been unbelievable! He did not go into hiding; on the contrary what led to his demise was that he was planning more acts.'[34]

Neil Herman, a modest man whose skill as an investigator and as an FBI supervisor has doubtless saved many lives, is concerned that all Muslims should not be tarred with the same militant brush. 'I think Muslims have got a bad rap,' he says. However, he remains quietly proud of his work. 'I think the thing that I'm most proud of is that all six of the defendants [in the WTC bombing] have been convicted on all counts.'

Several of the agents involved in the case have been commended for their investigative skill. Brian Parr was promoted within the Secret Service and became a senior member of the Presidential Detail based in Washington D.C. Chuck Stern was promoted to Supervisory Special Agent and Frank Pelligrino received the Attorney General's award; both are still on the FBI Joint Terrorist Task Force.[35] John Lipka was also promoted within the Bureau, while in Pakistan Rehman Malik was made Additional Director General of the Federal Investigation Agency and was given a special gallantry award by the President of Pakistan.

Malik, however, was not as fortunate as his American counterparts. He began investigating allegations of corruption levelled at the then former Pakistani Prime Minister Nawaz Sharif, and had been working on the task for several months when he narrowly survived an assassination attempt: gunmen tried to mow him down with a machine gun outside his Islamabad home. Nawaz Sharif was then re-elected as Prime Minister, and Malik was arrested on trumped-up charges and thrown into jail without being taken before a court. According to Pakistani intelligence sources scorpions and snakes were put into the cell of the high-ranking officer and he suffered two heart attacks before escaping with the help of friends. He continued his investigations from abroad, finally completing an explosive report in summer 1998, alleging that Sharif had amassed a fortune by siphoning money into offshore bank accounts.[36]

Neil Herman was awarded the FBI Directors' Award for excellence in managing the World Trade Center investigation, but admits he will carry memories of the tortured building for ever.[37] 'You never really get away from it. The buildings are such imposing figures. In some ways the WTC seems like yesterday and other ways it seems like a lifetime ago. I always stop and collect my thoughts on 26 February, and whenever I go down there it brings back memories.'

As the supervisor of one of the most important manhunts in FBI history, perhaps it is not surprising that Herman admits Ramzi Yousef has been a 'big part' of his life. Herman still has Yousef's arrest photograph in his office, and several more at home. 'Sometimes my daughter asks me "Who is that person?" She always refer to him as "that man". I sometimes think he might scare her a bit.'

However, there are still some aspects of the Tradebom investigation that trouble Neil Herman. 'It always haunts me with the Yousef case – how much didn't we know,' he said. 'That's always one of the things that's frustrating about these cases, unless you have the chance to sit down and talk with them [men like Yousef] you never really get a true picture of their lives, what motivated them, anything about them. There are gaps.' Questions, for example, still surround the accepted theory of Yousef's identity. His own passport, in the name of Abdul Basit Karim, listed him as being 5ft 8in. Yousef himself is a wiry 6ft.

Dr Laurie Mylroie proposes a controversial explanation. She believes the real 'Karim' was killed in Kuwait during the Iraqi occupation, and Iraqi intelligence agents then replaced his fingerprints in the Interior Ministry with those belonging to their agent: Ramzi Yousef. But Yousef applied for his passport in October 1984, when he was just 16, and it is not unheard of for late developers to sprout a few inches in their late teens.

Another query still hangs over Yousef's time in Swansea. Was he really there? Mylroie and some senior staff in Swansea Institute think not. They believe he took 'Karim's' identity after he was killed in Kuwait.

However, Neil Herman and the FBI are convinced Yousef and Karim are one and the same, and several former students remember and identify 'Ramzi', their 'temperamental' and 'volatile' former mate.[38] 'One minute he was your friend, and the next . . .' said one Welsh student. Another former student from South Wales remembers a mutual friend of his and Yousef's – a Briton from an Asian family – mentioning a political conversation the two men had. 'He's a real nutter,' the man was told. Another student cut out and kept newspaper articles from Yousef's trial. When Yousef was still on the run he remembers comparing the newspaper pictures with those in his albums. 'That's my friend Jane, she's a teacher,' he would say to friends looking at the albums, 'that's my friend Phil, he's an engineer, and then [turning to the articles] that's my friend Ramzi, the international terrorist and most wanted man in the world.'[39]

A few miles outside the little town of Florence, Colorado, about 100 miles south-west of Denver, a well-worn road, baked by the heat, snakes into the distance. Sunlight glinting off the glass of six large guard-towers alerts visitors to the Florence Correctional Institute, a sprawling complex comprising four federal prisons: a work camp, a medium-security facility, a maximum-security facility, and a United States Penitentiary called Administrative Maximum Facility (also known as 'Supermax', the 'Big One', and 'the Alcatraz of the Rockies').

Supermax is not like any other prison in the United States. It is not, in fact, like any other prison in the world. At a cost of more than £120 million, the prison is the successor to the US federal prisons at

Alcatraz in San Francisco Bay (which closed in 1963), and Marion, Illinois.

It is probably the most secure jail ever built, and it needs to be, because the 387 men who live there are among the most violent and dangerous felons in the world. More than 22 per cent of the prisoners are men who have killed fellow inmates in other prisons. More than 35 per cent have led or participated in violent attacks on fellow inmates or prison guards. It is there, on the ultra-high-security wing of the most secure prison in the world, that Ramzi Yousef will almost certainly spend the rest of his life.

Every morning Yousef wakes in a 12ft-by-7ft cell which contains a concrete slab and a thin mattress for a bed, a shower (with a timer to prevent flooding), a toilet, an electric light, an immovable concrete desk and stool, a polished steel mirror riveted to the concrete wall, a cigarette lighter and a 13-inch black-and-white television.

Motion detectors, cameras, 1,400 remote-controlled steel doors and 12ft razor-wire fences now guard Yousef. Cells are designed so inmates cannot see the ground outside: windows are set high up in the wall and angled pointing to the sky. This has the effect of discouraging dissent and breakouts, because prisoners are disorientated and unable to work out where they are being held in the prison.

'It will take Einstein's genius and more than a little luck to get out of this baby,' said John Quest, the architect who designed the 37-acre complex, much of which is built into the side of a mountain.[40] Laser-beams, pressure-pads and silent attack dogs, which can kill a man without barking, all guard the area between the prison walls and the surrounding razor-wire. Visitors and prisoners enter down a heavily guarded road tunnel into the mountain, discouraging attack and making it difficult even for visitors to judge where they are in the prison.

The security measures to ensure Yousef never escapes are astonishing: cells are staggered along green and maroon corridors so inmates cannot see each other, and each one is sound-proofed to prevent communication between prisoners by Morse code. Librarians check every single page of books withdrawn by prisoners to ensure no messages are left for other inmates.

For those inside life is simple. One of the few decisions Yousef can now make is his choice of food for his three daily meals, which are all served mechanically through a hatch in his climate-controlled home. Yousef spends 23 hours every day in the cell; for his one hour of exercise he pads slowly around a little exercise yard, his feet shackled together and his every move watched by at least two prison guards. On occasion he may be allowed to visit one of the cell-block's basic law libraries, medical offices or barber's shops.

The Bureau of Prisons has no doubt about Yousef's capacity for violence. 'Specifically, the Bureau of Prisons considers him to be one of the very highest security risk inmates in the entire Bureau of Prisons system,' was the conclusion of a 'threat assessment' by the Department of Justice.[41] Yousef has been placed in virtual solitary due to an assessment by the Bureau of Prisons that: 'in general population [he] would pose a serious threat to the safety of staff, inmates, himself, the institution, and possibly even the nation, because of his advanced technological background and expertise in bomb-making'.[42]

The inmates at Supermax, which opened in 1995, include the hitman Charles Harrelson, the father of Hollywood movie star Woody Harrelson, jailed for killing a federal judge. Other customers will eventually include Mafiosi John Gotti, Nicodemo 'Little Nicky' Scarface, John Walker, the Navy spy, Edwin Wilson, the arms smuggler, Jonathan Pollard, the Israeli spy, and Jeff Fort, the leader of the Chicago El Rukn gang, one of the first corporate-style 'supergangs'.

On the ultra-high-security wing of Supermax, Yousef has the delightful company of Theodore Kaczynski, the 'Unabomber' who plagued America with bombs for 17 years until his capture in a crude cabin in the Montana woods; and Juan Ramon Matta Ballestros, a notorious Medellin drug trafficker. Yousef was also joined by Timothy McVeigh, the Oklahoma City bomber, until July 1999, when McVeigh was moved to a new 50-bed death-row prison at Terre Haute, Indiana, to await his execution.

Kaczynski is in high security because he is a master bomb-builder; Ballestros is there because his men may try to spring him from jail; Yousef is there for both reasons – he has, according to sources in the FBI and Bureau of Prisons, the highest level security status in the entire American prison system. The terms of his incarceration are even more stringent than those of McVeigh and Kaczynski, and until December 1998 Yousef was allowed no human contact other than that of the omnipresent guards.

Despite Yousef's abhorrent crimes, it is, according to psychiatrists, a questionable form of punishment. 'It's a kind of mental torture,' according to Stuart Grassian, a psychiatrist on the Harvard Medical School faculty.[43] 'The sensory deprivation causes enormous psychological suffering and mental illness.' Philip Heymann, a Professor of Criminal Law at Harvard University, said: 'I think it could pose a substantial issue of cruel and unusual punishment.'[44] Yousef is a tough nut, but if he starts to crack the only redress available is a counselling service – and even that is conducted via a video camera.

Yousef's restrictions were loosened only when it became clear that Amnesty International was examining the legitimacy of Yousef's solitary incarceration on the grounds it may be 'cruel and unnatural punishment'; and when Yousef himself began suing the Federal prison system for $1 million (£625,000) for treating him more harshly than Timothy McVeigh, who faced the death penalty.

Yousef was then allowed to exercise together with McVeigh and Kaczynski, and the three men developed a bizarre friendship.[45] Yousef asked McVeigh for lessons on American slang, and the three men were heard discussing details of their cases and the films shown on Ted Turner's 'golden oldies' channel in their prison cells. Yousef is still complaining about his treatment.

However, the conditions of Yousef's incarceration cannot be considered without an understanding of his career, and his personal dedication to the cause of terrorism. According to sources in the FBI, the young mastermind may still be re-indicted for his plot to kill President Clinton, although some federal and intelligence officials think the case would be a waste of time: after all, Yousef will never leave prison alive. 'They may try to charge him alongside bin Laden when he's captured to increase the possibility of [bin Laden's] conviction,' said one source.[46]

Yousef deserves no pity. By claiming to represent Islam he has tarnished the image of Muslims around the world. He has shown no remorse and despite his crimes, seems to relish his position in the dark annals of history. 'Yousef thinks he should be congratulated,' according to one federal investigator. 'But he knows he'll never be released.'[47] He is surely right. For Ramzi Yousef was a one-man terror campaign, the like of which the world has never seen. Within the space of two years he corrupted and recruited dozens of young Muslims, and plotted a spate of bombings and assassinations that could have killed tens of thousands of people, destroyed the World Trade Center complex and brought the international airline industry to its knees. He is the herald of a new dawn of apocalyptic terrorism, and in Western eyes at least, Ramzi Ahmed Yousef has a legitimate claim to the title of most dangerous man in the world.

References

[1] GMA-7 Radio-Television Arts Network, 'Police Arrest Suspects Linked to New York Bomb', Quezon City, 22.30 GMT, 2 March 1995.

[2] Author interview with Benazir Bhutto.

[3] Dilip Ganguly, 'Muslim Group Wants World Trade Center Bombing Suspect Released', Associated Press, 30 July 1995.

[4] Author interview with Filipino investigator.

[5] Patricia Hurtado, 'Bomb Suspect to Defend Himself', *New York Newsday*, 31 May 1996.

[6] Author interview with American investigator.

[7] Stephen Handelman, 'Dense maze of clues blurs terror trial', *Toronto Star*, 31 July 1996.

[8] Gail Appleson, 'Three Convicted in Plot to Bomb US Airliners', Reuters, 6 September 1996.

[9] Author interview with Philip Kennedy.

[10] Author interview with Laurie Mylroie.

[11] Edward Smith, speaking in court, US v. Salameh et al. 24 May 1994.

[12] Author interview with an American investigator.

[13] Ramzi Yousef, speaking in court on 8 January 1998, before sentencing by Judge Kevin Duffy, S12 93 CR 180 (KTD).

[14] Judge Kevin Duffy, sentencing Ramzi Yousef.

[15] Gail Appleson, 'Parents of bomb defendant tearfully say son is innocent', Reuters, 16 August 1995.

[16] Frederic Bichon, 'Questions Remain', AFP, 3 April 1998.

[17] Letter from Mary Jo White, United States Attorney, SDNY, to Attorney Roy Kulcsar, 7 July 1997.

[18] Ibid.

[19] Ibid.

[20] Author interview with Pakistani investigator.

[21] Author interviews.

[22] Author interview with American investigator.

[23] Ibid.

[24] Most notably in 'The World Trade Center Bomb', *The National Interest*, No. 42, Winter 1995/96.

[25] James Fox, speaking in 1994, before Yousef's capture.

[26] Author interview with FBI investigator, and Laurie Mylroie, op. cit.

[27] Laurie Mylroie, op. cit.

[28] Author interview.

[29] Based on author interviews with US intelligence source, also Claro Cortes, 'The Gulf War', Associated Press, 19 January 1991.

[30] Author interviews with Pakistani and American investigators.

[31] Author interview with Neil Herman.

[32] According to Louis Freeh, Director of the FBI, in testimony to the Senate Commerce Committee, 25 July 1996.

[33] Author interview with Laurie Mylroie.

[34] Author interview with Neil Herman.

[35] Ibid.

[36] Author interview with Pakistani investigator.

[37] In April 1999, Herman was appointed as a Director of the American Anti-Defamation League.

[38] Author interview with Mylroie, four former and current staff at Swansea Institute, and fourteen former students who were directly traced by the author, or who responded to advertisements placed by the author in Welsh and British newspapers.

[39] Author interview. Names changed at interviewee request.

[40] 'Unabomber begins life sentence in "the Big One"', Reuters, 6 May 1998.

[41] Affidavit of Dominique Raia, staff attorney for the Department of Justice, Bureau of Prisons, assigned to the Metropolitan Correctional Center in New York, filed 2 June 1995, US District Court, SDNY.

[42] Ibid.

[43] Sharon Walsh, '"Proud" Terrorist gets 240 years in NY bombing', *Washington Post*, 9 January 1998.

[44] Ibid.

[45] Author interview with American investigator.

[46] Ibid.

[47] Ibid.

CONCLUSION

Future Terror

THE MEN and women who dominated international terrorism until the 1990s were a murderous bunch. Using plastic and home-made explosives, they blew up buildings, shopping centres, planes and trucks, killing thousands of innocent people and maiming many thousands more. But according to intelligence analysts they could be the terrorists of the past.

In the years to come, warn the experts, terrorists will not stop at blowing up a building, they will want to threaten an entire city, or even a whole nation, using weapons of mass destruction (WMD). Their arsenals will contain nuclear bombs, and biological and chemical weapons. It is the stuff of nightmares.

Rather than frighten the electorate, politicians and policemen have traditionally promised they have terrorism under control. No more: even senior politicians now admit that scenarios of madmen with dangerous chemicals, a batch of plague-inducing bacteria, or a crude nuclear bomb that can kill tens of thousands of people, are no longer far-fetched. William S. Cohen, the US Secretary of Defense, says: 'They are real – here and now.'[1]

With advanced technology and a smaller world of porous borders, 'the ability to unleash mass sickness, death, and destruction today has reached a far greater order of magnitude,' says Cohen, and the problem is increasing. Cohen admits that small amounts of weapons-usable plutonium and highly enriched uranium have already been 'diverted', probably from Russian nuclear facilities, and may soon fall into the hands of terrorists.[2]

This is enormously concerning. To make a crude atomic bomb

similar to the device dropped on Hiroshima in the Second World War, a terrorist needs no more than 18lbs of 94-per-cent plutonium-239 or 55lbs of uranium.[3] Making a bomb from plutonium may be difficult, because detonating the 18lbs requires about 800lbs of conventional explosives packed around the plutonium (which has to be fashioned into a near-perfect sphere), and then triggered with split-second precision by high-energy nuclear capacitors. But it is not beyond the limitations of a terrorist such as Osama bin Laden, who has dedicated followers and access to millions of dollars in funds.

Rather than using plutonium, however, terrorists are more likely to opt for enriched uranium. This is easier to detonate, because one carefully shaped chunk is simply fired into another, but enriched uranium is difficult to obtain. Until now, that is.

'Security for nuclear materials is a major proliferation problem, particularly in Russia,' admits Cohen.[4] The combination of lax security at many former Soviet nuclear facilities, poor economic conditions in the republics, and mushrooming organized crime has vastly increased the potential for theft or smuggling of nuclear material.

Terrorists have obtained chemical and biological weapons in the past, but until the 1995 sarin gas attack on the Tokyo underground by the Aum Shinrikyo (Supreme Truth) cult, when thousands were hospitalized, they had either been caught before their attacks or had not actually dared to use them. In 1972 members of The Order of the Rising Sun, an American fascist group, obtained 80lbs of typhoid bacteria cultures they planned to feed into the water supplies of several cities. In 1985 a small group of American neo-Nazis was arrested with 30 gallons of cyanide they were hoping to use to poison the water in New York and Washington D.C. Thousands of people would have died, but the groups did not 'cross the line' and use the weapons. Future terrorist groups will not always display the same restraint.

'Terrorists will use weapons of mass destruction as soon as they perfect the means of delivering them,' said Oliver Revell, the former Deputy Director of the FBI.[5] 'Both nuclear and chemical [weapons] are difficult [to deliver], but biological are much less so. They are readily available and can be delivered through many means. Where you have groups that have state support, then I think biological [weapons] pose a serious risk and that genie is already out of the bottle.'

According to Revell the world will soon see terrorists armed with WMD. 'Would they be able to wipe out the population of the United

States? No. But could they cause thousands, perhaps even hundreds of thousands of casualties? I think the answer is absolutely yes.' It is no longer a question of *if* terrorists will successfully use a weapon of mass destruction, but *when*.

To consider and study the likely future of terrorism, the Pentagon conducted a secret study, called 'Terror 2000', which was designed to help the intelligence world prepare to meet the threat. 'As I looked at the data it became evident to me that there were watershed changes underway, beginning with the collapse of the Soviet Union and international communism. We were very concerned about the future tracks that terrorism might take,' said Peter Probst, an expert on terrorism in the Pentagon's Office of the Assistant Secretary of Defense for Special Operations and Low-Intensity Conflict.

As supervisor of the study Probst approached Marvin Cetron, the President of Forecasting International, which conducts studies for hundreds of major corporations and 17 governments from its base in Arlington, Virginia, and asked him to investigate. 'I told the Pentagon, "We need the best people in the world", and I think we got them,' said Cetron.[6] More than forty experts were brought in, including Major-General Oleg Kalugin, the former KGB head of First Chief Directorate Operations in America; a senior official from Mossad; Brian Jenkins from international security company Kroll Associates; and Paul Wilkinson, Professor of International Relations at St Andrews University, Scotland – perhaps the best terrorism analyst in Europe, according to Probst.[7]

The group spent months investigating terrorism and turning its findings into a classified report that shocked the intelligence community. Terror 2000 suggested the terrorist threat was increasing. International terrorists would launch major attacks on the West, it predicted, home-grown terrorists would become a major headache, and – most worryingly – terrorists would increasingly turn to weapons of mass destruction, including chemical and biological agents.

The report was then presented to representatives from the CIA, FBI, NSA, Defense Intelligence Agency, State Department, and senior officials from the telecommunications, computer and banking industries.[8] It met with a barrage of cynicism.

'Some of the people thought it was right on – but most of them thought it was too far out,' said Cetron. 'Some of the people said, "My

God, how can you believe that, they can't get a hold of these things, where are they going to get chemical or biological weapons?" They thought it was too far-fetched, and that people wouldn't go that far.'

Yet Terror 2000 can be seen as almost prophetic in the accuracy of its warnings. One of the most important conclusions of the report was that rather than bombing a single target, terrorists would soon try to conduct simultaneous bombings and attacks, perhaps even in different countries, to maximize the devastation and publicity for their cause. When Ramzi Yousef was finally arrested in 1995, he was, of course, planning the simultaneous destruction of 11 airliners. In 1998 al Qaeda operatives simultaneously attacked US embassies in Kenya and Tanzania, and were foiled in attempts to bomb the US embassy in Uganda and other US targets around the world. Other massive simultaneous bombings have since been thwarted in India and the Middle East.

The team behind Terror 2000 was convinced that the world is witnessing the dawn of a new age of 'superterrorism', when men with no moral restrictions on mass killing will use weapons of mass destruction. 'We expect biological attacks in the future,' confirms Marvin Cetron.[9] 'You're talking about taking large numbers of people out because that becomes theatre, because it attracts attention.'

Peter Probst agrees: 'people talk in terms of chemical [weapons] being the most likely, and I think biological is as well. It's so readily available.' According to Probst there is a tremendous proliferation of knowledge, with details of biological, chemical and radiological weapons and agents now available on the Internet. '"How to create your own anthrax culture",' said Probst. 'It's really quite easy to do.'

Oliver 'Buck' Revell warns that terrorists are already using the Internet as a massive information resource: 'With the Internet, with Global Positioning Satellites, and with mobile communications a small terrorist group has more command, control, communications and intelligence capability than nation-states had, except for the great powers, ten years ago.'[10]

Some senior intelligence officials now accept these warnings. John C. Gannon, the Chairman of the CIA's National Intelligence Council, says terrorist groups seeking to develop or acquire chemical and biological weapons are 'proliferating'.[11] The threat, he adds, 'is real and growing', and 'agents of increasing lethality are being developed that have the potential to cause massive casualties . . .'[12] 'Rapid advances in biotechnology will yield new toxins or live agents, such as exotic animal viruses, that will require new detection methods and vaccines as well as other preventative measures.' The CIA is also extremely concerned, Gannon admits: 'that some states might acquire more advanced and effective CW agents, such as Russia's fourth-generation "Novichok" agents, which are more persistent and deadly.'[13]

This growing terrorist threat has given agents from Western intelligence agencies a new sense of purpose after the collapse of communism and the end of the Cold War. Five years ago politicians were talking about 'scaling back' intelligence operations; now they are eagerly voting through major budget increases to prevent massive terrorist attacks. The FBI's unclassified budget for counter-terrorism, for example, rose from $80 million in 1994 to nearly $400 million in 1997. Ten special Rapid Assessment and Initial Detection (RAID) teams were also established across the country, each comprising 22 experts and specialists in chemical and biological weapons (CBW), to provide a maximum four-hour response to any CBW attack.

According to several investigators and intelligence agents who have been involved in counter-terrorism for most of their working lives, this increase in funding is absolutely essential because terrorism is now in a transitional phase, crossing from a home-made operation into one that is more sophisticated.

Huge numbers of lives are threatened by the new breed of terrorist. 'It's happening because people are upset, and they don't mind if they kill their own people,' said Marvin Cetron.[14] It is also happening because religious terrorism is increasing, particularly Islamic terrorism, and new groups, such as Osama bin Laden's, have fewer restrictions on the use of weapons of mass destruction. 'Religiously motivated groups have no qualms about operations that cause mass casualties,' said Peter Probst. 'In fact they actively seek them. This, I believe, is because they have no constituencies which would really object to that. They report to a constituency of one, their God. Secular groups, although they may be very brutal, generally stay away from mass-casualty operations.'[15]

According to Probst, 'religious zealotry creates the will to carry out mass-casualty attacks, and proliferation provides the means. This marriage of will and means has forever changed the face of terrorism. These groups actively seek to maximize the carnage, believing that only by annihilating their enemy may they fulfil the dictates of their guru or God. The more non-believers they can lay on the altar, the better.'[16]

Bruce Hoffman, the highly respected former director of the Centre for the Study of Terrorism and Political Violence at Scotland's University of St Andrews, and the author of *Inside Terrorism*, agrees. 'Whenever religion is involved, terrorists kill more people,' he says.[17]

The ultimate reasoning is simple: terrorism works. 'Remember that one driver in one suicide attack against our Marines in Beirut turned American policy 180 degrees and drove the greatest world power out of Lebanon,' Probst observed.

Osama bin Laden knows that terrorism can be successful. He helped to beat the Soviets in Afghanistan, and now he wants to attack the West. 'Russia was the head of the communist bloc. With the disintegration of Russia, communism withered away in the Eastern Europe. Similarly if the United States is beheaded, the Arab kingdoms will wither away,' said bin Laden.[18] 'If Russia can be destroyed, the United States can also be beheaded. They are like little mice.' Bin Laden is as determined a terrorist as the West has ever faced. His belief is unshakeable. 'Next century', he says, 'is the century of the Muslims.'[19]

There can be little doubt that Osama bin Laden and international Islamist groups have already obtained weapons of mass destruction in the form of phials of botulism and anthrax, and possibly even code-protected nuclear suitcase bombs. The challenge for intelligence agencies is preventing the groups from perfecting a means of turning these raw materials into viable weapons and delivering them on to a target. 'It's certainly a credible threat,' said Peter Probst.[20]

The problem for the intelligence community, however, is that there is not just one single international terrorist gang that is keen to obtain and possibly use WMD, but several. The threat will not disappear when bin Laden is in handcuffs. Other terrorist groups, including Hamas, and white supremacist and militia groups in America, who have already been caught experimenting with the deadly poison Ricin, are interested in obtaining weapons of mass destruction. 'There are other Osama bin Laden's out there,' warns Probst.

The CIA agrees. Al Qaeda 'is just one of about a dozen terrorist groups that have expressed an interest in or have sought chemical, biological, radiological, and nuclear (CBRN) agents,' says George J. Tenet, the Director of Central Intelligence.[21]

Even as the world wakes to a new order of terrorist threat, intelligence agencies in Europe, Asia and America are finding militant groups increasingly difficult to stop or contain. The reason, put simply, is that these groups are planning and behaving less and less like the traditional terrorist gangs that were dominant during the 1970s and 1980s, such as the IRA or the Basque separatist group ETA. Those organizations realized they were being infiltrated and monitored by the police and security services, and they developed complicated cell structures. Information and instructions were restricted on a 'need to know' basis: for example, a terrorist within a four-man cell would be given specific instructions only about their individual role in a bombing, and might not even know the target, method or date of the attack. The groups then became extremely difficult to target and infiltrate.

The new breed of terrorist is even more dangerous, because the groups are less structured and hierarchical: the terrorists are more like members of a cult, receiving religious motivation and broad instructions via radio broadcasts, satellite television or, increasingly, via the Internet. Osama bin Laden can call on Islamic revolutionaries to attack America and Britain, and zealous young Muslims rise to the call, even those who were born in the West or who have lived there for many years. 'You just get them riled up and then they will go off and do their thing,' said Marvin Cetron.[22] 'They are almost impossible to infiltrate,' warns Oliver 'Buck' Revell.[23]

At the Pentagon, Peter Probst says he can foresee a day when the West will be facing terrorist groups 'where the terrorists will never actually meet, except perhaps to carry out a specific operation with the planning, the vetting of the individuals all taking place through the Internet. They will be very, very difficult to stop.'[24] Terrorism has changed, and the West has been slow to adapt. 'We have not been very good at anticipating change, and once we have identified change, we have not proved very adept at developing an effective response.'[25]

In truth, however, there is often little the authorities can do to prevent terrorist attacks, particularly those by religiously motivated terrorists. 'How do you stop a Mullah in a mosque in Kabul from preaching jihad?' said a senior British intelligence official involved in the current global investigations into Osama bin Laden.[26] 'We're not a global Gestapo. How can we stop them?'

It is for reasons such as these that the Western response to terrorism remains muddled. Many senior officials seem confused by the best method of preventing attacks and the spread of militancy, while their agencies are hindered by an over-reliance on technology. For two decades Western governments concentrated their money and resources on technological intelligence at the expense of human intelligence – men and women on the ground. High technology and satellites were useful tools during the Cold War, intercepting coded messages and giving great insight into the workings of the Soviet machine. But times have changed, and satellites prove useless when a man like bin Laden switches off his cellular telephone and relies on face-to-face meetings and emissaries to convey his wishes or demands.

'We've made a mistake and gone hi-tech and we've forgotten hi-touch,' confirms Marvin Cetron. 'We can fly over and we can check even tunnels, and we can read watches at so many miles above the earth, but we don't have the human intelligence in places where it's needed. We need them both.'

From his office in the Pentagon, Peter Probst tries to anticipate future terrorist tactics. His conclusion, after years of study, is that in the future small groups will pose the greatest terrorist danger. 'They may be religiously motivated, or they may be what I call single-issue terrorist groups, like the extremely violent anti-abortionists, extremely violent environmentalists, because they have an almost religious belief in their tenets they will be quite willing to carry out mass casualty operations. I can see some of these very radical anti-abortionists trying to blackmail the government.'

The London-based International Institute of Strategic Studies (IISS) issued a similar warning in May 1999 when it released its annual report: 'The new terrorists are likely to be more indiscriminate and more lethal than the old. Some are more sophisticated in technological, operational and other terms than earlier terrorists, and more capable of conducting operations at great distances.' According to Colonel Terence Taylor, the Assistant Director of the IISS: 'One-man or very small cells, motivated by extreme beliefs, can bring about large numbers of casualties. They only have to be lucky once to kill lots of people.'[27]

To counter this threat, particularly that posed by foreign groups, Probst says intelligence agencies must start working to separate hardcore terrorists from the members of their gang and from their recruiting pool. 'There are several ways to do that,' said Probst, who is now saying the previously unthinkable: 'Many terrorist groups have legitimate grievances. Where these grievances can be legitimately met, go ahead and try to meet them. Meet legitimate demands to try to steal the terrorist's thunder. It may be something like land reform, it may be taxation, it may be something like rampant corruption. It's a diplomatic and social response.'

Contrary to their popular gung-ho image, senior Western investigators, including FBI and British agents involved in the Ramzi Yousef and Osama bin Laden investigations, believe the only way to prevent future apocalyptic terrorist attacks is for a concerted international effort to create greater harmony between the West and the East. 'More emphasis has to be placed on breaking down barriers between religious groups,' said one senior serving FBI agent. 'Change starts with the small things.' For example, 'there's a very, very small percentile of individuals who are involved in terrorism. And a fraction of them happen to be Muslims. I've been trying to get the FBI for years to say, when you have a guy like Yousef, just to say that "today he was arrested", we don't need to mention that he's Muslim. When we arrest Christians we don't say they're Christians.'

But it may already be too late. Men like Yousef and bin Laden are not interested in the language of conciliation. On 10 June 1999, millions of Arabs heard Osama bin Laden calling for a holy war against America when the government of Qatar allowed an interview to be broadcast with him on its al-Jazeera satellite channel, the first time bin Laden had been heard interviewed in Arabic in the Middle East and Gulf. By mid-June 1999, Osama bin Laden was touting around draft copies of a book he has written in flowery Arabic, setting out his vision of the future. Sources in Pakistan who claim to have seen copies report that it bears the title *America and the Third World War*, and consists of a lengthy exhortation to Muslims to rise up and destroy the United States.[28] Terrorists such as bin Laden and Yousef no longer want reform, they no longer want to put a halt to corruption. They want to attack their enemies and annihilate the West.

The days when Carlos the Jackal bombed and shot his way around Europe in the fight for political revolution are over. The danger now is not political violence but a curious branch of religious anger that espouses the death of all non-believers. 'Carlos the Jackal and Abu Nidal were essentially fighting for a place at the table. They wanted recognition for their movement, they wanted recognition for their demands, whereas Osama bin Laden and Ramzi Yousef . . . want to punish and destroy, they're not looking for a place at the table – they want to destroy the table, and maximize casualties,' said Oliver 'Buck' Revell.[29]

The world must prepare for more deadly attacks from this new breed of militant. Ramzi Yousef – along with his plots to detonate a radiological bomb in New York, topple the twin towers and simultaneously destroy 11 airliners – may prove to be the first of several apocalyptic terrorists to attack the West. 'Judgement day shall not come until the Muslims fight the Jews, whereas the Jews will hide behind trees and stones, and the tree and the stone will speak and say, "Muslim, behind me is a Jew, come and kill him" . . .' says bin Laden.[30] 'We predict a black day for America and the end of the United States as United States . . . [It] will retreat from our land and collect the bodies of its sons back to America. Allah willing.' Ramzi Yousef is just the first of the New Jackals, and money from men like Osama bin Laden is now being used to prepare many more in terrorist training schools dotted around Pakistan, Afghanistan and the Middle East. The West will soon be facing militants armed with weapons of mass destruction, and there is little that can be done to prevent a disaster.

'Ramzi Yousef, after the World Trade Center bombing, became a well-known Muslim personality and all Muslims know him,' said Osama bin Laden.[31] 'I remember him as a Muslim who defended Islam from American aggression.' The world, warns bin Laden: 'will see many young men that will follow Ramzi Yousef.'

References

[1] Message of the Secretary of Defense, accompanying the Pentagon report 'Proliferation: Threat and Response, 1997'.
[2] Ibid.
[3] Author interview with a British weapons expert.
[4] Secretary of Defense, op. cit.
[5] Author interview with Oliver Revell.
[6] Author interview with Marvin Cetron.
[7] Author interviews with Marvin Cetron and Peter Probst.
[8] In June 1994.
[9] Interview with Marvin Cetron.
[10] Author interview with Oliver Revell.
[11] Gannon, remarks at the Hoover Institution's Conference on Biological and Chemical Weapons at Stanford University, 16 November 1998.
[12] Ibid.
[13] Ibid.
[14] Author interview with Marvin Cetron.
[15] Author interview with Peter Probst.
[16] Speech given by Probst at a US DoD anti-terrorism conference held in San Antonio, Texas, in 1997.

17 Bruce W. Nelan, 'The Price of Fanaticism', *Time*, 3 April 1995.
18 Hamid Mir, interview with Osama bin Laden, Pakistan, 18 March 1997.
19 Ibid.
20 Author interview with Peter Probst.
21 George J. Tenet, Director of Central Intelligence, testifying before the Senate Armed Services Committee, 2 February 1999.
22 Author interview with Marvin Cetron.
23 Author interview with Oliver Revell.
24 Author interview with Peter Probst.
25 Speech given by Probst, op. cit.
26 Author interview.
27 Colonel Taylor speaking in May 1999 at the release of the IISS's annual report. For more details of the report, see: Stuart Millar, 'Growing threat of the lone terrorist', *Guardian*, 5 May 1999.
28 Author interview with a Pakistani intelligence source.
29 Author interview.
30 Interviewed by John Miller, and quoted on *ABC News*, 28 May 1998.
31 Ibid.

APPENDIX ONE

Text of Osama bin Laden's fatwa urging a jihad against Americans, published in *Al Quds al-Arabi* on 23 February 1998:

Praise be to God, who revealed the Book, controls the clouds, defeats factionalism, and says in His Book 'But when the forbidden months are past, then fight and slay the pagans wherever ye find them, seize them, beleaguer them, and lie in wait for them in every stratagem (of war)'; and peace be upon our Prophet, Muhammad Bin-'Abdallah, who said 'I have been sent with the sword between my hands to ensure that no one but God is worshipped, God who put my livelihood under the shadow of my spear and who inflicts humiliation and scorn on those who disobey my orders.' The Arabian Peninsula has never – since God made it flat, created its desert, and encircled it with seas – been stormed by any forces like the crusader armies now spreading in it like locusts, consuming its riches and destroying its plantations. All this is happening at a time when nations are attacking Muslims like people fighting over a plate of food. In the light of the grave situation and the lack of support, we and you are obliged to discuss current events, and we should all agree on how to settle the matter.

No one argues today about three facts that are known to everyone; we will list them, in order to remind everyone:

First, for over seven years the United States has been occupying the lands of Islam in the holiest of places, the Arabian Peninsula, plundering its riches, dictating to its rulers, humiliating its people, terrorizing its neighbours, and turning its bases in the Peninsula into a spearhead through which to fight the neighbouring Muslim peoples.

If some people have formerly debated the fact of the occupation, all the people of the Peninsula have now acknowledged it.

The best proof of this is the Americans' continuing aggression against the Iraqi people using the Peninsula as a staging post, even though all its rulers are against their territories being used to that end, still they are helpless.

Second, despite the great devastation inflicted on the Iraqi people by the crusader–Zionist alliance, and despite the huge number of those killed, in excess of 1 million . . . despite all this, the Americans are once again trying to repeat the horrific massacres, as though they are not content with the protracted blockade imposed after the ferocious war or the fragmentation and devastation.

So now they come to annihilate what is left of this people and to humiliate their Muslim neighbours.

Third, if the Americans' aims behind these wars are religious and economic, the aim is also to serve the Jews' petty state and divert attention from its occupation of Jerusalem and murder of Muslims there.

The best proof of this is their eagerness to destroy Iraq, the strongest neighbouring Arab state, and their endeavour to fragment all the states of the region such as Iraq, Saudi Arabia, Egypt, and Sudan into paper statelets and through their disunion and weakness to guarantee Israel's survival and the continuation of the brutal crusade occupation of the Peninsula.

All these crimes and sins committed by the Americans are a clear declaration of war on God, his messenger, and Muslims. And ulema [religious scholars] have throughout Islamic history unanimously agreed that the jihad is an individual duty if the enemy destroys the Muslim countries. This was revealed by Imam Bin-Qadamah in 'Al-Mughni', Imam al-Kisa'i in 'Al-Bada'i', al-Qurtubi in his interpretation, and the shaykh of al-Islam in his books, where he said 'As for the militant struggle, it is aimed at defending sanctity and religion, and it is a duty as agreed. Nothing is more sacred than belief except repulsing an enemy who is attacking religion and life.'

On that basis, and in compliance with God's order, we issue the following fatwa to all Muslims: the ruling to kill the Americans and their allies – civilians and military – is an individual duty for every Muslim who can do it in any country in which it is possible to do it, in order to liberate the al-Aqsa Mosque and the holy mosque from their grip, and in order for their armies to move out of all the lands of Islam, defeated and unable to threaten any Muslim. This is in accordance with the words of Almighty God, 'and fight the pagans all together as they fight you all together,' and 'fight them until there is no more tumult or oppression, and there prevail justice and faith in God.'

This is in addition to the words of Almighty God 'And why should ye not fight in the cause of God and of those who, being weak, are ill-treated and oppressed – women and children, whose cry is "Our Lord, rescue us from this town, whose people are oppressors; and raise for us from thee one who will help!" '

We – with God's help – call on every Muslim who believes in God and wishes to be rewarded to comply with God's order to kill the Americans and plunder their money wherever and whenever they find it. We also call on Muslim ulema, leaders, youths, and soldiers to launch the raid on Satan's US troops and the devil's supporters ally-ing with them, and to displace those who are behind them so that they may learn a lesson.

Almighty God said 'O ye who believe, give your response to God and His Apostle, when He calleth you to that which will give you life. And know that God cometh between a man and his heart, and that it is He to whom ye shall all be gathered.'

Almighty God also says 'O ye who believe, what is the matter with you, that when ye are asked to go forth in the cause of God, ye cling so heavily to the earth! Do ye prefer the life of this world to the here-after? But little is the comfort of this life, as compared with the here-after. Unless ye go forth, He will punish you with a grievous penalty, and put others in your place; but Him ye would not harm in the least. For God hath power over all things.'

Almighty God also says 'So lose no heart, nor fall into despair. For ye must gain mastery if ye are true in faith.'

Statement signed by Sheikh Osama Bin-Muhammad Bin-Ladin; Ayman al-Zawahiri, leader of the Jihad Group in Egypt; Abu-Yasir Rifa'i Ahmad Taha, a leader of the Islamic Group; Sheikh Mir Hamzah, secretary of the Jamiat-ul-Ulema-e-Pakistan; and Fazlul Rahman, leader of the Jihad Movement in Bangladesh.

APPENDIX TWO

Osama bin Laden's US Government Fact Sheet, as prepared by the Co-ordinator for Counterterrorism, Department of State, 21 August 1998:

On August 20, 1998, the US military struck a number of facilities of the terrorist network associated with Osama bin Laden. Today bin Laden's network leads, funds and inspires a wide range of Islamic extremist groups that perpetrate acts of terrorism around the world.

The bin Laden network is multi-national and has established a world-wide presence. Senior figures in the network are also senior leaders in other Islamic terrorist networks, including those designated by the Department of State as foreign terrorist groups, such as the Egyptian al-Gama'At al-Islamiyya and the Egyptian Islamic Jihad. Bin Laden and his network seek to provoke a war between Islam and the West and the overthrow of existing Muslim governments, such as Egypt and Saudi Arabia.

Our decision to attack facilities belonging to Osama bin Laden's network is the result of convincing intelligence that his group, working with other terrorist groups, was behind the heinous attacks of August 7 against the US & embassies in Nairobi, Kenya and Dar es Salaam, Tanzania. Elements of bin Laden's network were also involved last week in a plot to attack other US embassies.

Moreover, on August 19, an Islamic front created by the bin Laden network, and calling itself the World Islamic Front for Jihad Against the Jews and Crusaders, praised the bombings of our embassies and warned that, 'America will face a black fate ... strikes will continue from everywhere, and Islamic groups will appear one after the other to fight American interests.'

These latest atrocities in Africa are not the first occasion in which members of bin Laden's network have carried out acts of terrorism against America and its friends.

The list is a long one:

- They conspired to kill US servicemen in Yemen who were on their way to participate in the humanitarian mission 'Operation Restore Hope' in Somalia in 1992.
- They plotted the deaths of American and other peace-keepers in Somalia who were there to deliver food to starving Muslim people.
- Bin Laden's network assisted Egyptian terrorists who tried to assassinate Egyptian President Mubarak in 1995 and who have killed dozens of tourists in Egypt in recent years.
- The Egyptian Islamic Jihad, one of the key groups in the network, conducted a car bombing against the Egyptian embassy in Pakistan in 1995 that killed over 20 Egyptians and Pakistanis.
- Members of bin Laden's network plotted to blow up US airliners in the Pacific and separately conspired to kill the Pope.
- His followers bombed a joint US and Saudi military training mission in Riyadh, Saudi Arabia, in 1995.

Bin Laden's network has publicly and repeatedly articulated a clear and violent anti-US agenda:

- In August 1996, bin Laden issued a 'declaration of war' against the United States.
- In February 1998, bin Laden stated 'If someone can kill an American soldier, it is better than wasting time on other matters.'
- In February of this year, the bin Laden network's World Islamic Front for Jihad Against the Jews and Crusaders declared its intention to attack Americans and our allies, including civilians, anywhere in the world.
- In May of this year, bin Laden stated at a press conference in Afghanistan that we would see the results of his threats 'in a few weeks'.

Bin Laden's Network

Bin Laden's goal in his own words is to 'unite all Muslims and establish a government which follows the rule of the caliphs', which he believes he can accomplish only by overthrowing nearly all Muslim governments, driving Western influence from those countries and eventually to abolishing state boundaries.

The bin Laden network supports terrorists in Afghanistan, Bosnia, Chechnya, Tajikistan, Somalia, Yemen, and now Kosovo. It also trains members of terrorist networks from such diverse countries as the Philippines, Algeria and Eritrea.

Additional Background

Bin Laden, the youngest son of a wealthy Saudi businessman, developed a world-wide organization in the 1970s to recruit Muslim terrorists for the war against the Soviets in Afghanistan. In 1988, he formed a network devoted to terror and subversion. He returned to his home in Saudi Arabia in 1989, but the Government of Saudi Arabia expelled him the following year for his continued support of terrorist groups.

Bin Laden then went to Sudan from which he carried on his support for terrorist operations. At the urging of the United States, and following the attempted assassination of President Mubarak of Egypt, in which bin Laden was involved and in which the Sudanese Government was complicit, the Government of Sudan expelled bin Laden in 1996. However, he has maintained considerable business interests and facilities in Sudan.

APPENDIX THREE

A letter from Ramzi Yousef and the other conspirators in the World Trade Center bombing, published as received by the *New York Times* four days after the February 1993 explosion:

We are, the fifth battalion in the Liberation Army, declare our responsibility for the explosion on the mentioned building. This action was done in response for the American political, economical and military support to Israel the state of terrorism and to the rest of the dictator countries in the region.

Our demands:
1 – Stop all military, economical, and political aids to Israel.
2 – All diplomatic relations with Israel must stop.
3 – Not to interfere with any of the Middle East countries interior affairs.

If our demands are not met, all of our functional groups in the army will continue to execute our missions against military and civilians targets in and out the United States. This also will include some potential Nuclear targets. For your own information, our army has more than hundred and fifty suicidal soldiers ready to go ahead. The terrorism that Israel practices (which is supported by America) must be faced with a similar one. The dictatorship and terrorism (also supported by America) that some countries are practising against their own people must also be faced with terrorism.

The American people must know, that their civilians who got killed are not better than those who are getting killed by the American weapons and support.

The American people are responsible for the actions of their government and they must question all of the crimes that their government is committing against other people. Or they – Americans – will be the targets of our operations that could diminish them.

We invite all of the people from all countries and all of the revolutionaries in the world to participate in this action with us to accomplish our just goals.

'... IF THEN ANYONE TRANSGRESSES THE PROHIBITION AGAINST YOU TRANSGRESS YE LIKEWISE AGAINST HIM ...'

AL-FARBEK AL-ROKN, Abu Bakr Al-Makee

BIBLIOGRAPHY

Adams, James, *The New Spies: Exploring the Frontiers of Espionage* (Pimlico, London, 1995)

Alexander, Yonah, 'Middle East Terrorism: Current Threats and Future Prospects', *International Library of Terrorism*, Vol. 5 (G. K. Hall & Company, London 1994)

Alexander, Yonah, and Dennis A. Pluchinsky, *European Terrorism Today and Tomorrow* (Brassey's, London, 1992)

Allison, Graham T., Owen R. Coté Jr, Richard A. Falkenrath, and Steven E. Miller, *Avoiding Nuclear Anarchy: Containing the Threat of Loose Russian Nuclear Weapons and Fissile Material* (Belfer Center for Science and International Affairs, John F. Kennedy School of Government, Harvard University, 1996)

Allison, Graham T., 'Loose Nukes, Nuclear Smuggling, and the Fissile-Material Problem in Russia and the NIS', hearing before the subcommittee on European Affairs of the Committee on Foreign Relations, 104th Congress, 104–253, 1995

Anti-Defamation League of B'nai B'rith, *ADL Special Background Report: Hamas, Islamic Jihad and the Muslim Brotherhood: Islamic Extremists and the Terrorist Threat to America* (Anti-Defamation League, New York, 1993)

Anti-Defamation League of B'nai B'rith, *ADL Special Report: The Militia Movement in America* (Anti-Defamation League, New York, 1995)

Barnaby, Frank, *Instruments of Terror: Mass Destruction Has Never Been So Easy . . .* (Vision, London, 1997)

Bell, J. Bowyer, *A Time of Terror: How Democratic Societies Respond to Revolutionary Violence* (Basic Books, New York, 1978)

Bowman, Stephen, *When the Eagle Screams: America's Vulnerability to Terrorism* (Birch Lane, New York, 1994)

Combs, Cindy C., *Terrorism in the Twenty-First Century* (Prentice Hall, London, 1996)

Corcoran, James, *Bitter Harvest: The Birth of Paramilitary Terrorism in the Heartland* (Penguin, New York, 1995)

Corbett, Robert, *Guerrilla Warfare from 1939 to the Present Day* (Orbis, London, 1986)

Counterterrorism & Security Report, *'Sudan: Terrorist haven'* (1997)

Crenshaw, Martha, ed., *International Encyclopaedia of Terrorism* (Fitzroy Dearborn, Chicago, 1997)

Davidson, Lawrence, *Islamic Fundamentalism* (Greenwood Press, Westport, Conn., 1993)

Dees, Morris, with James Corcoran, *Gathering Storm: America's Militia Threat* (HarperCollins, New York, 1996)

Dwyer, Jim, David Kocieniewski, Deirdre Murphy and Peg Tyre, *Two Seconds Under the World: Terror Comes to America* (Crown, New York, 1994)

Dyer, Joel, *Harvest of Rage: Why Oklahoma City is Only the Beginning* (Westview Press, New York, 1997)

Falkenrath, Richard A., Robert D. Newman, and Bradley A. Thayer, *America's Achilles' Heel: Nuclear, Biological, and Chemical Terrorism and Covert Attack* (Belfer Center for Science and International Affairs, John F. Kennedy School of Government, Harvard University, 1998)

Federal Bureau of Investigation, *Terrorism in the United States: 1993* (US Department of Justice, Washington D.C., 1994)

Federal Bureau of Investigation, *Terrorism in the United States: 1994* (US Department of Justice, Washington D.C., 1995)

Freeh, Louis J., 'Counterterrorism', statement before the Senate Appropriations Committee, US Senate, 13 May 1997 (FBI, Washington, D.C., 1997)

George, John, and Laird M. Wilcox, *American Extremists: Militias, Supremacists, Klansmen, Communists & Others* (Prometheus Books, New York, 1996)

Global Organized Crime Project, *The Nuclear Black Market* (Center for Strategic and International Studies, Washington D.C., 1996)

Grosscup, Beau, *The Newest Explosions of Terrorism: Latest Sites of Terrorism in the 1990s and Beyond* (New Horizon Press, Far Hills, NJ, 1998)

Guelke, Adrian, *The Age of Terrorism and the International Political System* (St. Martin's Press, New York, 1998)

Hamm, Mark S., *Apocalypse in Oklahoma: Waco and Ruby Ridge Revenged* (Northeastern University Press, Boston, 1997)

Hoffman, Bruce, *Inside Terrorism* (Victor Gollancz, London, 1998)

Hoffman, David, *The Oklahoma City Bombing and the Politics of Terror* (Feral House, Venice, CA, 1998)

Huband, Mark, *Warriors of the Prophet: The Struggle for Islam* (Westview, Colorado, 1998)

Hunter, Gaz, *The Shooting Gallery* (Gollancz, London, 1998)

Inbari, Pinhas, *The Palestinians Between Terrorism and Statehood* (Sussex Academic Press, Sussex, 1995)

Jaber, Hala, *Hezbollah: Born With a Vengeance* (Columbia University Press, New York, 1997)

Jones, Stephen, '*Others Unknown: The Oklahoma City Bombing Case and Conspiracy*', (Public Affairs, New York, 1998)

Juergensmeyer, Mark, 'The Worldwide Rise of Religious Nationalism', *Journal of International Affairs*, vol. 50, no. 1, summer 1996

Juergensmeyer, Mark, 'Terror Mandated by God', *Terrorism and Political Violence*, vol. 9, no. 2, Summer 1997

Karawan, Ibrahim A., *The Islamist Impasse* (Oxford University Press for the International Institute for Strategic Studies, Oxford, 1997)

Kerson, Adrian, *Terror in the Towers* (Random House, New York, 1993)

Keith, Jim, *Okbomb!: Conspiracy and Cover-Up* (Illuminet, New York, 1996)

Kessler, Ronald, *The FBI* (Pocket, New York, 1994)

Khatchadourian, Haig, *The Morality of Terrorism* (Peter Lang, New York, 1998)

Kushner, Harvey W., ed., *The Future of Terrorism: Violence in the New Millennium* (Sage, London, 1998)

Maley, William, ed., *Fundamentalism reborn? Afghanistan and the Taliban* (Hurst, London, 1998)

Marks, R., *America Under Attack* (Carlyle, New York, 1995)

Marsden, Peter, *The Taliban: War, Religion and the New Order in Afghanistan* (Oxford University Press, Oxford, 1998)

Mickolus, Edward F., with Susan L. Simmons, *Terrorism, 1992–95, A chronology of events* (Greenwood Press, Westport, Conn, 1997)

Miller, J., 'Faces of fundamentalism', *Foreign Affairs* 73, 123–42, November/December 1994

Mizell Jr, Louis R., *Target USA: The Inside Story of the New Terrorist War* (John Wiley & Sons, New York, 1998)

Mohaddessin, Mohammad, *Islamic Fundamentalism, the new global threat* (Seven Locks Press, Washington D.C., 1993)

Nacos, Brigitte L., *Terrorism and the Media: From the Iran Hostage Crisis to the World Trade Center Bombing* (Columbia University Press, New York, 1996)

Nasr, Kameel B., *Arab and Israeli Terrorism* (McFarland & Company, New York, 1997)

O'Ballance, Edgar, *Islamic Fundamentalist Terrorism, 1979–95: The Iranian Connection* (Macmillan, London, 1997)

Potter, William C., 'Before the Deluge? Assessing the Threat of Nuclear Leakage from the Post-Soviet States', *Arms Control Today* (October 1995)

Purver, Ron, *Chemical and Biological Terrorism: The Threat according to the Open Literature* (Canadian Security Intelligence Service, 1995)

Reich, Walter, ed., *Origins of Terrorism: Psychologies, Ideologies, Theologies, States of Mind* (Woodrow Wilson International Center for Scholars, Washington D.C., 1998)

Revell, Oliver 'Buck', *A G-Man's Journal: A Legendary Career Inside the FBI; From the Kennedy Assassination to the Oklahoma City Bombing* (Pocket, New York, 1998)

Roberts, Brad, ed., *Terrorism with Chemical and Biological Weapons: Calibrating Risks and Responses* (Chemical and Biological Arms Control Institute, Alexandria, VA, 1997)

Schweitzer, Glenn E. and Carole C. Dorsch, *Superterrorism: Assassins, Mobsters and Weapons of Mass Destruction* (Plenum, New York, 1998)

Snow, Donald M., *Distant Thunder: Patterns of Conflict in the Developing World* (M. E. Sharpe, New York, 1997)

Tanter, Raymond, *Rogue Regimes, Terrorism and Proliferation* (Macmillan, London, 1998)

Taylor, Maxwell, *Terrorist Lives* (Brassey's, London, 1994)

Tibi, Bassam, *The Challenge of Fundamentalism, Political Islam and the New World Disorder* (University of California Press, California, 1998)

US Department of Defense, *Proliferation: Threat and Response* 1997 (US Department of Defense, Washington, D.C., November 1997)

US Department of Defense, *Terror 2000: The Future Face of Terrorism* (US Department of Defense, Washington, D.C., 1994)

US Department of Justice, *Report on the Availability of Bomb-Making Information* (submitted to the US House of Representatives and US Senate, April 1997)

US Department of State, *Patterns of Global Terrorism 1996* (US Department of State, Washington, D.C., 1997)

Volkan, Vamik, *Blood Lines: From Ethnic Pride to Ethnic Terrorism* (Farrar, Straus & Giroux, 1997)

Wilkinson, Paul, and Brian M. Jenkins, eds., *Aviation Terrorism and Security* (Frank Cass, London, 1999)

Wilkinson, Paul, 'Terrorism: British Perspective', *International Library of Terrorism, No. 1*, (G. K. Hall & Company, London, 1994)

Yallop, David, *Tracking the Jackal: The Search for Carlos, the World's Most Wanted Man* (Random House, New York, 1993)

ACKNOWLEDGEMENTS

SINCE RAMZI Yousef was convicted for the 'Manila Air bombing' and then for his leading role in the 1993 bombing of the World Trade Center, he has been held in virtual isolation, banned from speaking to journalists and writers, and forbidden visits from anyone but his lawyer and immediate family members. Requests I made to interview Yousef were rejected, and letters I sent to him were seized by officials from the Bureau of Prisons.

Coupled with the isolation imposed on Osama bin Laden by the Taliban after the American embassy bombings of 1998, this could have made writing a book on the two men and the future of terrorism extremely difficult. I have been fortunate, however, to have had the generous help of sources who gave freely of their time to piece together the careers of Yousef and bin Laden, while simultaneously explaining their concerns about this new and dangerous era of terrorism.

One regret is that I cannot publicly acknowledge all those who offered assistance. Many are still serving with various investigative or intelligence agencies and asked not to be identified. They know who they are; I am indebted to each and every one.

Of those I can name, special thanks must go to Neil E. Herman, the FBI Supervisory Special Agent in charge of the FBI's New York Joint Terrorist Task Force at the time of the World Trade Center bombing, who spent many hours talking me through the intricacies of the WTC investigation, the subsequent Manila Air investigation, and the manhunt for Ramzi Yousef. Thanks also to John Lipka, a senior FBI agent who created the Joint Terrorist Task Force in the Washington Metropolitan Field Office, worked in the Counterterrorism section at FBI Headquarters, and is now a Supervisory Special Agent with the

FBI's International Terrorism section. I'm also grateful to those serving and retired FBI agents who were prepared to be interviewed off the record – particularly my new friend the coffee-addict.

Thanks to Oliver 'Buck' Revell, who was in charge of the FBI Counterterrorism section as Deputy Director of the FBI and is now President of the Washington-based Institute for the Study of Terrorism and Political Violence; to Donna Brooks from the FBI Fugitive Publicity Office; and to FBI officials and agents Joe Valiquette, Jim Margolin, Joyce Riggs, Susan Tully, Neal Schiff and Rex Tomb. I am indebted to the FBI and individual serving and retired agents for providing me with many of the photographs used in this book.

In the intelligence world I thank the British official who lectured me on the Afghan Arabs and then explained the growth of Osama bin Laden's al Qaeda organization. I am grateful to the contact who introduced me to a senior official from the German BND who offered advice and help. Particular thanks to those serving and retired employees of the American intelligence community who were willing to talk about bin Laden, Yousef and Afghanistan, including the one who remembered a useful snippet of information on his way to work one morning, and rang from the roadside to pass it on. I suspect that another source for this book, who said fewer words than most but imparted fascinating information every time, also works for the CIA, and for her time I am indebted.

I would like to express my gratitude to Benazir Bhutto, Prime Minister of Pakistan 1988–90 and 1993–96, for meeting and talking with me and for her kind hospitality. At the Pentagon I would like to thank Peter Probst, an expert on terrorism in the Office of the Assistant Secretary of Defense for Special Operations and Low Intensity Conflict, for his time, and Lieutenant-Colonel William Darley for his assistance. Thanks also to all those in Pakistan and the Philippines who offered help and assistance, particularly HG, BY, RY, and NP in Pakistan, and SB and FQ in Manila. Special thanks to the senior investigator who graciously bought me several meals while I was researching this book, allowed me to pick his brains and also lent me several useful documents.

The journalists Jonathan Calvert, Adrian Levy and Cathy Scott-Clark gave me excellent advice, while Marvin Cetron, the head of Forecasting International, who led a secret investigation into the future of terrorism for the US Department of Defense, kindly shared some of his findings with me.

Among other journalists, I would particularly like to acknowledge the excellent work of Mary Anne Weaver on the Afghan Arabs, the Middle East and Pakistan, and the writings of Jim Dwyer, David Kocieniewski, Deirdre Murphy and Peg Tyre, in their book *Two Seconds Under the World*. Thanks also to Laurie Mylroie, both for her analysis of Ramzi Yousef and for *Iraq News*, which she distributes through the organization Information for Democracy.

I would like to thank the London office of the Islamic Republic News Agency (IRNA); David Swartzendruber, a forensic investigator from Microsoft who examined Yousef's laptop computer; William Ploss, a Miami-based lawyer; Stanley Morris, the former head of the US Marshals Service and head of the US Treasury's Financial Crimes Enforcement Network (FinCEN) 1994–98; Stephen Jones, the Chief Defense Counsel for Timothy McVeigh, the bomber convicted of the April 1995 bombing of the Alfred P. Murrah federal building in Oklahoma; Andy Laine from the State Department's Diplomatic Security Service; David C. Rapoport, Professor of Political Science at the University of California in Los Angeles; Philip Kennedy, Professor of Middle Eastern Studies at New York University; John Sanders; Peter Yerkes and Allen Morrison at the Port Authority of New York and New Jersey; Brionie Huish and Neville McBain at the British Council; Lynn White in the office of Circuit Judge Stanley Marcus; Goro Kamata; Carol Saunders at South Wales Police; James Pelton; Philip Rushton; Richard Goodfellow and Sergeant Bob Grey at Thames Valley Police; Judy Arthur at HBO; Dick Mills; Marilyn Annan in the *New York Times* library; Marvin Smilon; Herbert Hadad; Joe Jordan; Sean McPhilemy; Sandy; John Daniels; Terri; Robert at the FCO; James Young; Mike Deaves; Stan Davies; Fran; Sue Baxter; Anthony Drake; Mike Thompson; Anthony Bye; Melanie Blair; Jill Griffiths and Steve; Chris Webb and Paul Smith. Thanks also to Walter in New York, EL, MW and BW, another MW, BRRM, MJ, AE, SA, JA, TL and EM.

In Wales, I am indebted to staff and students from Swansea University and the Swansea Institute, formerly known as West Glamorgan Institute of Higher Education, or 'Wiggy'. All those who were prepared to be interviewed for this book declined to be identified by their full names, but special thanks must go to those former students, including Alex and Bev, who spent hours talking with me, and then spent even more time tracing old college friends.

Sincere thanks to the ever-patient Beth Morgan, who was always there for me, bravely read all my drafts and offered endless encouragement. Thanks also to my agent Robert Kirby and Catherine Cameron at Peters, Fraser & Dunlop in London, Nicky Paris, Kerrin Edwards, Leslie Barbazette and the team at André Deutsch, Bill Frohlich, Barbara Lenes and Jill Bahcall at NUP, and my accountant Steven Sykes at the Blue Skies Partnership.

I am also grateful to friends, family and colleagues who helped me while I was researching and writing this book, particularly my brother James, Hugh Edwards and my parents, who all rallied round and read drafts, and Amar Qureshi, Bob Marsden, Charlotte Soussan, Danny Viala, David White, Dimitri Zenghelis, EL, Elspeth Williams, Francesco, Frank Kwame-Appiah, Gaia Cavallari, Ian, Jennifer Melville, JP Rosen, Julie Cohen, Martha Roberts, Maurice McLeod, Michael Hall, MJ, Monisola Omotoso, Naomi Pope, Nicola Davidson, Paul Service, Stuart Conway, Tim Hodgson, Tony Effik and Veronica Masters.

My thanks to them all.

Simon Reeve

Index